Teaching the Harlem
RENAISSANCE

AFRICAN AMERICAN LITERATURE AND CULTURE

Expanding and Exploding the Boundaries

Carlyle V. Thompson
General Editor

Vol. 16

PETER LANG
New York • Washington, D.C./Baltimore • Bern
Frankfurt am Main • Berlin • Brussels • Vienna • Oxford

Teaching the Harlem
RENAISSANCE

Course Design
and Classroom Strategies

EDITED BY
MICHAEL SOTO

PETER LANG
New York • Washington, D.C./Baltimore • Bern
Frankfurt am Main • Berlin • Brussels • Vienna • Oxford

Library of Congress Cataloging-in-Publication Data

Teaching the Harlem Renaissance:
course design and classroom strategies / edited by Michael Soto.
p. cm.—(African American literature and culture:
expanding and exploding the boundaries; v. 16)
Includes bibliographical references and index.
1. Harlem Renaissance—Study and teaching. 2. American literature—
African American authors—Study and teaching. 3. African Americans—
Intellectual life—20th century—Study and teaching.
I. Soto, Michael.
E184.7.T43   700.89'9607307471—dc22   2007008559
ISBN 978-1-4331-0391-9 (hardcover)
ISBN 978-0-8204-9724-2 (paperback)
ISSN 1528-3887

Bibliographic information published by **Die Deutsche Bibliothek**.
Die Deutsche Bibliothek lists this publication in the "Deutsche
Nationalbibliografie"; detailed bibliographic data is available
on the Internet at http://dnb.ddb.de/.

Cover design by Clear Point Designs

Cover image: Marjory Collins, photographer. Washington, D.C.
"Reading lesson in a Negro elementary school", March 1942.
Library of Congress, Prints and Photographs Division, FSA-OWI Collection.
[LC-USW3-000888-E DLC]

The paper in this book meets the guidelines for permanence and durability
of the Committee on Production Guidelines for Book Longevity
of the Council of Library Resources.

© 2008 Peter Lang Publishing, Inc., New York
29 Broadway, 18th floor, New York, NY 10006
www.peterlang.com

Printed in the United States of America

Table of Contents

Part I. The Harlem Renaissance in Context

Part II. Harlem Renaissance Writers and Texts

Part III.   Supplemental Material

List of Illustrations

Illustrations

Acknowledgments

I began studying the Harlem Renaissance long before I knew it, in grade school, when I was assigned a poem by Langston Hughes. Over many subsequent years, in high school, college, and graduate school, I encountered many thoughtful and supportive and inspirational teachers who shared with me their Harlem Renaissances. More recently, my students at Trinity University have opened my eyes to inventive ways of knowing—they keep the Harlem Renaissance as fresh and new as ever. I owe all of them my thanks.

I am also grateful to the wonderful scholars and teachers who have given of their time and insight and energy to this book. The librarians at Trinity University and at the University of Texas at Austin also deserve credit for their thoughtful and hard work. And the editors and design staff at Peter Lang have been a pleasure to work with. Thank you.

Finally, my wife, Celina Peña, and my son, Alejo Xoaquín, keep me on my toes, in my senses, and up for anything that life may bring. They have my gratitude and my love.

Timeline

The very first reference to a "renaissance" of African American literature and culture was probably that of William Stanley Braithwaite, who in the *Colored American Magazine* in 1901 longed for a "'Negroid' renaissance" on a par with the literary ferment then taking shape in Ireland and Canada. For the next twenty-five years or so, African American writers and critics pointed to a "Negro renaissance" always just around the corner. During the early 1930s, as the Great Depression reached its cruelest depths, these same writers and critics routinely dismissed the "renaissance" as a shortsighted fad or a cultural pipe dream. If Alain Locke's *The New Negro* (1925) marks the movement's buoyant heyday, then Richard Wright's "Blueprint for Negro Writing" (1937) represents its disillusioned swan song. (I trace the rise and fall of "renaissance rhetoric" in Harlem and elsewhere much more fully in *The Modernist Nation* [2004].)

Not surprisingly, scholars tend to differ over the precise dates of the Harlem Renaissance. To offer just two well-known examples: Nathan Irvin Huggins, in his *Harlem Renaissance* (1971), and David Levering Lewis, in his *When Harlem Was in Vogue* (1981), select for the start of their renaissances the triumphal march down Fifth Avenue of the all-black New York Fifteenth Infantry Regiment on February 17, 1919. (Lewis then backtracks to the race riots and war preparations of 1917.) But they bring their renaissances to a close in vastly different ways: Huggins's renaissance drifts to an inglorious end during the Great Depression, whereas Lewis's comes crashing to a halt with the Harlem riots of March 1935. Anthologists by and large shy away from a prescriptive set of dates for the Harlem Renaissance, although like Huggins and Lewis their textual preferences tend to favor the so-called Jazz Age centered in the 1920s. Lewis, in *The Portable Harlem Renaissance Reader* (1994), follows the historical contours of his study with work ranging in time from 1917 to 1935. *The Norton Anthology of African American Literature* (1997; rev. 2004) supplies dates (1919–1940) that suggest an interwar understanding of the period, although individual titles in the section span a somewhat different set of dates (1918–1961). In their revisionist anthology, *Double-Take* (2001), Venetria K. Patton and Maureen Honey identify work from as early as 1916 and from as late as 1937, but they also include previously unpublished titles, thus further extending the movement's parameters. Huggins, in *Voices from the Harlem Renaissance* (1976), looks back as far as 1917 and proceeds forward as far as 1973 (in a retrospective interview with Eubie Blake about the 1920s music scene).

Rather than propose a definitive beginning and end of the movement, this Harlem Renaissance timeline is meant to suggest a web of cultural and historical contexts for individual writers and texts. Some of the connections will be obvious, some less so—and still other events are supplied here in the hope that enterprising students and scholars might draw connections where none were previously seen to exist.

1865	Thirteenth Amendment abolishes slavery
	President Abraham Lincoln assassinated
1866	Ku Klux Klan (first version) founded in Tennessee
1868	Fourteenth Amendment grants citizenship to African Americans
1877	President Rutherford B. Hayes withdraws federal troops from the South, bringing Reconstruction to an end
1881	Tuskegee Institute founded by Booker T. Washington
1890	Census Bureau declares the Western frontier "closed"
1893	World's Columbian Exposition takes place in Chicago
1895	Booker T. Washington delivers "Atlanta Exposition Address"
1896	*Plessy v. Ferguson* upholds segregation and "separate but equal" principle
	National Association of Colored Women founded by Harriet Tubman, Frances E.W. Harper, and others
1901	Booker T. Washington, *Up From Slavery*
	William Stanley Braithwaite calls for a "'Negroid' renaissance" in the *Colored American Magazine*
1903	W.E.B. Du Bois, *The Souls of Black Folk*
1905	Niagara Movement launched by W.E.B. Du Bois and William Monroe Trotter
	"Madame" C.J. Walker founds hair care business in Denver
1908	Jack Johnson defeats Tommy Burns to win boxing's heavyweight world championship

1909   National Association for the Advancement of Colored People (NAACP) founded

1910   NAACP begins publishing *The Crisis* magazine (edited by W.E.B. Du Bois)

1911   National League on Urban Conditions Among Negroes (later the National Urban League) founded

1912   James Weldon Johnson, *The Autobiography of an Ex-Colored Man*

1913   Imagist movement launched in *Poetry* magazine

1914   World War I begins in Europe

1915   Ku Klux Klan (second version) founded in Georgia

1916   Marcus Garvey gives his first speech in New York City

1917   United States enters World War I
        Russian revolution abolishes Russian Empire
        United Negro Improvement Association (New York division) established by Marcus Garvey
        A. Philip Randolph and Chandler Owen begin publishing *The Messenger* magazine

1918   Georgia Douglas Johnson, *The Heart of a Woman*

1919   First Pan-African Congress meets in Paris
        New York Fifteenth Infantry Regiment marches down Fifth Avenue
        Marcus Garvey founds the Black Star shipping line
        "Red Summer" riots occur in several cities throughout the North and South
        Jessie Fauset assumes role as literary editor of *The Crisis* magazine

1920   Eighteenth Amendment prohibits the manufacture and sale of alcohol
        Nineteenth Amendment grants women the right to vote
        Eugene O'Neill, *The Emperor Jones*

1921   Second Pan-African Congress meets in Brussels, London, and Paris
        Colored Players Guild founded in New York
        Eubie Blake and Noble Sissle, *Shuffle Along*

1922   Soviet Union founded in aftermath of Russian revolution
        Georgia Douglas Johnson, *Bronze*
        James Weldon Johnson, ed., *The Book of American Negro Poetry*

1923   Third Pan-African Congress meets in Lisbon, London, and Paris
        National Urban League begins publishing *Opportunity* magazine
        Waldo Frank, *Holiday*
        Jean Toomer, *Cane*

1924   *Opportunity* Civic Club dinner celebrates "Debut" of African American artists

1925   *Crisis* and *Opportunity* host awards ceremonies
        Alain Locke, ed., *Survey Graphic* Harlem number and *The New Negro*
        Countee Cullen, *Color*
        Edward Christopher Williams anonymously publishes "The Letters of
        Davy Carr: A True Story of Colored Vanity Fair" (later *When Washington
        Was in Vogue)* in *The Messenger* magazine

1926   Langston Hughes, *The Weary Blues*
        Wallace Thurman, ed., *Fire!!*
        Carl Van Vechten, *Nigger Heaven*

1927   Fourth Pan-African Congress meets in New York
        Marcus Garvey deported
        A'Lelia Walker opens her "Dark Tower" salon
        Countee Cullen, *Copper Sun* and *The Ballad of the Brown Girl*; ed.,
        Caroling Dusk
        Langston Hughes, *Fine Clothes to the Jew*
        James Weldon Johnson, *God's Trombones* and reprint of *The Autobiography
        of an Ex-Coloured Man*
        Alan Crosland, dir., *The Jazz Singer* (first feature-length talking picture)

1928   Countee Cullen marries Yolande Du Bois (daughter of W.E.B. Du Bois)
        Jessie Fauset, *Plum Bun*
        Nella Larsen, *Quicksand*
        Claude McKay, *Home to Harlem*

1929   Stock market crash marks beginning of the Great Depression
        Negro Experimental Theatre, Negro Art Theatre, and National Colored
        Players founded
        Countee Cullen, *The Black Christ*

1930   James Weldon Johnson, *Black Manhattan*

1931   "Scotsboro Boys" tried for rape and convicted (later overturned, retried)
        George S. Schuyler, *Black No More*

1932   President Franklin D. Roosevelt launches "New Deal" social program
        Twenty young African Americans travel to Soviet Union to film *Black
        and White* (never completed)
        Sterling Brown, *Southern Road*
        Wallace Thurman, *Infants of the Spring*

1933   Langston Hughes, *The Ways of White Folks*

1934   Rudolph Fisher and Wallace Thurman die within one week of each
        other
        Apollo Theater opens
        Nancy Cunard, ed., *Negro*

1935   Harlem riots
        National Council of Negro Women founded by Mary McLeod Bethune
1937   Joe Louis defeats James Braddock to win boxing's heavyweight world
        championship
        Richard Wright, "Blueprint for Negro Writing"

Introduction: Teaching the Harlem Renaissance

MICHAEL SOTO

There's never been a better time to study or to teach the Harlem Renaissance. The last three decades of American literary scholarship have been profoundly influenced by the revisionist efforts of African Americanist and feminist scholars, and the Harlem Renaissance stands at the center of this important work. Indeed, the Harlem Renaissance now represents the most thoroughly historicized and theorized movement in African American cultural history. The Library of Congress currently lists well over 150 book titles under the subject heading "Harlem Renaissance," most of which have been published in the last decade, and the MLA International Bibliography lists roughly 400 titles under the same heading. Substantial biographies and critical studies of major Harlem Renaissance figures also line library shelves across the country and around the globe. Just as important, today's more wide-ranging studies of U.S. literary modernism find it difficult if not impossible to ignore the movement and its key players. The latest "encyclopedias of" and "dictionaries of" U.S. literature feature entries on the Harlem Renaissance, and all of the major anthologies of U.S. literature now include a significant representation of Harlem Renaissance writers.

This research interest very naturally impacts the classroom experience. Since the 1980s, the proliferation of Harlem Renaissance courses, anthologies, and reissued editions defies simple measure. Most college English departments offer a course on the subject, and the recent multicultural turn in public education has exposed countless high school students to Harlem Renaissance writers. A dozen or so Harlem Renaissance anthologies already exist, and these are regularly joined by new titles. What's more, the Harlem Renaissance has exploded online, with literally thousands of Web sites, many of them designed by teachers and students, devoted to the topic. In spite of this sea change in the study of American and African American literature and culture, until now there has existed no work devoted to teaching the Harlem Renaissance at the college and high school levels. This book is meant to fill in the void.

Teaching the Harlem Renaissance: Course Design and Classroom Strategies addresses the practical and theoretical needs of college and high school teachers, although it will also be of use to anyone generally interested in the topic. In this collection many of the field's leading scholars engage a wide range of issues and primary materials, from the role of slave narrative in shaping individual and collective identity; to the long-recognized centrality of women writers, editors, and critics within the "New Negro" movement; to the role of the visual arts and "popular" forms in the dialogue about race and cultural expression; to tried-and-true methods for bringing students into contact with the movement's poetry, prose, and visual art. *Teaching the Harlem Renaissance* also provides supplemental material for use in designing courses and preparing lectures and lesson plans. Although some may wish to read this book cover-to-cover, it is meant to be an ongoing resource for scholars and teachers as they devise a syllabus, prepare a lecture or lesson plan, or simply learn more about a particular writer or text. Before I address the contents of the book in more detail, though, let me say a word about the history of the Harlem Renaissance in the classroom.

FROM THE STREETS OF HARLEM TO THE CLASSROOM

The Harlem Renaissance, or the "Negro Renaissance" as it was known during its heyday, designates a moment of unprecedented artistic flowering in African American literary culture. Social changes stemming from the Great Migration, a massive influx of African Americans from the rural South to the urban North at the turn of the twentieth century, paved the way for more strictly cultural activities in the following decades. Although African American writers and critics began calling for a cultural renaissance at the dawn of the twentieth century, most scholars now agree that the Harlem Renaissance took shape during the so-called Jazz Age, beginning with the armistice in 1918 and ending around the time of the Great Depression in the 1930s.

Formulations of the movement's ideals vary almost as widely as the intellectuals who guided it, but a few merit special attention for their pivotal role in our understanding of African American cultural history. *The New Negro* (1925), a collection of essays, poetry, fiction, and visual art edited by Alain Locke, is widely recognized as a key record of the ideals and creative expression central to the movement. In important ways the phrase "Harlem Renaissance" can be misleading: In *The New Negro*, Locke, a Harvard-educated philosopher and critic who taught at Howard University, emphasized the artistic vitality, the youthful energy, and the national scope of the movement. Locke, together with W.E.B. Du Bois, Jessie Fauset, James Weldon Johnson, and a handful of additional critics, cemented the notion that an avant-garde of accomplished artists might pave the way for a broad program of social uplift. As Johnson optimistically put it in his famous preface to *The Book of American Negro Poetry* (1922), "The world does not know that a people is great until that people produces great literature and art. No people that has produced great literature and art has ever been looked upon by the world as distinctly inferior" (vii). The Harlem Renaissance, then, might be seen as a quest by African American writers and artists to achieve greatness, for themselves and for others. Social change would follow aesthetic appreciation.[1]

We can easily—perhaps too easily—dismiss the ambitious social program of Harlem Renaissance intellectuals as hopelessly naive. They viewed the literary marketplace as a promised land of recognition and respect—it offered neither— and they viewed the American reading public as an eager, open-minded audience—it was not. Nor was the increasingly professionalized community of literary critics and historians—those who offered the first courses and designed the first programs in American literature—hospitable to Harlem Renaissance writing. The institutionalization of American literary studies during the 1930s and 1940s, as Paul Lauter and David Shumway have shown, witnessed the disenfranchisement of African American and women scholars, as well as the dismissal of African American and women writers from the literary canon. During this time, even the scant attention that had previously been paid by literary anthologies to Negro spirituals and African American poetry vanished almost entirely. In 1947, John S. Lash, professor of English at Southern University, bemoaned the fact that the "typical anthologist of that version of American literature which is taught in our secondary schools and colleges has neglected the Negro author" (69). The following year, the National Council of Teachers of English (NCTE) conducted a survey of American literature in the college curriculum; according to Lauter, the survey shows that "by the end of the fifties, one could study American literature and read no work by a black writer, few works by women except Dickinson and perhaps Marianne Moore or Katherine Anne Porter, and no work about the lives or experiences of working-class people" (440). *American Literature*, an official publication of the Modern Language Association's American literature section, did not publish an article about an African American writer until 1971 (Lauter 445). *American Quarterly*, the official organ of the American Studies Association, hardly fares better: Its first article on African American literature did not appear until 1963.[2]

Much like the writers and critics of the Harlem Renaissance, the earliest teachers of Harlem Renaissance literature found it necessary to respond to the legacies of Jim Crow prejudice and pseudoscientific racism, an unfortunate and ubiquitous holdover from the previous century, and they had to carry out their work in an unfriendly, or at best oblivious, academic climate. The simultaneous rise of what we now call African American studies and the entry of Harlem Renaissance literature into the classroom during the 1930s is no simple coincidence. In 1940, left-leaning cultural critic V.F. Calverton, writing in the *Saturday Review of Literature*, reminisced that "in the 1920's to be a Negro writer was to be a literary son of God. It was like being a proletarian writer in the 1930's" (3). Calverton, who hobnobbed with Langston Hughes and Jessie Fauset during the Jazz Age, is merely repeating the familiar refrain that (as Hughes put it in his autobiography that same year) the "Negro was in vogue" for a brief and dissatisfying moment. Even so, the Harlem Renaissance did represent a time of relative celebrity for African American writers, in part because the movement's leaders strategically publicized the efforts of their protégés in new and moderately effective ways.[3] In other words, by the 1930s, when the Harlem Renaissance drew to a close, and when courses in "Negro History" and "Negro Literature" entered the college curriculum on a modest scale—first at historically black colleges and universities (HBCUs), and somewhat later at predominantly white schools—faculty could rely on the critical reputations of writers such as Countee Cullen and Claude McKay. Indeed, many of the key figures behind the Harlem Renaissance—such as Sterling Brown, W.E.B. Du Bois, James Weldon Johnson, Alain Locke, and Kelly Miller—were also among the founders of African American studies. They presided over a cultural movement *and* invented an academic discipline.[4]

The fate of the Harlem Renaissance in the classroom mirrors its place in academic criticism. Courses specifically titled "Harlem Renaissance" did not exist until the latter part of the twentieth century, first appearing in the late 1960s and early 1970s,[5] gaining currency in the 1980s, and spreading vigorously in the 1990s. (At my own institution, Trinity University, the course made a somewhat belated appearance in the *Courses of Study* catalog in 1997, along with a survey course in African American literature.) This is not to say that Harlem Renaissance writing wasn't important in the classroom before 1970; in fact, the movement was central to the institutionalization of African American literary studies in HBCUs. As early as 1933, one review of college course catalogs identified courses on "Negro literature" at seven HBCUs, and courses on "the Negro in American literature" at four (Moton 401). A more comprehensive 1934 survey of 58 HBCUs found that 45 (77.5%) offered courses in "Negro history," and 28 (48.2%) in "Negro literature" (Dabney 280, 282).[6] But what were teachers teaching in these courses?

The 1934 survey, conducted by Thomas L. Dabney, mentions a handful of textbooks by name (Dabney 283); all of these titles (including *The New Negro* and *Book of American Negro Poetry*) prominently feature the work of Harlem Renaissance writers. Anecdotal accounts further illustrate the importance of the Harlem Renaissance in the classroom at this crucial juncture in the institutional history of African American studies. In 1941, Nick Aaron Ford, who was then assistant professor of English at the Oklahoma Colored Agricultural and Normal University (present-day Langston University), described his curriculum for a three-hour course in "Negro Literature" for *College English*, the journal of the NCTE. Much of the nonfiction, most of the fiction, and all of the "major poets" (535) making up the course have long been closely associated with the Harlem Renaissance, even though Ford does not consider the field-organizing relevance of the movement label. For Ford, Harlem Renaissance literature simply *was* "Negro literature."[7]

In 1947, Lash singled out the Harlem Renaissance in answering the question posed by his *College English* essay title, "What is 'Negro Literature'?":

> At the beginning of the twenties "Negro literature" was the sum of the combined expression of Negro writers in America, but was losing its quantitative connotation to a cause more narrowly racial. In 1921 [*sic*], James Weldon Johnson published his *Book of American Negro Poetry*, with a prefatory essay on the Negro's creative genius which was to establish a theory for a "Negro literature." … The Negro authors who followed were a part of that prolific period of literary composition called "The Harlem Renaissance." Johnson's essay was given the force of a racial prophecy as Langston Hughes crooned into the stanzas of his poetry the plaintive melody of the blues, as Sterling Brown captured in verse the spirit of the garrulous folk tales, as Johnson himself catechized in the stentorian sermons of the old-time preacher. These three, more than any others, embodied a racial strain in their authentic reproductions of voices which were lucid in the cadences of a racial tradition. Other writers were preoccupied with militancy and brute realism and primitivism. New theories of culture, new experiments with the racial theme, were born and expired amid the tinsel and glitter of a fabulous era. (40)

Lash not only celebrates the Jazz Age mystique that fills Harlem Renaissance courses with eager students, he also anticipates the Black Arts Movement aesthetic that would ultimately reshape the academy and resurrect the fortunes of Harlem Renaissance figures such as Zora Neale Hurston and Jean Toomer. But similar ideas had already found their way into the first extensive scholarly study of the Harlem Renaissance, a *Revue de Paris* article by French historian Franck L. Schoell, published in 1929; and into the first graduate school monograph on the topic, Melvin B. Tolson's 1940 master's thesis at Columbia University; and into Hughes's still-influential memoir, *The Big Sea* (1940). By Lash's account, there was no "Negro literature" before the Harlem Renaissance, just "literature written by Negroes." After the Harlem Renaissance, as we have just seen, things changed dramatically: The movement's writers and critics taught us not only *what* to read, what counts as literature, but also *how* to read, why African American literature counts as literature—and how literature might also be *African American*.

It is fitting, then, that courses titled "Harlem Renaissance" began to appear as the Black Arts Movement was in full swing, at the same time as book-length analyses of the movement, beginning with Nathan Irvin Huggins's seminal *Harlem Renaissance* (1971). The earliest of these courses appears to have been a Yale graduate seminar taught by Arna Bontemps in 1969, the year he assumed the role of curator of the James Weldon Johnson Collection there (Wall 74 n. 6).[8] Since then, colleges and high schools have grown much more attentive to the intellectual needs of increasingly diverse student and faculty populations. At the same time, the Harlem Renaissance classroom experience has undergone profound changes, with effects that have redrawn the contours of the U.S. educational landscape. We can expect the change to continue, both inside and beyond the classroom. I sincerely hope that this book will foster transformation in the best traditions of Harlem Renaissance studies.

ABOUT TEACHING THE HARLEM RENAISSANCE

This book has been divided into three distinct but complementary sections. The first part, "The Harlem Renaissance in Context," brings into view some of the most important historical and theoretical developments informing contemporary Harlem Renaissance scholarship. The first four essays delve back and forth into the spatial and temporal dimensions of the movement. Dorothea Löbbermann focuses her keen eye on the question of how Harlem came to be identified as the paradigmatic African American urban experience, and how the showcasing of Harlem as "Mecca of the New Negro" transforms cultural expression. Exploring how Harlem Renaissance writers negotiate their place in literary history, Claudia Stokes pays particular attention to the quintessential African American literary genre—slave narrative—and how it provides Harlem Renaissance writers and thinkers with an indispensable (and unavoidable) model for understanding individual and collective identity. William J. Maxwell surveys the social pressures exerted upon modern African American artists and intellectuals and discusses the debate informing Harlem Renaissance aesthetics and cultural expression, including intra- and inter-racial conflict and cooperation within modernist and avant-garde circles. And Martha Jane Nadell addresses the role of visual artists in Harlem salon culture and in the literary marketplace, with a particular emphasis on how artists and writers engaged in an important dialogue about the role of race in cultural expression and identity.

The last three essays in part 1 have been profoundly shaped by recent developments in feminist and gender studies research. Amber Harris Leichner demonstrates that African American women, long ignored in Harlem Renaissance scholarship, were central to the movement as writers and critics and helped negotiate modernity for African American culture and society. Laura Harris asks teachers and students to reexamine long-held views of the African American experience in light of recent (and not so recent) additions to our understanding of key figures' public and private sexualities. And Maureen Honey considers the role of women poets in Harlem Renaissance cultural production and interpretation, both during the movement's heyday and more recently.

Part 2, "Harlem Renaissance Writers and Texts," represents the "bread and butter" of *Teaching the Harlem Renaissance*, with individual chapters devoted to a single figure or book. The contributors to this section, who together have amassed well over a century of classroom experience, share refreshing textual approaches along with personal teaching triumphs, not to mention a few pitfalls to avoid. In his suggestions for teaching Sterling Brown's poetry, James Smethurst considers Brown's impact not just on modern verse, but also on African American studies as an emergent discipline. It is not possible, and it's unwise, Smethurst suggests, to separate literary expression from its discursive, disciplinary, and institutional contexts. Patrick Bernard looks at the productive tensions between individual and collective identity—between "I" and "we"—in his essay on teaching Countee Cullen's poetry. Susan Tomlinson's essay on teaching Jessie Fauset's *Plum Bun* (1929) locates the novel in terms of its formal and thematic genres. *Plum Bun* "confounds genre, movement, and meaning," Tomlinson concludes, but where there is confusion (to borrow from another Fauset title), there might also be found insight. In her discussion of Waldo Frank's *Holiday* (1923), Kathleen Pfeiffer reflects on the novel's curious composition and publishing history, as well as on its painful themes (including gruesome, racialized violence) and its lyrical form. The poetry of Langston Hughes represents one of the unbridled successes of the Harlem Renaissance, and Anita Patterson reveals valuable approaches for stepping beyond the deceptive simplicity of Hughes's verse forms. Also looking at Hughes is Hans Ostrom, who provides useful direction for considering *The Ways of White Folks* (1934) in the context of Hughes's career trajectory and in terms of the short story collection's most important recurring themes. Lawrence J. Oliver's essay on teaching James Weldon Johnson's *The Autobiography of an Ex-Colored Man* (1912) considers the proto-Renaissance novel (first published anonymously as bona fide nonfiction) in its richly vexed social and cultural contexts. Emily Hinnov's approach to teaching Nella Larsen's *Quicksand* (1928), informed by a cultural studies critique of primitivism, offers useful advice for bringing student readers into contact with the challenging ethics of the novel. Bringing in a discussion about contemporaneous films, Tom Lutz surveys many of the key issues—such as "arguments about jazz, primitivism, assimilation, incrementalism, [and] representation"—that animate Claude McKay's *Home to Harlem* (1928) and the varied responses to the novel. My essay on *The New Negro* suggests a variety of ways to use the anthology for different levels of students, including seven specific (but hopefully not prescriptive) approaches to the book. The topic of Rita Keresztesi's essay is George S. Schuyler's *Black No More* (1931), a science-fiction satire that Keresztesi positions alongside Schuyler's nonfiction prose (especially his famous "Negro-Art Hokum" essay) to illustrate his geography- and class-based critique of racial identity politics. Successfully teaching Jessie Fauset's *Plum Bun* (1929), Elisa Glick emphasizes, requires attention to the novel's many and multifaceted genre patterns. Nathan Grant similarly deploys questions of genre (specifically, expectations that attend reading a novel) in his suggestions for teaching Jean Toomer's genre-bending *Cane* (1923). Taking as her starting point the vexing title of Carl Van Vechten's *Nigger Heaven* (1926), Emily Bernard steers us through the novel's linguistic minefields and its other fascinating conundrums. And Adam McKible, whose diligent recovery work helped bring Edward Christopher Williams's *When Washington Was in Vogue* (1926) back from obscurity, shares his insights into the role the novel might play in the classroom.

The classroom approaches described in these important new essays, diverse as they are, do not even begin to circumscribe the range of methods and the variety of theoretical developments informing Harlem Renaissance scholarship and pedagogy. For this reason, part 3, "Supplemental Material," presents maps of Jazz Age Harlem, a sampling of course syllabi, and a bibliography of recent, important scholarship on the movement as well as on individual writers and texts. Together, these apparatuses might recommend a wider range of classroom activity and scholarly investigation.

As fruitful as the last generation of Harlem Renaissance studies has been, no one can predict where the next generation's scholars will take us. Just as feminist scholars in the 1980s and 1990s repositioned women writers at the forefront of the Harlem Renaissance, in the twenty-first century literary critics and historians have only just begun to take stock of important issues. These include the transnational dimensions of Afro Diaspora cultural and social networks, and the cosmopolitan rhetoric inspired by dialog across national borders; the connection between performance (onstage and off) and social identity; the role of gay and lesbian writers on the Harlem Renaissance margins and in its mainstream; and, as Hughes and Hurston were right to insist decades ago, on the role of popular forms in the African American imagination. No doubt tomorrow's students of African American literature will explore as-yet-unimagined avenues for scholarly inquiry. What is clear is that the Harlem Renaissance will remain at the front and center of American and African American studies for the foreseeable future.

NOTES

1. This notion of cultural uplift, remarkable though it may be, must be understood in the context of the more politically radical alternatives offered by (for example) the accommodationist Booker T. Washington and the separatist Marcus Garvey.
2. However, before the 1960s *American Quarterly* did publish several studies of slave culture, along with a handful of articles on the history of jazz.
3. For more on the publicity efforts of Harlem Renaissance intellectuals, see Hutchinson and Mott.
4. According to Scott Zaluda, the first cataloged course in African American history at Howard University was taught by Carter Woodson in 1919 (251).
5. In a survey of Black studies curricula conducted between 1968 and 1970, William P. Smith lists a history course titled "Harlem Renaissance."
6. On the rise and spread of African American studies curricula during this period, see Crouchett. As Zaluda has shown, students at HBCUs had already been writing term papers on such topics as "The Legal Position of the Negro" and "Negro Labor in Atlanta" as early as the 1890s (246).
7. Ford went on to a distinguished career as professor and chair of English at Morgan State University, where he was the inaugural Alain Locke professor of Black studies.
8. According to Cheryl Wall, "Only a handful of such [Harlem Renaissance] courses existed in 1971. The very idea of a 'period' course in black literature seemed anomalous, even at Howard University, where I had been a student—and a most fortunate one—having taken 'Literature By and About Negroes' with Sterling Brown. Professor Brown was a heroic figure to me, and I had bought *Negro Caravan* as well as his critical studies, originally published by a Negro press in Washington in the late 1930s and reissued as a joint volume. But as much as I learned from them, those studies were not models for me. *Harlem Renaissance* was" (63).

WORKS CITED

Calverton, V.F. "The Negro and American Culture." *Saturday Review of Literature* 22.22 (1940): 3–4, 17–18.

Courses of Study 1997–1998. San Antonio: Trinity University, 1997.

Crouchett, Lawrence. "Early Black Studies Movements." *Journal of Black Studies* 2.2 (1971): 189–200.

Dabney, Thomas L. "The Study of the Negro." *Journal of Negro History* 19.3 (1934): 266–307.

Ford, Nick Aaron. "I Teach Negro Literature." *College English* 2.6 (1941): 530–41.

Huggins, Nathan Irvin. *Harlem Renaissance*. New York: Oxford UP, 1971.

Hughes, Langston. *The Big Sea: An Autobiography.* New York: Knopf, 1940.

Hutchinson, George. *The Harlem Renaissance in Black and White.* Cambridge: Harvard UP, 1995.

Johnson, James Weldon. *Book of American Negro Poetry.* New York: Harcourt, 1922.

Lash, John S. "The Anthologist and the Negro Author." *Phylon* 8 (1947): 68–76.

———. "What is 'Negro Literature'?" *College English* 9.1 (1947): 37–42.

Lauter, Paul. "Race and Gender in the Shaping of the American Literary Canon: A Case Study from the Twenties." *Feminist Studies* 9.3 (1983): 435–63.

Moton, R. R. "Negro Higher and Professional Education in 1943." *Journal of Negro Education* 2.3 (1933): 397–402.

Mott, Christopher M. "The Art of Self-Promotion: Or, Which Self to Sell? The Proliferation and Disintegration of the Harlem Renaissance." *Marketing Modernism: Self-Promotion, Canonization, Rereading.* Eds. Kevin J. H. Dettmar and Stephen Watt. Ann Arbor: U of Michigan P, 1996. 253–74.

Schoell, Frank L. "La 'renaissance nègre' aux États-Unis." *Revue de Paris* 36 (January–February 1929): 124–65.

Shumway, David R. *Creating American Civilization: A Genealogy of American Literature as an Academic Discipline.* Minneapolis: U of Minnesota P, 1994.

Smith, William P. "Black Studies: A Survey of Models and Curricula." *Journal of Black Studies* 10.3 (1971): 269–77.

Tolson, Melvin Beaunorus. *The Harlem Group of Negro Writers.* 1940. Ed. Edward J. Mullen. Westport, CT: Greenwood, 2001.

Wall, Cheryl A. "Histories and Heresies: Engendering the Harlem Renaissance." *Meridians: Feminism, Race, Transnationalism* 2.1 (2001): 59–76.

Zaluda, Scott. "Lost Voices of the Harlem Renaissance: Writing Assigned at Howard University, 1919–31." *College Composition and Communication* 50 (1998): 232–57.

Part I. The Harlem Renaissance in Context

CHAPTER ONE

The Renaissance's Harlem: Representing Race and Place

DOROTHEA LÖBBERMANN

The fact that the New Negro movement went down in history as the Harlem Renaissance is interesting in itself and reveals much about the importance of place in African American cultural memory. Up until then, epochs in African American history and culture had received names that signified displacement and institutionalized racism rather than a place of identification: the Middle Passage, slavery, the Great Migration. "Tuskegee" had already established itself as a place that counterbalanced slavery's "down river," but with "Harlem" black Americans created a symbol that in a much more radical way broke with the tradition of slavery.

It matters little that the New Negro Movement was not limited to a neighborhood in uptown New York City. Many of its protagonists resided elsewhere: Alain Locke in Washington, Claude McKay in Europe, Dorothy West in Boston, and Sterling Brown in Chicago; and the Chicago jazz scene predated and rivaled Harlem's (Lewis 171ff.). In addition, that Harlem's reality often did not live up to its reputation—an observation that writers have made since the early 1920s—had little impact on the importance of place. On the contrary, looking at Harlem from the perspective of its symbolic value sharpens the awareness that a city is always more than abstract topography, or the "mere" materiality of streets and buildings. It is also a "state of mind," as sociologist Robert E. Park phrased it in 1915 (1).[1] Harlem and the Renaissance evolved together: There was no place readily awaiting black artists and intellectuals. Rather, the social, material, and symbolic aspects of Harlem developed in a close net of interconnections.

On the one hand, Harlem is a good example of the fact that place is made and remade by the people who live in it and who are, in turn, influenced ("made") by the place: Harlem's diverse history leads from the Dutch village to the upper-class suburb, to the "Mecca of the New Negro," to the black ghetto of the 1940s onwards, and to its contemporary economic revival. Given the malleability of a place such as Harlem, and given the heterogeneity of this urban space even within these diverse periods, it becomes difficult to grasp the identity and meaning of place: Which of its historical moments are we thinking about, and which of its aspects?

On the other hand, place radiates an aura of "authenticity," and place becomes a metonym for identity: It provokes feelings of "home," of local pride or shame. To be "from" a certain place has a tremendous meaning for identity formation. It is in this sense—and in consideration of place in African American cultural history—that Harlem has become a symbolic place for black America. Yet while symbolic status brings about visibility and self-assurance, its oversignification also brings about problems. For whom is Harlem a symbol, and what does it symbolize? What is the real Harlem, what is its myth? As early as the 1920s, these questions proved difficult to answer.

THE MAKING OF BLACK HARLEM

The making of black Harlem has been impressively documented by James Weldon Johnson, Gilbert Osofsky, and others (see De Jongh 1–14). One important aspect of Manhattan is its never-easy multiculturalism: After an artificial European colonial homogeneity (uniting the Dutch and English against the Native Americans), new immigrants of the nineteenth century formed "Little Italies" and "Little Russias" that existed well into the twentieth century. Railroad and subway development led to housing speculation in Harlem and a subsequent bust made it necessary for the white real-estate owners, at the beginning of the twentieth century, to sell or rent out to black Americans.

For the black middle class, who moved to Harlem from downtown Manhattan, Harlem meant an end to the segregation they had endured in the crowded areas of Five Points (today's City Hall), Little Africa in Greenwich Village (today's Little Italy), and the Tenderloin District (West Side between the 20s and 60s). They were happy to pay disproportionately high rents in exchange for the cleanliness and spaciousness of Harlem. When their arrival in Harlem eventually led to a mass exodus of white people, black, predominantly working-class migrants from the Southern states and the Caribbean crowded the space. What had started out as a movement away from the black ghettos led to the formation of a new, albeit larger and more diverse, black neighborhood. In 1914, 50,000 African Americans lived in Harlem; in 1920, the number had reached 73,000; and by 1930 they were

164,566 (Osofsky 123, 130). The black neighborhood in Harlem, which centered around 135th and 145th Streets between 5th and 8th Avenues, had by 1930 spread out until Central Park to the south and the Harlem River to the north and east.

Harlem illustrates the forced segregation into ghettos as much as the triumphant "control" of a neighborhood. Many African American organizations were involved in this process: The wealthy black congregations that built churches and other buildings moved their flocks to Harlem and invested in real estate; the social clubs, fraternities, and other social and political organizations (National Association for the Advancement of Colored People, Universal Negro Improvement Association, etc.) that followed them uptown; and newspapers such as *The Crisis*, *The Messenger*, or *The New York Age* that both attracted writers and disseminated the image of New York as a center of racial uplift.

The social took place not only in or through organizations: Sharing the space of Harlem led to new, often improvised forms of social interaction. Because of crowded living conditions, much of the social life was moved to the streets. "Strolling in Harlem," Johnson observed, "does not mean merely walking along Lenox or upper Seventh Avenue or One Hundred and Thirty-fifth Street; it means that those streets are places for socializing" (162). The frequency of parades and protest marches, and the speakers' corner on Lenox Avenue and 135th Street, contributed to the street's function as a space of social interaction. Apartments also rose to fame, both through the entertainment that was held in the private parlors of the middle class and through the institution of the rent party.[2] Here family, friends, and strangers mingled, sharing home-cooked food and moonshine drinks. These symbolic social institutions arose from the material and historic conditions of Harlem and, in turn, shaped its perception.

HARLEM'S POSITION IN THE CULTURAL IMAGINARY

Descriptions of Harlem were rarely "realistic." Rather, they projected onto Harlem the longings that resulted from a history of African American spatial and social discrimination and thus saw Harlem as "prophetic," as Locke phrased it in "The New Negro" (1925), rather than as typical. Locke's famous manifesto is the starting point of an analysis of Harlem's importance for the African American cultural consciousness, touching upon the "promise" of Harlem, its urbanity, its function as a "home" and a "center," as well as the problems of its representation. Locke writes about Harlem:

> Here in Manhattan is not merely the largest Negro community in the world, but *the first concentration in history of so many diverse elements of Negro life*. It has attracted the African, the West Indian, the Negro American; has brought together the Negro of

the North and the Negro of the South; the man from the city and the man from the town and village; the peasant, the student, the businessman, the professional man, artist, poet, musician, adventurer and worker, preacher and criminal, exploiter and social outcast. ... Proscription and prejudice have thrown these dissimilar elements into *a common area of contact and interaction*. Within this area, race sympathy and unity have determined a further fusing of sentiment and experience. So what began in terms of segregation becomes more and more, as its elements mix and react, *the laboratory of a great race-welding*. ... In Harlem, Negro life is seizing upon its first chances for group expression and self determination. It is—or promises at least to be—a race capital. (6–7, italics mine)

This seminal quotation combines (welded in modernist technological metaphor) key concepts of the Harlem Renaissance, developed out of the notion of the modernity and urbanity of Harlem. Locke's Harlem is an urban "common area of contact and interaction," a center of international migration, yet it is also the *promise* of such a "contact zone."[3] Projecting into the future, Locke simultaneously alludes to a black cultural spatial history that explains the specific hopes for Harlem.

THE PROMISE

Harlem, Locke writes, promises to be a race capital ("All hit do is promise," says a character in Rudolph Fisher's short story "The Promised Land" [54]). As already indicated, the materiality and the symbolic value of Harlem stand in a close and reciprocal relationship. It was to a large extent its *reputation* that attracted the masses of migrants who, in the end, shaped the new, black Harlem. Intellectuals such as Locke and Johnson, as well as jazz musicians, writers, artists, and other multipliers, circulated a picture of Harlem that was based less on its visible reality than on its possibilities; they attracted the people who made Harlem the center of black America. And it was these people's dissatisfaction with the social conditions of a racialized city that led to the 1935 riots and to the violence against the material structure of the neighborhood subsequently left to decay. Decades of neglect by the city and by corporate America are responsible for the large number of historical buildings that have not been demolished in the course of economic progress, and that are now being renovated, attracting tourists and investors alike. Tourism, which has become an important economic branch of Harlem, produces new myths about the place—that now mainly project into the past, much as the myths of the 1920s had projected into the future.

Scholars of the Harlem Renaissance have long argued about the relationship between the promise of Harlem and the contrasting social conditions, either highlighting the importance of consciousness and racial pride (Baker) or condemning the illusionary hocus-pocus, describing Harlem as a "theater" produced for a white clientele (Huggins). Yet another way of interpreting the Renaissance is to look at the interconnectedness of race, urbanity, and spectacle, and to look at the diversity of Harlem's inhabitants not only as a source of class and inter- and intra-ethnic conflict, but also as the possibility and potential described by Locke. Taking place in the age of reproduction, in the modernity of the 1920s, the making of the "New Negro" had to be a spectacle—not only for white slummers but also for black Americans themselves, whether in Harlem or elsewhere.

THE CITY

For Locke, one major importance of Harlem is its urbanity. Although African Americans had lived in towns and cities before, with few exceptions they had lived at their peripheries. Harlem, however, was localized centrally. Johnson placed Harlem in "the heart of Manhattan" (4). Harlem's buildings, streets, and infrastructure met modern standards, and trains connected its inhabitants easily with the rest of the city; and this city was New York, whose skyscrapers and artists celebrated the modern age. As early as 1925, Johnson wrote:

> In the make-up of New York, Harlem is not merely a Negro colony or community, it is a city within a city, the greatest Negro city in the world. It is not a slum or a fringe, it is located in the heart of Manhattan and occupies one of the most beautiful and healthful sections of the city. It is not a "quarter" of dilapidated tenements, but is made up of new-law apartments and handsome dwellings, with well-paved and well-lighted streets. ("Making" 635)

But the city was important not only as a source of comfort and security but also as a place that signified arrival in the modern world, a world characterized by technology, mobility, diversity, community, and individualism. The "thrill of the urban" (Balshaw 14) that can be traced through Harlem Renaissance writing strongly differs from the negative images of American cities that we know from both nineteenth- and twentieth-century cultural criticism, especially the dystopic understanding of the black inner city as it has developed since the Depression. In the 1920s, however, the Chicago School of sociology had ventured a new and optimistic understanding of the urban as a quintessentially modern form of existence; industrial as well as humane, technologically constructed as well as "the product of human nature," the city was understood as both a "physical mechanism" and a "state of mind" (Park 1). As Maria Balshaw reminds us, the Chicago School saw the city as the place of the evolution of a civic consciousness inspired by the diversity of people who brought their various talents and cultures into a dynamic and exciting urban space, much in the spirit of Locke's contemporaneous concept of a "race-welding." As George Hutchinson has shown, Harlem Renaissance scholars were deeply influenced by the Chicago School's urbanism, which they appropriated for the description of a particularly black place (50–60).

A HOME?

In African America's symbolic geography, Harlem takes up a significant position.[4] This symbolic geography can be characterized by three elements: the notion of displacement, the journey north (from slavery to freedom), and the search for a home. Place, in the African American cultural memory, was a highly ambivalent concept: It meant movement rather than permanency (the Middle Passage, the Underground Railroad, the Great Migration); if it did offer homes, these homes were in constant danger of being destroyed. Clearly, not all black Americans were Southerners or descendents of slaves; however, as the impact of *The Souls of Black Folk* (1903) by W.E.B. Du Bois (from Massachusetts) or *Cane* (1923) by Jean Toomer (from Washington, D.C.) suggests, Southern slavery has become the traumatic, primeval site of American blackness. Against this ambivalent "anti-home," the escape to freedom in the North has become a second African American "site of memory" (to borrow Pierre Nora's phrase). Robert Stepto has shown that nineteenth-century African American narrative typically describes a northern movement (in which "north" connotes freedom) both in a political and a spiritual sense. The "ascent" to the north figured also as an ascent to heaven. Lucy Ariel Williams's poem "Northboun'" (1926) famously testifies to this symbolic geography:

> Huh! De wurl' ain't flat,
> An' de wurl' ain't roun',
> Jes' one long strip
> Hangin' up an' down–
> Since Norf is up,
> An' Souf is down,
> An Hebben is up,
> I'm upward boun' (Balshaw 14)

Titles of Harlem Renaissance fiction such as Carl Van Vechten's *Nigger Heaven* (1926) and Rudolph Fisher's "City of Refuge" (1925) testify to Harlem's symbolic value, as does Claude McKay's *Home to Harlem* (1928). In light of the history of displacement, Harlem offered to be a home to black America. Yet most fictional representations describe the disillusionment of the protagonists who had arrived full of hopes. Maybe this is less the problem of Harlem, which turned out to be another black neighborhood within a society dominated by racist ideologies, and more the problem of the notion of home. With the onset of modernity, "home" had become an idea fraught with nostalgia. If twentieth-century African American literature has constructed an idea of home, it is that of the South, even if the South, as the site of slavery, has always been an extremely ambivalent home.[5] Harlem, it turned out, did not solve this problem; to the contrary, the continuing discrimination proved even harder for the urban masses. Nevertheless, the question about Harlem as "home" remains interesting, since it points to the fundamental complexity of notions such as place, race, culture, and belonging. In a paradoxical way, Harlem has become a symbolic place for black urban America *and* has revealed that "home" is an extremely complex, heterogeneous, and ambivalent concept. If Harlem has become a "home," then this home is "anti-illusionary" and professes not to be nostalgic, but "authentic" and "real" (iconized in the figure of the street-smart ghetto youth). At the same time as Harlem has problematized the meaning of "home," it has created a new urban myth of belonging.

THE CENTER

A further general aspect of place is its relationship to other places—places that Harlem's inhabitants come from and that they reach out to. Harlem can be perceived as a place defined not only as a topographical territory (even if these boundaries, as long as they connote "Black Harlem," are expanding), but also as a focal node of movements going in and out of that territory. Just as the Harlem Renaissance was "prophetic" (Locke), reaching out into the future through themes and modes that would speak to people for a long time to come, it also reached out geographically. As the quotation from Locke illustrates, Harlem was the geographic destination not only of the Southern migration, but also of migrants from Africa, the Caribbean, and Latin and Central America. These people brought with them their languages, traditions, food, and music and met with the great interest of Harlem artists and intellectuals (much as European modernism took inspiration from vernacular cultures, be it Picasso's discovery of African masks or Dvořák's use of [African] American folk tunes). Finally, Harlem was the goal of white Americans who were fascinated with black culture or were eager to have a good time in the exotic spaces of Harlem nightclubs.

If Harlem was an international, interethnic place, it was furthermore connected to many places in the world, since most Harlemites were dedicated to travel. Not only was there a constant to and fro between the South and Harlem, but also most of the artists and writers of the period (not to mention the jazz and blues musicians in whose nature it is to tour) were eager travelers: Locke had studied in Britain, France, and Germany and spent his summers in Europe; Du Bois studied in Berlin; Langston Hughes and Zora Neale Hurston undertook anthropological field trips to the South and the Caribbean, and Hughes and other Harlemites spent months in the Soviet Union working on a never-realized film project; Nella Larsen grew up and studied in Denmark. McKay, the Jamaica-born author of *Home to Harlem*, never made Harlem his home for more than a few months at a time; in fact, he never really settled anywhere and spent the 1920s to the 1940s in Britain, Germany, the United States, France, and the Soviet Union. Marcus Garvey's Back-to-Africa movement transported the imagination, if not the physical bodies, of many to Africa. And, reciprocally, the Harlem Renaissance was most influential for the development of Africa's *négritude* movement. As James De Jongh demonstrates, between the 1920s and the 1940s, Harlem was sung about in French, Spanish, and Portuguese by poets from Africa, Latin America, and Brazil (48–70).

REPRESENTATION

The number of publications by African American writers was unprecedented at the moment of the Harlem Renaissance. This is especially important because, as Stepto and others have argued, "freedom" was—historically and symbolically— inseparably connected to "literacy," both in the sense of black education and of black literary representation. Considering that the Middle Passage defied representation from the perspective of its victims (with few exceptions), and that the centuries of slavery could almost only retrospectively be put into writing, the considerable amount of published fictional (and non-fictional) writing of the Harlem Renaissance was remarkable. New York's role as a publishing center certainly plays no small part in this development, as do patrons and go-betweens such as Van Vechten, Charlotte Osgood Mason, and others. After centuries of silence, and a century of slowly growing literary output, the sudden literary visibility of black life—and a new, urban experience thereof—must have had a strange effect on readers and writers. The myriad representations of Harlem were emancipatory as they gave expression to black experience and documented black existence. But at the same time, the expectations of readers and publishers; the repercussions of exoticism and the exploitation of blackness; and the pressures of the market as well as the abundance of literary, visual, and musical representations of Harlem in journalism, sociology, fiction, poetry, jazz, blues, painting, and photography made Harlem's writers extremely aware of the distorting effects of representation. Wallace Thurman went farthest when he accused the Harlem Renaissance of being nothing but a publicity fad. Fisher, who once said that he would like to be remembered as "Harlem's interpreter" (xxxvi), was acutely aware of the singular moment of global attention to Harlem and its consequences; yet instead of fighting the phenomenon, he tried to put into language the place and the ironies of its representation.

"CITY OF REFUGE"

In his short story "City of Refuge," Fisher captures many of the elements discussed above. This story is an ideal starting point for an analysis of the Harlem Renaissance, because it evokes the history of slavery and institutionalized Southern racism, the story of the Great Migration, the story of the promises and dangers of the city, and the ironies of Harlem as a "city of refuge." Coming from his native North Carolina because of all the good things he has heard about Harlem ("In Harlem, black was white" [4]), King Salomon Gillis experiences a rebirth in the modern city when he emerges from the overpowering subway like "Jonah emerging from the Whale" (3). The Harlem he faces is busy and urban; it is peopled by Southern and northern African Americans of all kinds as well as by Jamaicans and Italians, all of whom Fisher characterizes through their vernacular speech. The city street crowded with predominantly black people is a spectacle to the newcomer:

> Gillis set down his tan cardboard extension case and wiped his black, shining brow. Then slowly, spreadingly, he grinned at what he saw: Negroes at every turn; up and down Lenox Avenue, up and down 135th Street; big, lanky Negroes, short, squat Negroes; black ones, brown ones, yellow ones; men standing idle on the curb, women, bundle-laden, trudging reluctantly homeward, children rattle-trapping about the sidewalks; here and there a white face drifted along, but Negroes predominantly, overwhelmingly everywhere. There was assuredly no doubt of his whereabouts. This was Negro Harlem. (3)

The naive country-boy, a fugitive from a law he has no reason to trust in the South, is conned into drug dealing in Harlem and is finally arrested. Yet while this rendition of the plot would simply lead to a negation of the story's title ("Harlem is no City of Refuge"), its ending has an additional twist: Ever since his arrival in Harlem, the spectacular figure of a black policeman has enthralled Gillis. Unthinkable in the South, the black policeman guarantees civil rights; he is proof to Gillis that indeed "in Harlem, black was white."

This is why, at the end of the story, he stops resisting his arrest when a black policeman approaches him. Although in fact Harlem turns out to be no city of refuge for Gillis (the law catches up with him), in a larger sense it fulfills its promise since it guarantees Gillis the reassurance and protection of a black policeman. In this sense, Fisher subtly describes Harlem's promise as both an illusion and a reality.

SYMBOLIC PLACES IN HARLEM

In "The New Negro," Locke had described Harlem as a place where the heterogeneous mixture of class, nationality, and culture was not a reason for conflict, but a source of a new racial consciousness. Harlem Renaissance writers have found many ways of narrating this notion of tension and unity, and conspicuously many found the images for this notion in the streets of Harlem themselves. Harlem, in fiction, is thus never only a locale, but always also a motif, as De Jongh reminds us (1, 15). While my examples of urban symbolic spaces—the grid, the airshaft, and the cabaret—are all images for Locke's notion of "union out of diversity," they are also able to concretize and problematize Locke's ideal. A particularly apt fictional counterpiece to Locke's manifesto is a vignette by Fisher that combines topography with representation. The beginning of the short story "Blades of Steel" describes Harlem as a site of class struggle, evoking Seventh and Lenox Avenues as the location of (respectively) rich and poor Harlemites; but Fisher expresses the idea of unity through a connecting street (135th Street), an image that, given the grid of Manhattan's topography, spells an "H," for Harlem, Heart, and possibly Home:

> Negro Harlem's three broad highways form the letter H, Lenox and Seventh Avenues running parallel northward, united a little above their midpoints by east-and-west 135th Street.
>
> Lenox Avenue is for the most part the boulevard of the unperfumed; "rats" they are often termed. Here, during certain hours, there is nothing unusual in the flashing of knives, the quick succession of pistol shots, the scream of a police-whistle or a woman.
>
> But Seventh Avenue is the promenade of the high-toned dickties and strivers. It breathes a superior atmosphere, sings superior songs, laughs a superior laugh. Even were there no people, the difference would be clear: the middle of Lenox Avenue is adorned by street-car tracks, the middle of Seventh Avenue by parking.
>
> These two highways, frontiers of the opposed extreme of dark-skinned social life, are separated by an intermediate any-man's land, across which they communicate

chiefly by way of 135th Street. Accordingly 135th Street is the heart and soul of black Harlem; it is common ground, the natural scene of unusual contacts, a region that disregards class. It neutralizes, equilibrates, binds, rescues union out of diversity. (132)

Typically for Fisher, this scene personifies urban space: The streets are almost as important as the people. Also typically, the excerpt abounds in exaggeration and stereotypes, mocking the public's expectations and sensationalism. Fisher thus succeeds in signaling his awareness of Harlem's mythical status while simultaneously expressing an original image of conflict and communication that is itself grounded in Harlem's topography. In this vignette, Harlem writes its own story, it spells its own name.

Fisher created many "contact zones" such as 135th Street, the most inventive of which is the airshaft, a place that is featured in many of his stories.[6] The airshaft, a quintessentially urban space, connotes the simultaneity of community and separation: Sounds, smells, and views abound in this narrow space, although their producers are separated by it. In "The City of Refuge," the airshaft is a conglomeration of acoustic and olfactory waste, "a sewer of sounds and smells" (6)—something like a parody of Locke's idea of Harlem as the "concentration [...] of so many diverse elements of Negro life." In "The Promised Land," Fisher uses the airshaft as the place within which the various generations and their different musical cultures are contrasted and reconciled as "two futile prayers": "The one was a prayer for the love of a man, the other was a prayer for the love of God: 'blues,' and a spiritual" (48). The airshaft helps us recognize the urban condition and the potential of literary representation; this is especially true for the voyeurism that the illuminated windows allow, which in itself transforms the neighbor into a spectacle (for instance, the woman arranging her hair in "The City of Refuge" [6]).

Yet another important symbolic place in Harlem is the cabaret. Günter H. Lenz has analyzed the cabaret as a liminal space in which social order is suspended and new relationships can be explored (321–24). More than streets and airshafts, the cabaret is a place that is characterized as authentically African American: Patrons and musicians come here for the communal experience of jazz. While everyday life might have little to do with the Harlem Renaissance, the cabaret is a site in which black culture finds triumphant expression. There is hardly a text about Harlem in the 1920s that does not mention the cabaret. Most of them celebrate its modern expressiveness, the rhythmic dynamics, the interaction between men and women (and same-sex couples), the racial interaction between blacks and whites. However, writers have not only celebrated the place, they have also problematized it, exposing the illusion.

Sexually, it is important to recognize the cabaret as a place not only of heterosexual freedom, where Victorian morals were suspended, but also of homosexuality that was treated with singular openness during the 1920s.[7] But if the cabaret was a place to explore heterosexual, gay, lesbian, or nondefined sexual identity, it was also a place of anxiety and repulsion. Larsen, for example, in her novel *Quicksand* (1928), portrays the cabaret from the perspective of Helga Crane, a middle-class woman who feels threatened by the licentiousness of the place that to her is nothing but a repetition of the sexual and racial exploitation she experiences daily. Helga's reaction echoes that of Ray in Claude McKay's novel *Home to Harlem*. In contrast to his friend Jake, who enjoys Harlem as a sexualized place, Ray feels threatened by the gender roles he sees himself confined to. In order to evade the pressure of becoming a "Harlem nigger strutting his stuff" (264), he leaves Harlem for Europe. Both Helga and Ray love and hate Harlem, both of them experience it as claustrophobic. For Helga, Harlem is "too cramped, too uncertain, too cruel" (96); and McKay writes, "Harlem! How terrible Ray could hate it sometimes. Its ... promiscuous thickness" (267).

In terms of race, the cabaret proved also more complicated than advertised. The segregation in classy cabarets such as the Cotton Club, where white patrons were exclusively permitted to listen to black musicians, demonstrated that racist spatial politics did not stop at Harlem. Even without segregation, the white fascination for blackness created ambivalent reactions. Again, Fisher puts into words the complex dynamics between white visitors and black Harlemites. In his 1927 article "The Caucasian Storms Harlem," he mockingly describes how the white slummers, with their craze for black dancing, push him and other black regulars from the ballroom floor. But instead of bemoaning that blacks are only spectacular objects in the white gaze, as Nathan Huggins would, Fisher uses the cabaret as his own laboratory and turns the gaze around: "Now Negroes go to their own cabarets to see how white people act" (81). The white fascination for and exotization of blackness is transformed into a black fascination for and amusement with white people who act black, dancing the "black-bottom" better than the author himself. Fisher's essay comments on the possible social consequences of slumming, consequences that suggest the idea of communication and mutual respect, if not the abolishment of racial boundaries. At the end of his essay, Fisher expresses the hope that white people might gain awareness through participation in black culture: "Maybe these Nordics have at last tuned in on our wavelength. Maybe they are at last learning to speak our language" (82). Even so, the generally critical tone of his essay makes him sound rather doubtful. When Fisher envies the white dancers, it is not only because they dance better than him, but also because their blackness is a game ("we see them play Negro games" [81]) that has no consequences for their everyday experience of race.[8]

PLACE AND AUTHENTICITY

I would like to conclude with a consideration of the problem of place and authenticity. After all, place is not only the hybrid space where often highly contradictory things happen simultaneously; place also—and in some contradiction to its other character—radiates the notion of authenticity. In the light of what has been called Harlem's Second Renaissance (for instance, by then-mayor Rudy Giuliani), the question of whom Harlem "belongs" to—for whom Harlem is the "authentic" place—is of no little importance. The gentrification of Harlem that has been going on since the 1980s signifies two contradictory things: On the one hand, it registers the economic consolidation of the neighborhood, the long overdue restoration of buildings, and a return of Harlem to public consciousness beyond the connotations of inner city ghetto and criminality; on the other hand, it means the displacement of thousands who can no longer keep abreast of the rising real estate prices. Harlem has attracted not only international tourists, but also new Harlemites: an African American middle class and young urban professionals from all ethnic backgrounds, along with a new wave of Caribbean and African immigration.

In many ways, the contemporary changes in Harlem are as drastic as those of the 1920s, and in this respect, the moniker "Second Harlem Renaissance" might have its validity. And while a thorough discussion of contemporary Harlem would be a digression, the changes pose important theoretical questions about the nature of place that throws light on the ongoing making and remaking of Harlem. Did the Harlem of the Renaissance belong to African Americans? Had it belonged to European Americans before that? To whom does it now belong? These are questions about place as much as about race. In light of the history of Harlem, and in consideration of the theoretical problems of racial essentialism (a very non-"Renaissance" idea at that), the notion of "ownership" must be rejected. Claiming that Harlem belongs to African Americans is as problematic as claiming that the country club belongs to European Americans. Yet it is exactly the racialization of space, in which prime real estate predominantly signifies whiteness (in which the country club remains "white"), that makes it necessary for African Americans to continue to fight for Harlem.

Theoretically, the example of Harlem underscores the fact that space is both "lived" and "signified" (Keith 529); it is both the ground on which history takes place and always already a cultural sign (in this case, a sign for black urban culture). Michael Keith writes that "places are both the conditions of possibility and the expressive modality of identities" (529). As such, Harlem has been and continues to be both the place where the Renaissance historically could and did happen and a site that expresses urban black identities. During the Harlem Renaissance, these two aspects were already well developed. In reading Harlem Renaissance writing, it is worthwhile and fascinating to acknowledge and identify these two aspects of (racialized) place.

NOTES

1. Wallace Thurman, in his novel *Infants of the Spring* (1932), took up the expression but reversed Park's optimism: "Harlem has become a state of mind, peopled with improbable monsters" (222).
2. The artists of Harlem found their own spaces, including galleries and literary salons; of these, A'Lelia Walker's "Dark Tower" was one of the classiest, and "Niggerati Manor"—a rooming house for artists sponsored by Iolanthe Sidney, possibly the most notorious (see Watson 140–144). Rents, always higher for blacks than for whites, doubled between 1919 and 1927. A 1928 sample shows that Harlem families paid 45% of their wages for housing (Osofsky 137).
3. The term "contact zone" is of course taken from Mary Louise Pratt.
4. I am borrowing the term "symbolic geography" from Robert Stepto's *From Behind the Veil*, without following his detailed application of Victor Turner's anthropology (66–69).
5. Stepto's symbolic geography concludes with the "journey of immersion," the turning away from the northern cities and the return South, an immersion into the "roots" of African American culture.
6. See "City of Refuge," "The Promised Land," "Guardian of the Law," "John Archer's Nose," and the unpublished story "Across the Airshaft," which is paraphrased in Deutsch.
7. For an analysis of Harlem as a "queer Mecca," see my "Looking for Harlem."
8. For a more thorough analysis of the various interethnic gazes in 1920s and 1930s Harlem tourism, see my "Making Strange."

WORKS CITED

Baker, Houston A. *Modernism and the Harlem Renaissance.* Chicago: U of Chicago P, 1987.

Balshaw, Maria. *Looking for Harlem: Urban Aesthetics in African-American Literature.* London: Pluto, 2000.

De Jongh, James. *Vicious Modernism: Black Harlem and the Literary Imagination.* Cambridge: Cambridge UP, 1990.

Deutsch, Leonard J. "Rudolph Fisher's Unpublished Manuscripts." *Obsidian* 6 (1980): 82–97.

Fisher, Rudolph. *The City of Refuge. The Collected Short Stories of Rudolph Fisher.* Ed. John McCluskey. Columbia: U of Missouri P, 1987.

———. "The Caucasian Storms Harlem." *Voices from the Harlem Renaissance.* Ed. Nathan I. Huggins. New York: Oxford UP, 1995. 74–82.

Huggins, Nathan I. *Harlem Renaissance.* New York: Oxford UP, 1971

Hughes, Langston. *The Big Sea.* 1940. New York: Hill and Wang, 1993.

Hutchinson, George. *The Harlem Renaissance in Black and White.* Cambridge: Harvard UP, 1995.

Johnson, James Weldon. *Black Manhattan.* New York: Knopf, 1930.

———. "The Making of Harlem." *Survey Graphic* 6 (March 1925): 635–39.

Keith, Michael. "Identity and the Spaces of Authenticity." *Theories of Race and Racism.* Ed. Les Back and John Solomos. New York: Routledge, 2000. 521–38.

Larsen, Nella. *Quicksand* and *Passing*. 1928, 1929. New Brunswick: Rutgers UP, 1986.

Lenz, Günter H. "Symbolic Space, Communal Rituals, and the Surreality of the Urban Ghetto: Harlem in Black Literature from the 1920s to the 1960s." *Callaloo* 11 (Spring 1988): 309–45.

Lewis, David Levering. *When Harlem Was in Vogue*. New York: Oxford UP, 1981.

Löbbermann, Dorothea. "'Looking for Harlem': (Re)Konstruktionen Harlems als *queer Mecca, 1925–1995*." *Amerikastudien/American Studies* 46.1 (2001): 55–69.

———. "'Making Strange' in Tourism: Harlem through European Eyes in the 1920s and 1930s." *Comparative Sites of Ethnicity: Europe and the Americas*. Eds. Carmen Birkle et al. Heidelberg: C. Winter, 2004. 63–78.

Locke, Alain. "The New Negro." 1925. *The New Negro*. Ed. Alain Locke. New York: Atheneum, 1992. 3–16.

McKay, Claude. *Home to Harlem*. 1928. Boston: Northeastern UP, 1987.

Osofsky, Gilbert. *Harlem: The Making of a Ghetto. Negro New York, 1890–1930*. New York: Harper, 1966.

Park, Robert E. "The City: Suggestions for the Investigation of Human Behavior in the Urban Environment." *The City*. Eds. Robert E Park et al. 1915/1925. Chicago: U of Chicago P, 1967. 1–46.

Stepto, Robert. *From Behind the Veil: A Study of Afro-American Narrative*. Urbana: U of Illinois P, 1979.

Thurman, Wallace. *Infants of the Spring*. 1932. Boston: Northeastern UP, 1992.

Watson, Steven. *The Harlem Renaissance: Hub of African-American Culture, 1920–1930*. New York: Pantheon, 1995.

CHAPTER TWO

Literary Retrospection in the Harlem Renaissance

CLAUDIA STOKES

In 1925, book collector and Harlem Renaissance patron Arthur A. Schomburg began the essay "The Negro Digs Up His Past," published in Alain Locke's landmark anthology *The New Negro* (1925), by proclaiming that the "American Negro must remake his past in order to make his future. ... So among the rising democratic millions we find the Negro thinking more collectively, more retrospectively than the rest, and opt out of the very pressure of the present to become the most enthusiastic antiquarian of them all" (231). These words might be surprising to the beginning student of the Harlem Renaissance, seduced by the period's ebullience and transgressive energies into perceiving the period as heralding a decisive, refreshing break from the past rather than as the product of revitalized retrospection. However, as any introductory discussion of the definition and connotations of the word "renaissance" must inevitably reveal, a renaissance typically entails the return to and reengagement with the texts of the past as a way of inspiring fresh considerations of the present and the future. The Harlem Renaissance is no exception to this paradigm, as visible not only in the frequency with which Harlem Renaissance writers directly discussed their literary forebears, among them Frederick Douglass and Paul Laurence Dunbar, but also in the publication of such works as *The Book of American Negro Poetry* (1922), edited by James Weldon Johnson, which made the black literary past newly available to interested readers. Just as courses in literary modernism cause students to reconsider the basis of the modern in the less-than-modern, classroom pedagogy of the Harlem Renaissance must also negotiate the period's avant-garde innovations with its "antiquarian" impulses, whether in its frequent use of the literary past as source material or in its adaptation to the conditions of the Harlem Renaissance present.

Some of these products of literary retrospection are more immediately recognizable as such, as with Langston Hughes's celebrated poem "The Negro Speaks of Rivers" (1921), whose black persona ruminates on ancient civilizations and rivers "ancient as the world and older than the / flow of human blood in human veins." Harlem Renaissance writers often turned to the more recent past with the frequent recruitment of oral narrative and blues lyrics. For example, Sterling Brown's 1927 poem "Odyssey of Big Boy" took this conscription as its starting point, as with its opening identification with black folk heroes—"Lemme be wid Casey Jones, / Lemme be wid Stagolee"—to craft a black American riff on Homer's *Odyssey*, albeit one traveling the migratory trajectory of North-bound blacks. Similarly, Zora Neale Hurston's *Mules and Men* (1935) may (and probably should) be construed as an anthropological revisitation of the same narrative terrain mined by Joel Chandler Harris to such acclaim in the late nineteenth century, a derivation made explicit by Franz Boas in the introduction to his former student's work.[1] However, in narrative texts that elect a less vernacular voice, this engagement with the African American literary past may be less readily visible to beginning students of literature, though the influences on such texts are no less powerful and important. By way of explication, I turn to two autobiographies central to the Harlem Renaissance, despite the fact that both texts were published at the historical periphery of the period: James Weldon Johnson's *Autobiography of an Ex-Colored Man* (1912) and Langston Hughes's *The Big Sea* (1940).[2] Both works demonstrate the necessity of reading texts of the Harlem Renaissance with an eye toward the black literary past, a practice especially germane in the study of autobiography of the period, which often references its generic antecedents in the slave narrative.

At first glance, the slave narrative genre might seem too historically remote, too staid and scripted to have exerted much influence on the heady, improvisatory modernism of the Harlem Renaissance. However, Johnson's 1912 novel—despite its foray into the glittering world of popular music, nightclubs, and crossings, both racial and geographical, that we typically associate with the Harlem Renaissance—tells another story. Even students lacking a working knowledge of the basic conventions of the slave narrative genre quickly alight upon the novel's curious style: its flat, matter-of-fact tone; its emotional detachment, despite its claim to be an intimate chronicle of a man's painful journey through racial socialization and resocialization; its episodic organization; its quick, shallow depictions of character; its projection outward toward a social panorama at the expense of the narrator's interiority and consciousness. All of these stylistic features can make for a productive class discussion of the emotional and even narratological consequences of the white supremacy the novel's narrator endures, and yet these features also identify to the trained eye and ear the stylistic fingerprint of the slave narrative, the nineteenth-century (and even earlier) literary organ of abolition that employed one person's experience solely as a window onto a wider culture of race-based oppression and whose obsessive emphasis on the evidentiary produced a near-robotic authorial voice.

Points of contact between the *Autobiography* and the slave narrative abound. Johnson's novel quickly situates itself in relation to this genre with the first words of the third paragraph, "I was born in a little town of Georgia" (5), words that echo the signature slave narrative opening, repeated in the opening of Henry Bibb's 1849 narrative, "I was born May 1815, of a slave mother, in Shelby County, Kentucky" (441). Typical of the slave narrative, the narrator of Johnson's novel is the product of an illegitimate union between a black mother and a white father he hardly knows and recollects with shadowy imprecision. The narrator's recollection of his childhood cleverness in helping an obtuse student cheat in a spelling bee right under the teacher's nose revises a conventional scene of the slave narrative, in which the author typically recounts her or his resourcefulness in acquiring literacy despite the legal injunction against it; one has only to recall Douglass's 1845 account of his learning the alphabet from maritime shipping notations and the white children he'd transformed into unwitting pedagogues to see the antecedents of this episode in Johnson's novel. The tense scene in which the narrator passes for white while onboard a train evokes Douglass's own escape from slavery by passing as a white sailor traveling north by train, recounted in *The Life and Times of Frederick Douglass* (1893). And like the slave narrative, Johnson's novel commences with a prefatory letter of endorsement, simply signed "The Publishers," vouching for its authenticity and importance, and rapidly closes upon the narrator's escape from the culture of racial oppression he has painstakingly documented.

Despite these many similarities, teachers of the Harlem Renaissance may also find it productive to invite students to consider the equally numerous points at which Johnson's novel seems to diverge from the slave narrative, to subvert, invert, and revise the conventions of the genre. This is particularly apparent in the novel's refusal to do the work of the slave narrative in allaying many common apprehensions of white readers; instead, the novel only seems to exploit prevalent anxieties—among them, the fears of race suicide and black male sexual predation of white women—exhorted in the white supremacist press and to dramatize the fulfillment of those fears. So, too, does the novel refrain from combating widespread anxieties about the black work ethic with an industrious, morally unimpeachable protagonist. Instead, Johnson's Ex-Colored Man is an indolent, itinerant spendthrift gambler and nightclub habitué whose election of stable employment coincides with his decision to suppress his racial heritage, a concurrence that throws into question the promises of a reliable black workforce offered in the nineteenth century by the slave narrative and in the early twentieth century by Booker T. Washington. The conservative ethical core of the slave narrative is nowhere visible in Johnson's novel and is replaced by a detachment and malaise that speak more to modernist sensibilities than to the fervent political evangelism of abolition. What to make, too, of the novel's foggy vagueness and lack of detail (names, places, and dates), which seem to be at odds with the evidentiary responsibilities of the slave narrative genre? Though Johnson's novel no doubt deviates from this generic convention, it may be productive to consider whether Johnson employs what Robert Stepto has termed the "rhetoric of omission" that he deems characteristic of Douglass's 1845 narrative, in which Douglass, like Johnson's narrator, claims to withhold identifying data to avoid incriminating others (105).[3] In this respect, Johnson may be imitating one slave narrative while diverging from others, and these other generic deviations at once reference and modernize the narrative and ideological conventions of the earliest forms of African American self-expression.

Johnson's enlistment of the slave narrative genre shouldn't come as much of a surprise. Though the viability and political utility of the slave narrative ended with Emancipation, the genre saw somewhat of a revival in the first years of the twentieth century with the publication of *Up from Slavery* (1901), the first autobiography of Johnson's early sponsor, Booker T. Washington, and a text that adhered to many of the conventions of the genre.[4] Indeed, in his introduction to the 1927 reissue of the *Autobiography*, Carl Van Vechten, impresario of the Harlem Renaissance, remarked upon the similarities of Johnson's novel to Washington's autobiography, presuming this more recent example of the genre to be Johnson's primary source of influence (26). Attentive readers can also detect references to Douglass scattered throughout the novel, as with the protagonist's boyhood adoration of Douglass and the portrait of Douglass that hangs in the nightclub that occupies a central role in the novel. It is worth mentioning, too, that Johnson's own genuine autobiography, *Along This Way* (1933), not only elaborates at length on the "worshipful awe" he felt for Douglass and his reading of Douglass's narratives (201) but also begins with a kind of slave narrative itself, recounting his family origins in the slave trade in Haiti and Nassau during the early nineteenth century. Though the book eventually comes to discuss his involvement in the Harlem Renaissance and the writing of such works as the *Autobiography of an Ex-Colored Man* and *Black Manhattan* (1930), its commencement with Johnson's own family's origin in slavery suggests that the history of the black present must necessarily begin with a discussion of slavery, an organizational premise that may be useful for teachers and students attempting to gloss his earlier adaptation of the slave narrative genre in 1912.

A discussion of the generic sources of Johnson's novel may also help teachers address the common misconception among students that the novel is in fact

Johnson's own autobiography. Johnson himself orchestrated this mistaken belief in 1912 by suppressing his authorship and passing the novel off as an authentic auto-biography, a ploy designed to stimulate sales by generating speculation about the identity of the incognito author (Levy 126–27). This generic confusion between autobiography and novel, between fact and fiction, plays on the preoccupations and devices of the very earliest examples of black narrative and self-expression in the American nineteenth century. Johnson's calculated entanglement of fact with fiction would have bedeviled authors and publishers of slave narratives, for whom nothing could have been worse than the allegation of similar confusion. To rebut these accusations from slavery's defenders, slave narrative authors and publishers bent over backwards to evince their texts' total facticity by providing a wealth of verifiable data and corroborating documents. What's more, the first black-authored published novel, William Wells Brown's *Clotel, or The President's Daughter* (1853), plaited together fact and fiction by prefacing the novel with an abbreviated account of Brown's previously published autobiographical slave narrative, *Narrative of William W. Brown, a Fugitive Slave, Written by Himself* (1847). Though clearly indebted to its own generic antecedents—Stowe's *Uncle Tom's Cabin* (1851), for instance—Brown's novel imaginatively elaborates upon the enduring rumor of Thomas Jefferson's sexual relationship with his slave Sally Hemming, thereby further entwining the fictional with the factual. In deliberately exploiting his readers' confusion, Johnson's novel, then, may be construed as pay-ing homage to the form and reception history of black-authored narrative in the United States.

Renowned for its lively portraits of many of the central figures of the Harlem Renaissance, Langston Hughes's 1940 autobiography, *The Big Sea*, however, begins by announcing its denunciation of such literary history. Rather than starting with the conventional "I was born" opening that threads through black autobiography well into the twentieth century or even with the familial slave prehistory that opens Johnson's own 1933 autobiography, Hughes begins by relating an anecdote in which he, at age twenty-one, tossed overboard the *S.S. Malone* "all the books [he] had had at Columbia [where he'd briefly been a student], and all the books [he] had lately bought to read" (3). "It was like throwing a million bricks out of my heart," he wrote, "for it wasn't only the books that I wanted to throw away, but everything unpleasant out of my past. … I wanted to be a man on my own, control of my own life, and go on my own way. I was twenty-one. So I threw the books in the sea" (98). A supreme gesture of anti-antiquarianism, as it were, this stunning opening scene prepares the reader for an unconventional narrative that at once documents a writer's struggle to find his own way outside the literary tradition he dramatically ejects and itself employs unconventional technique to tell that story. To a degree, *The Big Sea* fulfills both expectations, as with Hughes's unlikely career as a seaman and his employment of some unconventional literary devices, such as his beginning paragraphs with the exclamation, "Listen, everybody!" (201).

As such, Hughes's autobiography would seem a far cry from the historicist sensibility Schomburg imputed to the Harlem Renaissance as well as the highly conventional, formulaic slave narrative, which required authors to demonstrate at every turn their familiarity with and adherence to literary custom. However, this opening gesture can be construed as deriving from the very literary traditions that the twenty-one-year-old Hughes claimed to eschew. His explanation for jettisoning his library—"I wanted to be a man on my own, control of my own life, and go on my own way"—equates manhood and self-determination with literary control and independence, a long-standing formulation also espoused by writers and publishers of slave narratives in the nineteenth century. Abolitionist presses famously wielded an iron editorial grip to prevent fugitive slave authors from exerting too much independence in their narratives or from emphasizing their own private experiences at the expense of the wider panoramic commitments of the genre. In this way, the struggle for literary control and the literary expression of selfhood underwrites the genre of the slave narrative, a struggle that found its most celebrated articulation in Douglass's 1845 narrative, as he resisted the conventions of the genre—either through his silences or through generically irregular poetic flights such as the famous apostrophe to the ships on the Chesapeake—to stake out a highly individualized voice among the hordes of nearly identical narratives. That is, Douglass experienced the same intertwined struggle for literary and personal independence as Hughes, but was more successful than most of his fellow slave authors in resisting editorial control for the expression of selfhood. Moreover, Hughes's equation of manhood with literary independence revises Douglass's 1845 renowned remark, "You have seen how a man was made a slave; you shall see how a slave was made a man" (60), a transformation enabled by Douglass's resistance to supervisory authority, both immediate (in the figure of Mr. Covey) and literary. For both men, the assumption of manhood is contingent on the assumption of literary control and self-determination, and Hughes's autobiography communicates the endurance of this struggle for black writers well into the twentieth century.

The Big Sea also modifies other conventions of the black-authored autobiography inaugurated by the slave narrative, among them the family structures typical of fugitive slave authors. Though Hughes's father is not the absentee white plantation owner common to such narratives, he nonetheless assumes the trappings of this role by his near-total absence throughout Hughes's life and his oft-stated contempt for people of color, having internalized the white supremacy he'd fled by moving to Mexico. Similarly, Hughes commences his autobiography, as many slave narratives had, with a scene of travel between Africa and North America. However, whereas earlier texts, among them James Albert Ukawsaw

Gronniosaw's narrative of 1772 and Olaudah Equiano's of 1789, began with the authors' memories of Africa and passage to North America, Hughes's autobiography reverses this trajectory, with his journey from North America to Africa, Dakar in particular. Hughes's joyful recounting of this trip also markedly contrasts with the grief expressed by fugitive slave authors upon recalling their own travels. His trip backtracks over the crossings of his generic forebears, only to find no homecoming among Africans who regard him purely as an American because of his family's interbreeding with Native Americans and whites.

Teachers of the Harlem Renaissance might ask their students to consider the consequences of these generic legacies and modifications. Do they communicate the ineluctability of generic history or even race history? The enduring fingerprint of slavery in African Americans' lives and narratives, despite its abolition long before? The impossibility of making a definitive rupture with one's own cultural, narrative, and political history? The pursuit of these questions should by no means be limited to a discussion of these two texts, Johnson's *Autobiography of an Ex-Colored Man* and Hughes's *Big Sea*. To consider the generic customs for narrating black female experience, class analysis of such canonical novels as Hurston's *Their Eyes Were Watching God* (1937) or Jessie Fauset's *Plum Bun* (1929) would profit from a comparison to female-authored narratives such as Harriet Jacobs's *Incidents in the Life of a Slave Girl* (1861) to examine the literary history of black women's self-expression and the ways in which Harlem Renaissance female writers employ or revise the techniques originated by female fugitive slaves. And to consider the multiple layers of generic influence on the literature of Harlem Renaissance, teachers may urge students to examine how such novels as Wallace Thurman's *The Blacker the Berry* (1929) and George Schuyler's *Black No More* (1931) display a clear debt to Johnson's 1912 novel, revising and elaborating on his thematics of color and narrative premise, a circuit of influence that renders these later texts, however improbable it may at first seem, second-generation adaptations of the slave narrative. Such a line of inquiry may cause students to awaken to the historical significance of literary genre, which brings about the interface of texts separated by time and space,[5] and to observe that even innovations have their antecedents. In this way, students themselves may develop their own intellectual antiquarian habits.

NOTES

1. Boas wrote, "Ever since the time of Uncle Remus, Negro folklore has exerted a strong attraction upon the imagination of the American public." He differentiated Hurston's work from Harris's, however, with the qualifier that in prior collections of folklore "the intimate setting in the social life of the Negro has been given very inadequately" (xiii).

2. Though published several years before the formal commencement of the Harlem Renaissance, Johnson's novel enjoyed a second life once reissued by Carl Van Vechten in 1927, whereupon it received the critical acclaim and attention it failed to receive fifteen years earlier. Also, there is some discrepancy in the spelling of the novel's title: Though originally spelled "Ex-Colored," the novel's title changed with the 1927 Van Vechten reissue, which elected the more Anglophilic "Ex-Coloured." To honor Johnson's own orthographic choice, literary critics traditionally use the original spelling of the novel's title, a decision I have concurred with.

3. Johnson's narrator explains the omission of specifics on the grounds that "there are still people living there who would be connected with this narrative" (5).

4. According to Johnson's biographer, Eugene Levy, Johnson played Du Bois and Washington against each other to his own careerist advantage, refraining from joining Du Bois's Niagara Movement, joining the Washington-aligned National Negro Business League, and landing his ambassadorial post because of Washington's influence (103–05).

5. For a more fully elaborated discussion of this dynamic, see Dimock.

WORKS CITED

Bibb, Henry. "Narrative of the Life and Adventures of Henry Bibb." 1849. *Slave Narratives*. Eds. William L. Andrews and Henry Louis Gates, Jr. New York: Library of America, 2000. 425–566.

Boas, Franz. Preface. *Mules and Men*. By Zora Neale Hurston. 1935. New York: Harper, 1990.

Brown, Sterling. "Odyssey of Big Boy." *The Collected Poems of Sterling A. Brown*. Ed. Michael S. Harper. New York: Harper, 1980. 20–21.

Dimock, Wai Chee. *Through Other Continents: American Literature across Deep Time*. Princeton: Princeton UP, 2006.

Douglass, Frederick. "Narrative of the Life of Frederick Douglass, an American Slave." 1845. *Frederick Douglass: Autobiographies*. Ed. Henry Louis Gates, Jr. New York: Library of America, 1994. 1–102.

Hughes, Langston. "The Negro Speaks of Rivers." *The Collected Poems of Langston Hughes*. Ed. Arnold Rampersad. New York: Vintage, 1994. 23.

———. *The Big Sea*. 1940. New York: Hill and Wang, 1963.

Johnson, James Weldon. "Autobiography of an Ex-Colored Man." 1912. *James Weldon Johnson: Writings*. Ed. William L. Andrews. New York: Library of America, 2004. 5–124.

———. "Along This Way." 1933. *James Weldon Johnson: Writings*. Ed. William L. Andrews. New York: Library of America, 2004. 125–606.

Levy, Eugene. *James Weldon Johnson: Black Leader, Black Voice*. Chicago: U of Chicago P, 1973.

Schomberg, Arthur A. "The Negro Digs Up His Past." *The New Negro*. Ed. Alain Locke. 1925. New York: Macmillan, 1992.

Stepto, Robert B. *From Behind the Veil: A Study of Afro-American Narrative*. Urbana: U of Illinois P, 1979.

Van Vechten, Carl. Introduction [to *The Autobiography of an Ex-Coloured Man*.] 1927. *Critical Essays on James Weldon Johnson*. Eds. Kenneth M. Price and Lawrence J. Oliver. New York: GK Hall, 1997.

CHAPTER THREE

Harlem Polemics, Harlem Aesthetics

WILLIAM J. MAXWELL

At first glance, the Harlem Renaissance challenges the reigning wisdom among academic literary critics that conceptual categories such as periods and movements are unable to capture the genuine texture of cultural history. The idea of a renaissance of African American culture headquartered in black New York between the world wars was an idea of that place and of that time. When writers such as Countee Cullen, Langston Hughes, Zora Neale Hurston, Nella Larsen, Claude McKay, and Jean Toomer allowed their poems and stories to be reprinted in Alain Locke's signal 1925 anthology, *The New Negro*, they were aware they would be grouped together as evidence of a black rebirth starring Harlem-connected artists. When we today employ the classification of the Harlem or the New Negro Renaissance to refer to many of the highlights of African American literary modernism, we thus reflect the self-classification accepted, however strategically or fitfully, by most of the figures associated with the movement.

To the eye trained by American and European artistic modernisms, the Harlem Renaissance in fact looks like an example of the least deniable, most voluntary of early twentieth-century artistic groupings: the avant-garde. Like Dadaism, futurism, surrealism, and the rest of the experimental avant-garde "-isms," the Harlem Renaissance declared itself a striving, collective, and metropolitan enterprise with a taste for the new in article after manifesto. (The Harlem movement's love affair with novelty was indeed strong enough to inspire real and imaginary bodily makeovers: Among other things, the idea of a New Negro was an ideal of embodied avant-gardism in which making it new reached past the page to the author's physical presence.) If Harlem's renaissance did not always target the romantic idea of the solitary, inspired artistic genius, it undoubtedly bet that Harlem's sponsorship of an unprecedentedly large community of black artists would kill off the isolating doctrine of "one black writer at a time," a doctrine that had affected consumption patterns of African American literature since the eighteenth century. Again like the modernist avant-gardes, convinced of the far-reaching social effects of enfolding art back into the practice of everyday life, the ultimate aims of the Harlem Renaissance vaulted well beyond the artistic realm. Although the Renaissance was less optimistic than its European counterparts about the revolutionary potential of smashing the glass case surrounding the true, beautiful, and autonomous middle-class artwork, it aspired to extend artistic reform and innovation into the brutal arena of American racial politics.

To view Harlem's renaissance solely through the lens of the avant-garde, however, would be to neglect many of its other crucial understandings of itself: namely, its response to specifically African American economic, political, and artistic histories; its claims to unveil a previously repressed, specifically black, African, or African American style or quintessence; and its commitment to the *rebirth* of a specifically black cultural power announced in the Renaissance's very name. The Harlem Renaissance, then, was an avant-garde movement with a critical difference. The innovation of its proponents was generally less interested in producing shocking goodbyes to a toxic Western past than in fashioning reconnections with modes of African culture interrupted only by the deadly economics of racial slavery and imperialism. Yet the effort to recuperate the past of Africa and Africanness was in many Renaissance hands the furthest thing from primitivism. For all the talk of "ancestral arts" and of African alternatives to the alienations of industrial capitalism, the movement's recovery of a mighty and subtle continent before the fall into European bondage was designed to aid the growth of a proudly fresh, proudly modern African American self.

In this we find a partnership of past and present stemming from what black British theorist Stuart Hall would term an act of "imaginary reunification." All the same, it would be a mistake to envision the Renaissance's creation of a usable African past as freely chosen. As Hall himself reminds us, cultural "identities are the names we give to the different ways we are positioned by, and position ourselves in, the narratives of the past"; while neither unchanging cores nor inevitable destinies, these identities "come from somewhere, have histories" (225). Harlem Renaissance thinkers composed tales of the ties between modernizing Afro-America and premodern Africa in part because they were compelled to correct racists whose narratives of black identity had insisted that people of African descent either had no past or lived completely bound by it. Such correction of intellectual racism was a painful yet obligatory concern of the Harlem movement, and this concern was addressed most successfully in the Renaissance's rebuttal of eighteenth- and nine-teenth-century Euro-American charges that blacks were fundamentally incapable of producing literature. Henry Louis Gates Jr. has argued that such charges were directly linked to the burning question of black humanity and, therefore, to the morality of African slavery. "Philosophers and literary critics, such as Hume, Kant, Jefferson, and Hegel," Gates notes, "seemed to decide that the absence or presence of a written literature was the single measure of the potential, innate humanity of a race" (25). With its galaxy of talented, sometimes best-selling black writers and its insistence on their reproducibility, the Harlem Renaissance made it that much harder even for committed white supremacists to deny that African Americans had written themselves into the Enlightenment family of Man. Seemingly an entire generation of educated blacks had at once escaped commodity status through their possession of the humanizing commodity of literacy.

The onerous existential weight placed on the display of literary mastery exerted strong pressure on the work of the Harlem movement's two most influential historians from the Civil Rights years through the mid-1990s: David Levering Lewis, more recently the author of a massive, prize-wining biography of W.E.B. Du Bois, and the late Harvard professor Nathan Irvin Huggins. One of the few unambiguous successes Lewis was willing to grant the movement was what he called its demonstration of "the considerable creative capacities of the best and the brightest of a disadvantaged racial minority" (xliii). For his part, Huggins avowed that the Renaissance remained a "principal emotional resource" for African Americans, one "verifying" nothing less than "our manliness and womanliness" (4). Whatever its other late-twentieth-century meanings, then, the Harlem Renaissance continued to be regarded as an avant-garde saddled with an errand only racial slavery could demand—the burden of authenticating the full humanity of a people through singing prose and elegant couplets.

Those who have read more than a few books of Harlem Renaissance literature are probably suspicious of the definite article—the singular "the"—placed before the words "Harlem Renaissance." While the status of the term as a collective self-description may indicate that the movement is more than the concoction of later critics, it does not mean that there was or is solid consensus about the movement's causes, extent, nature, or significance. Huggins and Lewis, for their part, periodized the movement somewhat differently. The former opted for the most common dating of the Renaissance—from the close of World War I to the coming of the Great Depression—while the latter argued for the more precise bookends of 1917 through the March 1935 Harlem riot. More significant are their differences regarding the Renaissance's preconditions, motivations, and goals. Huggins, who gave the Harlem Renaissance to a 1970s shaped by the transatlantic renewal of black nationalisms and Pan-Africanisms, described a movement that played a role in the global challenge to European empire and cultural hegemony that followed the crack-up of World War I. He claims that the Harlem Renaissance was not an isolated African American development, "but part of a worldwide phenomenon" (8). In his view, the emergence of a determinedly new black artist in postwar New York was a partial consequence of what the philosopher Hegel called the irony of history. America and the European powers, seeking only to employ black troops as cannon fodder in another war to end all wars, inadvertently created conditions for the emergence of an international, anticolonial black consciousness. "[P]ulled out of their various traditional contexts and introduced to a world-view that had been previously available to only a few of them," explains Huggins, black troops "became conscious of one another—colonials with similar experiences under English-, French-, Portuguese-, or German-speaking masters" (6). Returning to Western capitals including New York, they built Pan-Africanist institutions and stoked a "voice of emerging black self-assertion" (6) that would cohere into cultural drives like the Harlem Renaissance.

David Levering Lewis, meanwhile, seemed intent on narrowing any international frame for the Renaissance. He laid down the definitional law in a single rich sentence: "The Harlem Renaissance was a somewhat forced phenomenon, a cultural nationalism of the parlor, institutionally encouraged and directed by the leaders of the national civil right establishment for the paramount purpose of improving race relations in a time of extreme national backlash, caused in large part by economic gains won by Afro-Americans during the Great War" (xv). Instead of a spontaneous upsurge of black fellow-feeling, we here find a Renaissance cooked up in an elite cultural laboratory; instead of a Pan-Africanism instigated by foot-soldiers, we have a cultural nationalism of the salon; instead of a willful seizing of the international anticolonial opportunities provided by World War I, we have a defensive and tightly national response to white racial backlash in the war's wake. These substitutions should not be attributed mainly to a cynical turn of mind. Writing well after Huggins's generation had retreated from high hopes about black nationalism at home and Pan-Africanism around the world, Lewis is concerned to account for the political disappointments of not one, but two Renaissances: Harlem's in the 1920s and the Black Arts Movement of the late-1960s and early 1970s that called itself "Renaissance II."

Lewis's conviction that these Renaissances had largely failed is, of course, dependent on a generous sense of their potentials. Lewis held the Harlem Renaissance to a torturously high standard: its success in winning acknowledgment not merely of black humanity but also of the final collapse of American racism. As literary historian George Hutchinson has noted, it's "hard to know how to respond to a critique for which the [measure] of an artistic movement is its effectiveness in ending centuries of oppression" (22). Yet Lewis's critique finds a basis in the movement's own secular faith that black writing might in itself be antiracist fighting. One of the points on which Lewis and Huggins agree is that Harlem Renaissance literature was African American politics by other means. Lewis draws on the psychoanalytic vocabulary to describe the Renaissance as a "cultural sublimation of civil rights" (xxiv), a formula that posits a deeply political black unconscious expressing itself in the socially acceptable language of art-making. Drop the words "civil rights" from the formula and add "black self-determination," and you have coined a phrase that would fit neatly into Huggins's work. Both Lewis and Huggins present movement histories in which the specifically artistic Harlem Renaissance oddly enough owes much to the first American "Red Scare," in which the black nationalist Marcus Garvey and the black socialists at the *Messenger*, the *Crusader*, and other radical Harlem journals were pressured, squelched, jailed, or deported along with other subversives in the early 1920s. "In an atmosphere of [severe] political repression," reasons Huggins, "the aggressive, optimistic, self assertive 'New Negro'" who had absorbed the anticolonial lessons of World War I "could best thrive as a cultural being, not as a political force" (9). As Lewis conceives it, however, thriving as a New Negro cultural being did not mean abandoning the terrain of American racial politics, but instead reconceiving it as ripe for artistic intervention. With a spoonful of scorn, Lewis describes a Renaissance program of "civil rights by copyright" presided over by Alain Locke and other liberal intellectuals associated with racial uplift groups such as the National Association for the Advancement of Colored People (NAACP) and the National Urban League (NUL). "It was the brilliant insight of the men and women associated with the NAACP and the NUL," Lewis writes, "that, although the road to the ballot box, the union hall, the decent neighborhood, and the office was blocked, there were two untried paths that had not been barred, in large part because of their very implausibility, as well as irrelevance to most Americans: arts and letters" (xxvi). Lewis never quite claims that Harlem Renaissance culture was a political gambit built to order for a tiny directorate of the black bourgeoisie, but he comes very close. What he says outright is that the confusion of racial art and racial politics was the Renaissance's foremost failing.

Even Lewis was forced to admit, however, that Renaissance literature would never have arisen had it not been for a massive relocation of the black working class voting with its feet against the Jim Crow South. Another proposition on which Lewis and Huggins agree—along with virtually every other historian of the Harlem Renaissance—is that the movement's New York affiliation and over-all metropolitan spirit were dependent on the Great Migration, the name given to the voluntary relocation of a large portion of the African American population from the South to the urban north that began in earnest with the industrial labor shortages of World War I. Between 1910 and 1930 alone, over 1,200,000 blacks abandoned the South for the cities of the Northeast and Midwest, ensuring that their numbers in the north increased by almost 300 percent. With the move northward came ample distance from the historical and symbolic ground of slavery, the transition of a majority of blacks from something like a peasantry to an urban (though not uniformly industrial) working-class, and the stimulating prospect of black electoral power. New York City was fertile soil for the invention of an artistic movement that would express and address these epochal changes of black urbanization. The growth of Manhattan's African American population was especially explosive: "in 1890, one in seventy people" there was black; "in 1930, one in every nine" (Douglas 73). The city boasted a long history of black performance in the arts, and a well-built community of new apartment houses, wide avenues, and elevated urban vistas—Harlem—that had just been opened to black residents. It was also the greatest crossroads of diasporic blacks on the planet, filling not only with migrants from Dixie, but with English- and French-speaking West Indians and the largest collection of African-born blacks in the New World. As George Hutchinson observes, the whole of Manhattan provided an unusual freedom of interracial relationships in addition to a concentration and diversity of black racial consciousness. In the New York of the 1920s, Harlem's Renaissance circle, Dorothy Parker's Algonquin Round Table, and Greenwich Village's bohemian-socialist scene were only a cab ride away from each other, and the residents of each took advantage of this fact. The relative ease of black-white contact helped to provide Harlem writers with unprecedented entree into an American publishing industry which had come to center in the city, ensuring that the Renaissance's key books would receive national distribution and a chance at an interracial mass audience. Altogether, then, the unique material and social conditions black intellectuals met in the New York of the late-teens and 1920s should leave us asking not why the explosion of modern African American writing was identified with a small section of uptown Manhattan, but how it could be associated with any other locale. The culture of African American transnationalism that Brent Hayes Edwards and other influential comparativist scholars now see as the Renaissance's greatest legacy could only be Harlem-born, if not Harlem-bound.

When it comes to their concentration on the Great Migration and the special circumstances of black New York, Huggins's and Lewis's accounts of the Harlem Renaissance are difficult to second-guess. Nevertheless, scholarship in the past decade by critics such as Paul Allen Anderson, A.B. Christa Schwarz, J. Martin Favor, Barbara Foley, Martha Jane Nadell, Marlon Ross, Joyce Moore Turner, Cheryl A. Wall, and myself has suggested that new models of the Harlem Renaissance are necessary given at least two decisive developments in African American intellectual life. The first development is the shuffling and expansion of the canon of Renaissance works caused by the rediscovery and republication of texts by authors such as Helene Johnson, Georgia Douglas Johnson, and Richard Bruce Nugent, once-ignored women, uncloseted gays and lesbians, radicals of nationalist and socialist stripes, and cultural producers in interartistic or supposedly subliterary genres. The second development is the emergence of a postmodern or "postsoul" black cultural theory which has challenged the interpretive criteria of combative social realism, and has questioned the possibility and desirability of speaking on behalf of a single, generic black identity.

I'd like to close by identifying four enabling problems that are fundamental in the ongoing reconception of the Harlem Renaissance that these developments in black intellectual life have forced, four of the intellectual hubs that the newer scholarship circles around as it revisits and redefines the movement. The four are as follows: first, the problem of the black self or subject of the Renaissance; second, the problem of the white friend of the Renaissance; third, the problem of the relations between Renaissance literature and vernacular culture; and fourth, the problem of the Renaissance's internal variety and competition. The first hub, that of the black self or subject of the Renaissance, has been made unignorable by black feminisms, black gay studies, and disparate post-structural currents flowing within black criticism. Simply put, it involves the annoyance some may feel when encountering Huggins's judgment that the Renaissance was a creation of *the* African American and *his* self-assertion, upholding the assumption that African Americans are a singular and at least emblematically male population. Speaking of "*the* black experience" before, during, and after the Harlem Renaissance has often been a way for African Americans to surmount ethnic, cultural, and gender differences in their community and to build black movements strong enough to contest a deeply rooted national racism. Yet as many Renaissance intellectuals understood, it is one of this racism's deepest predicates that black people all think, write, love, and look alike, and one of the few features of this racism that black art is supremely suited to remedy.

The second intellectual problem, that of the white friend of the Renaissance, involves related issues of "essence" and singleness. One of the longstanding criticisms of the Harlem Renaissance is that it was seduced and abandoned by its white fans and patrons, surprisingly bold neurotics bent on remaking the black artist as a point-by-point alternative to the supposedly rational and repressed modern Western individual. (This longstanding criticism was in fact coined in immediate post-Renaissance black writing and can be found near the heart of distinguished works such as Langston Hughes's short story collection *The Ways of White Folks* [1934] and Richard Wright's influential critical pronouncement "Blueprint for Negro Writing" [1937].) To active scholars led by George Hutchinson, however, this line of attack relies on a reductive understanding of white interest in the New Negroes and their art. No one suggests that Carl Van Vechten and other white inspectors of the Renaissance were selfless and colorblind, or always capable of transcending the underdevelopment of racial thought circa 1920. Rather, the developing consensus has it that picturing Van Vechten as a Jazz Age version of the (pre-Buddhist) Beastie Boys and categorizing all white interest under the headings of "appropriation" and "primitivism" neglects the complexity of the interracial interactions that helped to jump-start the Harlem movement. Such narrow coding also fails to explore the actual impact of white patronage on Harlem writers. It's telling, Hutchinson testifies, that Langston Hughes and Zora Neale Hurston, black authors linked to the Renaissance's most imperious white patron, the wealthy Charlotte Osgood Mason, were also those most convinced of the health and autonomy of common black culture. More often than not, commitments to racial self-assertion and to sometimes thorny interracial exchanges were entwined in the literary and emotional lives of Harlem intellectuals.

Let's now move to the third intellectual problem around which newer accounts of the movement often revolve, that of Renaissance literature and the black vernacular, or the ordinary, nonliterate culture of what the (pre-solo) Sly Stone called everyday people. In some classic studies of the Harlem movement, the Renaissance qualifies as the moment when elite black literature finally embraces the music and the folklore of the black masses, thus distancing itself from the suspicion of popular culture seen in the so-called high modernism of contemporaries T.S. Eliot and Ezra Pound. In other classic studies, including Lewis's, however, the Renaissance is remarkable precisely for *rejecting* the black vernacular, thus missing the chance to forge an indigenously black literature and to build an alliance of elite desires and popular energies. Perhaps the only thing these two types of studies share is the assumption that the stories, songs, and oral signifying of working-class African Americans offer direct access to the best, truest, and least racially compromised elements in black culture. As Lewis encapsulates the idea, music is central and vital in black life, whereas literature, however impressive, is decorative and marginal. Without second-guessing the consequential genius of black music in the modern world or its great importance in the making of black communities, newer studies of the Renaissance recognize the crudeness of metaphors of a flour-white literary crust and a chewy, authentic, whole-wheat vernacular center. (This forced metaphor doesn't accurately explain most bread, let alone the Harlem Renaissance.) The movement in fact witnessed a two-way commerce between African American writers and musicians. Duke Ellington's long residence at the Cotton Club certainly helped to shape the jazz poetry of Langston Hughes; but it's no less true that Ellington went on to envy Hughes's informal title of "Shakespeare in Harlem" and to write musical histories of black America—and of Shakespeare—inspired in part by Hughes's many works for children. It's also not an accident that the literary Renaissance was concurrent with the adoption of black blues and jazz by the white-capitalized recording industry. Ironically, ideas of the racial authenticity and authority of black music were honed by its new mass availability in the form of "race records" such as Mamie Smith's "Crazy Blues" (1920), the inaugural hit of the 1920s blues boom, and Louis Armstrong's "Heebie Jeebies" (1926), the first memorable appearance of scat singing on wax—records bought in the hundreds of thousands by whites and blacks alike.

The fourth and final intellectual problem frequently addressed in newer accounts of the Harlem Renaissance is that of the movement's internal variety and competition. If we try to acknowledge the plurality of modern black selves and communities, the complexity of white interests in the movement, and the mutual influence of black literature and black vernacular forms, we create a Renaissance characterized by heterogeneity and conflict, not a stable, consistent unit. In my book, this is not a bad thing, given the differences that David Levering Lewis, for example, must explain away when offering his one-sentence definition of the movement. Just a roll call of the Renaissance's operative stances indicates the problem of synthesis: The movement featured important writing in realist, naturalist, romantic, regionalist, and high- and folk-modernist modes; its creators' cultural politics ranged from an Afrocentric rejection of all things Western, to black cultural nationalism, to cultural pluralism, to outright assimilationism; and their electoral politics ran from Garveyism, to Communism, to artsy indifference, to tenacious support for the party of Lincoln. (One of the Renaissance's most insightful intellectual gadflies, George Schuyler, would in fact become a lonely African American advocate of Barry Goldwater's campaign against the Great Society.) Burgeoning black diversity was one of the things that brought writers to Harlem in the first place, and it is a rare Renaissance novel set in New York City that doesn't spend several pages enthusing over the many different shades of Harlem life. Consider this passage from Nella Larsen's engrossingly shifty novel *Quicksand* (1928), in which skin color and other physical differences glimpsed in a basement nightclub challenge the logical coherence of racial thinking and open up onto the cultural multiplicity of black Manhattan:

> For the hundredth time, she marveled at the gradations within this oppressed race of hers. A dozen shades slid by. There was sooty black, taupe, mahogany, bronze, copper, gold, orange, yellow, peach, ivory, pinky white, pastry white. There was yellow hair, brown hair, black hair; straight hair, straightened hair, curly hair, crinkly hair, wooly hair. She saw black eyes in white faces, brown eyes in yellow faces, gray eyes in brown faces, blue eyes in tan faces. Africa, Europe, perhaps a pinch of Asia, in a fantastic motley of ugliness and beauty, semibarbaric, sophisticated, exotic were here. (87)

Should this carnival of Harlem differences sound like a conceptual mess or a tired postmodern cliché, it's worth recalling that much newer scholarship assumes that there was indeed one definable project on which the various tendencies of the Harlem Renaissance agreed. In my opinion, and that of a good number of other active critics, the Renaissance is most accurately seen as a self-conscious, Harlem-centered field of sometimes overlapping, sometimes contradictory attempts by black artists to link African American identity and history to the idea and material circumstances of an increasingly worldly U.S. modernity. These attempts occasionally took the (characteristically modernist) form of nostalgia for a superior premodern past, but the underlying focus was on racializing the modern, and vice versa. Beneath the clashing voices of New Negroes at the Savoy Ballroom, the offices of the NAACP, and the bohemian parties of hair-care heiress A'Lelia Walker, the many factions of the Renaissance were dedicated to imagining the blackness of a young and still auspicious twentieth century.

WORKS CITED

Anderson, Paul Allen. *Deep River: Music and Memory in Harlem Renaissance Thought.* Durham: Duke UP, 2001.

Douglas, Ann. *Terrible Honesty: Mongrel Manhattan in the 1920s.* New York: Farrar, Straus and Giroux, 1994.

Edwards, Brent Hayes. *The Practice of Diaspora: Literature, Translation, and the Rise of Black Internationalism.* Cambridge: Harvard UP, 2003.

Favor, J. Martin. *Authentic Blackness: The Folk in the New Negro Renaissance.* Durham: Duke UP, 1999.

Foley, Barbara. *Spectres of 1919: Class and Nation in the Making of the New Negro.* Urbana: U of Illinois P, 2003.

Gates, Henry Louis, Jr. *Figures in Black: Words, Signs, and the "Racial" Self.* New York: Oxford UP, 1987.

Hall, Stuart. "Cultural Identities and Diaspora." *Identity: Community, Culture, Difference.* Ed. Jonathan Rutherford. London: Lawrence and Wishart, 1990. 222–37.

Huggins, Nathan Irvin. *Harlem Renaissance.* New York: Oxford UP, 1971.

Hutchinson, George. *The Harlem Renaissance in Black and White.* Cambridge: Harvard UP, 1995.

Larsen, Nella. *Quicksand.* 1928. New York: Penguin, 2002.

Lewis, David Levering. *When Harlem Was in Vogue.* 1981. New York: Viking, 1988.

Maxwell, William J. *New Negro, Old Left: African-American Writing and Communism between the Wars.* New York: Columbia UP, 1999.

Nadell, Martha Jane. *Enter the New Negroes: Images of Race in American Culture.* Cambridge: Harvard UP, 2004.

Ross, Marlon B. *Manning the Race: Reforming Black Men in the Jim Crow Era.* New York: New York UP, 2004.

Schwarz, A.B. Christa *Gay Voices of the Harlem Renaissance.* Bloomington: Indiana UP, 2003.

Turner, Joyce Moore. *Caribbean Crusaders and the Harlem Renaissance.* Urbana: U of Illinois P, 2005.

Wall, Cheryl A. *Women of the Harlem Renaissance.* Bloomington: Indiana UP, 1995.

CHAPTER FOUR

Visual Art of the Harlem Renaissance

MARTHA JANE NADELL

Ask an African American literature course, an interdisciplinary Harlem Renaissance seminar, or a Jazz Age history class to list major Harlem Renaissance writers. Hands will shoot up and voices will call out Countee Cullen, Langston Hughes, Zora Neale Hurston, Claude McKay, and Jean Toomer. Ask students what they know of musicians and other performing artists of the period and the names of Josephine Baker, Duke Ellington, Paul Robeson, and Bessie Smith will pop of out each corner of the classroom. Try this exercise with Harlem Renaissance visual artists or, for that matter, with African American visual artists in general; there will be silence in the classroom, as students know very little, if anything, about the visual field.

In *The Art of History*, Lisa Gail Collins writes of the "visual conundrum" and the "visual paradox at the center of African American thought" (2). Contemporary critic Michele Wallace too describes "the problem of the visual in Afro-American culture" (43). Collins and Wallace are referring to a puzzling aspect of scholarship about African American arts and letters. Scholars, critics, and other intellectuals have been concerned with the high visibility of people of African descent in American culture and, hence, as Collins tells us, have "expended an enormous amount of time, energy, and resources attempting to influence visual terrain" (2). Yet these same scholars and critics have neglected and devalued African American visual artists and their work.

This is the root of the problem in the classroom. In conceiving of the Harlem Renaissance as a primarily literary and musical movement, scholars and teachers fail to explore the wide range of African American painting, photography, sculpture, and graphic arts. They neglect important artists such as Aaron Douglas, Palmer Hayden, Sargent Johnson, Archibald Motley, Augusta Savage, Hale Woodruff, and others. When they do attend to the visual arts of the period, they often elide differences among artists and across media by casting African American art as a unitary and aesthetically singular project. The challenge, then, is both to familiarize students with the visual arts of the Harlem Renaissance and to guide them toward an understanding of the importance and complexity of this work and the ramifications this complexity has for studies of the movement as a whole.

I have organized this essay around a number of key thematic, historical, formal, and conceptual questions. I begin with the historical background for the Harlem Renaissance and for its painting, sculpture, and graphic art. I then move to a series of questions grouped under the general rubric of "Representations of," including representations of the New Negro (with a special emphasis on women), of place (Africa, the South, and Harlem or the city, with attention to depictions of jazz), and of history (of the Great Migration and of African American history). Students may also investigate the debates about the nature of the New Negro and New Negro art, about patronage and the institutional contexts of the visual arts, and about the implications that a study of the arts has for the temporal and spatial parameters of the Harlem Renaissance. Because of the diversity of the visual arts emerging during the 'twenties and 'thirties, I encourage instructors to pay attention to the formal aspects of painting, sculpture, photography, and the graphic arts. Throughout this essay, I refer to a number of artists and objects, reproductions of which can be found in two valuable and accessible resources: Sharon F. Patton's general history *African-American Art* and the exhibition catalogue for *Rhapsodies in Black* contain stunning reprints of a large number of works.

Question 1: Who are the major visual artists of the Harlem Renaissance? What are the key terms used to describe their work?

Aaron Douglas (1898-1979) was a Topeka-born artist who was drawn to Harlem upon reading the New Negro number of *The Survey Graphic*. Friends with a number of black intellectuals and writers, including W.E.B. Du Bois, Alain Locke, Cullen, and Hughes, he contributed a large number of images for magazines, including *The Crisis, Opportunity*, and the single-issue little magazine *Fire!!*. In addition, Douglas provided illustrations or covers for the anthology *Ebony and Topaz: A Collectanea* (1927), James Weldon Johnson's *God's Trombones* (1927), Langston Hughes's *Fine Clothes to the Jew* (1927), Claude McKay's *Home to Harlem* (1928), and Paul Morand's *Black Magic* (1929). Perhaps the most important text he illustrated was Locke's *The New Negro: An Interpretation* (1925). There and in other venues, Douglas used a cubistic style that relied on the contrast of black and white and collage-like compositions, with bodies and shapes layered on and next to each other. He referred to the stylization of African masks and Egyptian art in his use of silhouettes. In 1934, Douglas produced his most famous work, the mural *Aspects of Negro Life*, which includes the panels *The Negro in an African Setting* (Powell 76), *From Slavery through Reconstruction* (Powell 78-79), *An Idyll of the Deep South* (Powell 74), and *Song of the Towers* (Patton 142). This work uses complex compositions, vibrant colors, and reference to African and African American folk culture in a narrative of African American history. Douglas is known as a modernist because of his formal experimentation and references to African and Egyptian art.

Douglas was encouraged to turn to an African- or Egyptian-inflected style by Winold Reiss (1886-1953), a German-born and -trained artist who arrived in New York City in 1922. Reiss is a major contributor to the visual arts of the Harlem Renaissance in his own right. He provided illustrations and portraits for the New Negro number of the *Survey Graphic* and *The New Negro*. His Harlem Renaissance portraits are some of the most recognizable images of the era (see Powell 54-57).

Born in Virginia, Palmer Hayden (1893-1973) painted in a range of styles, including landscape, seascape, and genre painting. In 1926, he won a Harmon Award for his work *Fétiche et Fleurs* (1926), which does not use the abstraction and stylization of African art but instead treats it thematically, by placing a Fang mask from Gabon and Bakuba raffia cloth from the Congo in "a traditional still life" (Patton 120-22). Other well-known paintings include *Midsummer Night in Harlem* (Patton 136), which shows an urban street scene, and *Nous Quatre à Paris* (Patton 137), which depicts four African Americans (including Woodruff and himself) playing cards with a Cézanne-like palpability and an African art-inspired (or Douglas-inspired) stylization in physiognomies.

Sargent Claude Johnson (1887-1967) was born in Boston but lived in California, where he attended art school. A sculptor and painter, he exhibited with the Harmon Foundation from 1926 to 1935. Although he was not a Harlem resident, he is known for the lithograph *Lenox Avenue* (1938) and for his sculptures that draw on Southern folk culture (Powell 53).

William H. Johnson (1901-1970) came to New York from South Carolina in 1918 or 1919. He studied at the National Academy of Design for five years, after which he went to Paris. He returned to New York in 1926 but a mere three years later he left for Europe. Johnson's work includes a number of portraits and self-portraits (see Powell 126-29) and, later, paintings that he called primitivist because, with their use of primary colors and with their flatness, they echoed an untrained folk art style (see Patton 153).

Jacob Lawrence (1917-2000) was thirteen years old in 1930 when he arrived in Harlem. There, he trained with African American artists Charles Alston, painter of *Girl in a Red Dress* (Powell 143), and Augusta Savage. He crafted a number of narrative series that employ vivid primary colors; best known of these is *The Migration of the Negro* (1941), a sixty-panel work that documents the history of the Great Migration. Although he was much younger than other artists, scholars often consider him as part, if not as the "concluder of a Harlem Renaissance and as the convener of another, yet-to-be recognized cultural 'rebirth'" (Wintz 273; Powell 32).

Archibald Motley (1891-1981) was born in New Orleans and raised in Chicago, where he studied at the Art Institute. He was the first African American to be featured in a one-man exhibit, which took place at The New Gallery in New York. In 1928, he won a gold medal from the Harmon Foundation; a year later, he used a Guggenheim Fellowship to study in Paris. He returned to Chicago in 1930. His best known works include *Mending Socks* (1924) and *Woman Peeling Apples* (1924), both studies of African American women engaged in domestic work (Patton 48; Powell 173). He also painted a number of portraits that were realist images of mixed-race women (see *The Octoroon Girl* [1925] in Patton 122). These portraits indicate the class status of their subjects through their interior setting and the clothing that the women wear. In the late 1920s and 1930s, he painted scenes of nightlife in Paris and Chicago, including his 1929 painting *Blues* (Powell 111), his 1935 painting *Saturday Night* (Patton 139), and *Saturday Night Scene* (Powell 116). Motley is known for his use of vibrant colors, his layering of figures, and his portrayal of the performative and musical aspects of African American culture. Richard J. Powell writes something that can be applied to Motley and others: They "visually excavated the rhythmic and emotional dimensions of black performance by placing it on the level of aesthetic prototype" (Powell 23). This was part of a "blues aesthetic," the use of the formal qualities and cultural significance of African American music as part of a visual aesthetic.

Hale Woodruff (1900-1980), like Douglas, was familiar with the Harlem scene and, like Douglas, worked with *Crisis*, though as an editorial cartoonist. He left Harlem for Paris in 1927, where he developed a more abstract style, inspired by the use of form he observed in the work of Cezanne and Picasso and in African art. Consider his work *The Card Players* (1930), which depicts figures playing cards. As Patton tells us, "form and space were converted into areas of color that emphasized the two-dimensional surface of the painting" (125). Woodruff modified his style when he turned to murals in the 1930s. The composition, molding, and colors of his *Mutiny Aboard the Amistad* (1939) were inspired by Mexican realists (Patton 145).

Like Motley, Richmond Barthé (1901-1989) studied at the Art Institute of Chicago. He arrived in New York City in 1929. He sculpted a range of African,

African American, and other black figures including *Fera Benga* (1935) (Patton 131). Although inspired by African figures, his work is more in a realist vein.

Born in Florida, Augusta Savage (1892-1962) studied art at Cooper Union in New York City in the 1920s, when she became known as a portraitist of the participants in the Harlem Renaissance. Her famous works include *Gamin*, a bust of her nephew (Patton 52), which won the Rosenwald Foundation award. She too studied in Paris. In 1932, she opened the Savage Studio of Arts and Crafts in Harlem; her school guided younger African American artists (Patton 130).

Author of the controversial *Nigger Heaven* (1926), patron of Harlem Renaissance writers, and regular in Harlem's salons and speakeasies, Carl Van Vechten (1880-1964) provided a photographic album, so to speak, of many of the era's important figures. His portraits of Hurston (1935) and Bessie Smith (1936) (Powell 124-25) not only capture the likeness of their subjects but also impart a sense of the tensions between their interior lives and their public personas. These photographs play with shadow, background, and light to call attention to their staging; they raise questions about performance and the tensions between realism and abstraction.

Settling in Harlem in 1906, James Van Der Zee (1886-1983) is perhaps the best known African American photographer. In 1917, Van Der Zee opened a portrait studio on 135th Street. There and in locations across Harlem, Van Der Zee recorded a range of Harlem public and private life. He did portraits of Harlem's well-known residents, as well as of unknowns. He photographed weddings, funerals, interiors and exteriors. As an extraordinarily prolific artist, his images form a visual record and a visual staging of New Negro identity. One of his most famous photographs is *Couple, Harlem* (1932), which depicts a man seated in an automobile in front of a Harlem brownstone. Standing next to the car is a woman. Both are wearing raccoon coats (Powell 131).

Miguel Covarrubias (1904-1957) was a Mexican caricaturist who came to Harlem in 1924. Taken with the music of Harlem, he drew caricatures of African American dancers, waiters, dandies, and others. He used bodily exaggeration to depict these figures in his 1927 book *Negro Drawings* and in his illustrations for *Vanity Fair* and other magazines and books. He was a controversial figure; Du Bois wrote, "I am frank to say, however, that I think I could exist quite happily if Covarrubias had never been born" (Williams 271-72). Hughes, on the other hand, appreciated his work, declaring that it had the "blues touch."

A number of terms are associated with the range of visual arts of the Harlem Renaissance: realism, modernism, primitivism, folk, and a blues aesthetic. Artists whose styles are different—albeit related—such as Douglas, Motley, and Hayden are often grouped together under the term modernist. Motley is sometimes called a realist and at other times a modernist. William H. Johnson and Sargent

Johnson both refer to folk art; both are considered modernist. These terms have general meanings, accessible in any dictionary of critical terms for art history. More important, however, is attention to the idiosyncratic aesthetics of each object. What we learn from sustained reading of particular paintings, sculptures, or photographs is that there was no single aesthetic stance, despite the common vocabulary, for the visual artists of the Harlem Renaissance.

Question 2: How were African Americans represented in earlier times?

Particularly useful are a set of images that reside in mid- to late-nineteenth-century American print culture. Although fine artists, such as the white artists Thomas Eakins and Winslow Homer and the African American artist Henry Ossawa Tanner (see *The Banjo Player* [1893] in Patton 99), painted dignified scenes and portraits of African American life, caricatures and stereotypes of African Americans surfaced in newspapers, lithographs, novels, post cards, and advertisements—the media that formed an important element of American popular culture of the time.

These images were part of what is known as the Graphics Revolution, when visual images became readily available and easily reproducible in print. Teachers may want to locate Currier and Ives "Darktown" lithographs, an immensely popular series that cast African Americans as farcical figures; using bodily and behavioral exaggeration, these extraordinarily popular lithographs lampooned African American political and literary aspirations, among others. Illustrator of Mark Twain's *The Adventures of Huckleberry Finn*, E.W. Kemble's "coon" drawings used the same type of virulent racist caricature (see Gates for a visual essay that includes examples of postcards and advertisements employing caricature).

Instructors may balance this discussion by introducing the manner in which, as Anne Carroll reminds us, "African American writers, artists, and editors have long used written and visual texts to counteract derogatory assumptions about African Americans" (7). Carroll describes how Phillis Wheatley, Frederick Douglass, and Sojourner Truth used visual images—in publications and advertisements—to control and to make positive images of themselves. In 1900, Booker T. Washington's *A New Negro for a New Century* used a large number of portraits of African American leaders as an attempt "to 'turn' the new century's image of the black away from the stereotypes scattered throughout plantation fictions, black-face minstrelsy, vaudeville, racist pseudo-science and vulgar Social Darwinism" (Gates 326-27). It is helpful to bear in mind Gates's comment: "Black Americans sought to re-present their public selves in order to reconstruct their public, reproducible images" (319).

Question 3: Who was the New Negro? How did visual arts represent him (or her)?

In December 1924, *Vanity Fair* heralded the New Negro in a piece entitled "Enter, The New Negro, a Distinctive Type Recently Created by the Coloured

Cabaret Belt in New York." With images by Mexican caricaturist Covarrubias and text by West Indian author Eric Walrond, this two-page spread proclaimed:

> The effortless New York public, revolving always with the fairest wind, has recently discovered a new brand of Negro entertainer. Not the old type, of course. The lullaby-singer is gone. Also the plantation darky. And, out of the welter of sentimentality which the old types created, the Negro now emerges as an individual, an individual as brisk and as actual as your own next-door neighbor. He no longer has to be either a Pullman car porter, or over-fond of watermelon, in order to be a successful type on our stage. He is a personality, always, and frequently an artist. (Williams 61)

Covarrubias's figures were identified with phrases that referred to types, or, some would say, "stereotypes" of Harlem's denizens: "The Sheik of Dahomey" and "That Tearin' Yalla Gal." Other captions referred to the place where one might encounter such a type: A young man looking for work is identified as "8 A.M. on Lenox Avenue"; a young, dancing woman is identified as "2 A.M. at the Cat and the Saxophone." These sketches bear the hallmark of caricature: bodily and physiognomic exaggeration.

In March 1925, Locke, the Harvard- and Oxford-educated philosopher and dean of the Harlem Renaissance, published a number of essays in the Harlem number of *The Survey Graphic*. In "Enter the New Negro," Locke celebrated the new persona emerging from the shift in the African American population from rural to urban, from South to North, and from pre-modern to modern. Reiss provided images for the magazine and for the anthology that grew out of it. Reiss's images included types (portraits of unknown individuals) and representatives (portraits of major cultural and political leaders). Presented in black and white in the magazine and in color plates in the anthology, the faces of these subjects were depicted in an almost photographic manner. The images of Cullen, Toomer, James Weldon Johnson, and others are recognizable because they bear a strong resemblance to subjects themselves; their clothing and other indicators of social standing were rendered in outline or with great attention to line, shape, and color (see Powell 54-57). On a formal level, then, these images suggest a tension between the realism of the earlier efforts to combat caricature and a move toward abstraction.

An introductory and thought-provoking exercise is to compare Covarrubias's and Reiss's images, which form a vital part of the representational field of the 1920s despite the fact that neither artist was African American. Students may explore the ideas about the New Negro embedded in the conjunction of image and text in *Vanity Fair* and *Survey Graphic*: Was the New Negro a jazz musician, a writer, or a worker? The images also throw into relief the formal strategies used by these artists and raise the question of the role of non-African Americans in black image-making.

Students may also examine the nature and role of Aaron Douglas's images in *The New Negro*, which grew out of *The Survey Graphic*. Images such as *Rebirth* (Patton 117) employ a black and white contrast, a layering in a collage-like manner, and a hard line, all of which flatten the figure into two dimensions and suggest closeness to a loosely defined African aesthetic. Teachers may ask how Douglas's illustrations suggest a New Negro identity rooted in both an African past and a modern(ist) world.

Photography offers another rich arena for depictions of the New Negro. Van Der Zee offers a record of Harlem from every quarter. His famous image *Couple* reminds of us a number of issues: the rise of the middle class in Harlem, the importance of the urban landscape, changes in transportation and technology, and the diversity of experience within Harlem. His depictions of both public and private life help students envision a time that is quite distant from their own. Savage's sculpture *Gamin* also raises questions along these lines. Is the New Negro one of the nameless denizens of Harlem, rather than the elite or bohemian editors, critics, and writers?

Visual images of women offer another fascinating arena for discussion. Motley's series of mulatto women raises questions about respectability, sexuality, color distinctions, and class in addition to formal issues. What Cherene Sherrard-Johnson tells us of *A Mulatress* can be applied to Motley's other portraits: They "derive [their] lineage not from the architecture of portrait art but from literary, legal, and anthropological discussions of race" (xvi). Consider Motley's *The Octoroon Girl* (1925), a dignified portrait of a light-skinned mixed-race woman in a sitting room and *Brown Girl (After the Bath)* (1931), which depicts a nude woman in a dressing room, sitting in front of a mirrored vanity, whose reflection stares at the viewer from the mirror (Patton 122; Powell 113). Instructors may ask a number of questions of these two images: Are women sexualized or respectable (or can they be both)? Are they subjects in their own right or gendered and racialized objects? What are the racial and class dimensions of the way in which beauty is coded? What ideas about race, performance, class, sexuality, and womanhood inform the formal strategies of these images? Are these images re-visioning of earlier ideas New Negro womanhood?

It would be fruitful to juxtapose Motley's portraits with earlier ones, such as those in Washington's *A New Negro for a New Century* and John H. Adams's "A Study of the Features of the New Negro Woman" (1901) (see Gates 330-31), and with contemporary and later ones, such as those of Reiss's portraits, Covarrubias's caricatures, Paul Colin's lithograph of Josephine Baker from *Le Tumulte Noir* (Powell 86), and Charles Alston's *Girl in A Red Dress* (1934) (Powell 143). Motley's paintings, as well as the other images, work well against Jessie Fauset's *Plum Bun* (1928), Nella Larsen's *Quicksand* (1928) and *Passing* (1929), and Jean Toomer's depiction of women in *Cane* (1923).

Question 4: How did the visual arts represent Africa, the South, and Harlem?

A useful frame with which to discuss the visual arts of the Harlem Renaissance is the idea of place. Certainly, Harlem itself was of importance to the artists, writers, and intellectuals who gathered there in the heady days of the movement. Yet the idea of Harlem as "prophetic," as a "race capital," and as a "nascent center of folk-expression," as Locke writes, is equally important in the construction of the New Negro ("New Negro" 7). Harlem served as the literal and figurative center for the "migrating peasant" and the "new generation" of African America ("Negro Youth" 49). Africa and the South were also important loci in African American thought at that time. Locke cast Africa as an ancestral home and a source for inspiration. In the South resided African American folk culture; it was the inspiration for literary works such as Toomer's *Cane* and the staging point of the Great Migration.

A comparison of the individual panels from Douglas's mural, *Aspects of Negro Life*, serves well here, as the entire mural follows a narrative trajectory from Africa to the South and then to Harlem. Students may explore the range of African American culture portrayed in each of these three areas. They may consider the way in which African American creativity is represented by exploring the dancing in *The Negro in an African Setting*, the music in *Slavery Through Reconstruction*, and the saxophone player at the emotional and compositional center of *Song of the Towers*. Students may compare the depiction of the atrocities of slavery in the South with the freedom in Africa and Harlem, or rather this unnamed urban area.

The city in general demands attention in a number of other paintings. Even though they are not set in Harlem itself, Motley's 1930s images of Paris and Chicago nightlife, including *Blues*, *Saturday Night*, and *Saturday Night Street Scene* are evocative of a number of themes of urban life: its density, the importance of music and performance, the construction of sexuality, and the dynamic between public and private life.

One of the most important aspects of these works is that they refer to and represent jazz. Motley's paintings are genre scenes that evoke jazz and the blues, key aspects in representations of the city. Set against the music of the Harlem Renaissance, they become useful in interdisciplinary courses that address the variety of arts that emerged in the period. Students may consider *Blues*, which focuses on a dancing couple who are framed by other couples, musicians, and a waiter. The colors, especially of the women's dresses, are vibrant. The depiction of the figures is suggestive of collage, in which bodies are layered on top of bodies, both linked and somehow separate. *Saturday Night* is similar in its focus on the interior of a speakeasy or nightclub and its denizens. Students may investigate the visual depiction of music and performance, the representation of women, and the dynamic between black performers and white patrons. *Saturday Night Scene* likewise refers to music and performance in its depiction of a street on which musicians play their instruments while others dance. This painting does not have the close focus that *Blues* does, so it raises ideas about the physical space of urban life and the compositional relationship among figures. Instructors may pose questions about the details of the painting: What do students make of the figures who gaze at the vibrant street from their apartment windows? What do they make of the position of the white policeman in the foreground of the image?

Hayden's *Midsummer Night in Harlem* offers a good comparison to Motley's work, as it too represents the meeting of the public and the private in urban street life. The painting depicts crowds of people gathering on stoops, individuals leaning out of their apartment windows, a car full of passengers on the asphalt, and in the background a church from which worshippers appear to exit. Hayden's figures are stylized and have much in common with nineteenth-century caricatures. Instructors may ask students about the nature of these representations. While they evoke urban life, do they reinforce negative images of African Americans or use the exaggeration as an ironic comment on them? It would be useful to juxtapose these images with Rudolph Fisher's "City of Refuge" (1925), a short story about recent migrants' initial encounters and disorientation with Harlem.

Sargent Johnson's *Lenox Avenue* approaches the idea of urban life and the importance of music with an aesthetic that is quite different from that of Hayden and Motley. Rather than rely on colorful genre scenes, Johnson's lithograph uses a gray scale to present a collection of abstract references to city life—the piano, a smokestack—that coalesce into a face. The attention here is on line and shade, while the figurative is subsumed.

The centrality of visual depictions of and formal strategies inspired by music is part of what scholars call a "blues aesthetic." African American visual artists and writers used black music to formulate black modernisms; the blues and jazz became the basis for a central visual and literary aesthetic of formal experimentation; cross fertilization of the arts; and vibrant, complex accounts of modern African American life. In pursuit of these issues, instructors may find it useful to compare visual, literary, and musical compositions; to discuss different formal strategies for addressing the modernity and complexity of African American urban life; and to imagine a visual soundtrack, so to speak, for African American urban life. Van Der Zee's images present a record of Harlem in that time period, including funeral scenes, parades, and interiors (see Powell 134-41). These images suggest the range of African American urban experiences, foregrounding the heterogeneity of the population and its experience of urban life.

Question 5: How did the visual arts represent the New Negro's history?

Along with the representation of place in the visual arts, the representation of history provides a useful avenue into important artistic productions of the Harlem

Renaissance. Douglas's murals, discussed above, form a narrative of African American history, beginning in an in idyllic African past and culminating in the Great Migration, indicated by a figure holding a suitcase in hand. Students may compare the scale of the murals, which constructs this history as monumental and epic, with the details of individual panels: the reading of the Emancipation Proclamation, depictions of stylized African American leaders, and the Ku Klux Klan in the second panel, or the skyscrapers and smoke in the fourth panel.

Lawrence's *The Migration of the Negro* is a counterpoint to Douglas's murals. In small, individual panels Lawrence constructs a detailed narrative, including the push and pull factors of the Great Migration (the epidemics of lynching and boll weevils of the South, the physical experience of the migration, and the vibrancy of Northern life). Using primary colors and flattened shapes and relying on historical and sociological research, he strips away shadow and variations from his figures and landscapes, thereby crafting a vast and epic history (see Patton 154-55). Rudolph Fisher's "The South Lingers On" (1925) would be a useful juxtaposition with this visual text.

These historical narratives in both large and small scale are useful in classes as they envision history using differing formal choices made by the artists. They raise questions about the contours of African American history; the role of Africa and the South in the rise of a black, urban population; and the experience of the city. Instructors may ask questions of these works: How does Douglas represent, both formally and thematically, the cultural and historical links across continents? How do Douglas and Lawrence conceive of African American origins, social oppression, and political resistance? How do they construct contemporary life?

Question 6: How did critics debate about the visual arts of the Harlem Renaissance?

Throughout the 1920s intellectuals argued often and in print about the nature of African American arts and letters. In 1926, Du Bois sponsored a symposium in print in a number of issues of *The Crisis*. In "The Negro in Art: How Shall He Be Portrayed?" Du Bois wrote, "There has long been controversy within and without the Negro race as to just how the Negro should be treated in art—how he should be pictured by writers and portrayed by artists" (Wintz 347). Relying on the language of painting, Du Bois asked a number critics, publishers, and novelists—African American and non-African American alike—to respond to questions about the nature, demands, and parameters of racial representation.

Hughes and George Schuyler too argued about the nature of African American arts. In 1926 they published "The Negro Artist and the Racial Mountain" and "The Negro-Art Hokum" in the pages of *The Nation*. The short-lived, fine little magazine *Fire!!* was in many respects part of a generational debate between the elder Harlem Renaissance critics and the younger members of the movement. Douglas,

Hughes, Hurston, Wallace Thurman, and others collaborated on a magazine that resisted admonishments to confine African American letters to the respectable.

Amidst these debates it is one critic who stands out as the most important theorist of Harlem Renaissance visual arts: Alain Locke. Locke was responsible for editing the seminal New Negro number of the *Survey Graphic* and the anthology that grew out of it, *The New Negro*. Throughout the 1920s and later, he produced a number of essays that dealt specifically with the visual arts, including "The Legacy of the Ancestral Arts," "To Certain of Our Philistines," and *Negro Art: Past and Present* (1936). It is also possible to read Locke's editing of the *Survey Graphic* and *The New Negro* as an implicit commentary on the role of the visual arts in the period.

Locke called for a distinctive Negro art, one that would both combat earlier and inadequate representations and form a new, modern, and racial tradition. Yet Locke also recognized the difficulty in producing this visual art. African American visual arts had not yet caught up to the innovations of literature and music. An African American visual art that wrestled with African American individuals and culture was, in essence, belated. Consider the following remarks:

> The Negro is a far more familiar figure in American life than in European, but American art, barring caricature and *genre* reflects him scarcely at all. ("Legacy" 262)

> Of all the arts, painting is most bound by social ideas. And so, in spite of the fact that the Negro offers, in the line of the human subject, the most untouched of all the available fields of portraiture, and the most intriguing, if not indeed the most difficult of technical problem because of the variety of pigmentation and subtlety of values, serious painting has all but ignored him. ("Philistines" 155)

> Social conventions stand closer guard over painting than most of the other arts. It is for that reason that a new school and idiom of Negro portraiture is particularly significant. ("Philistines" 155)

> We ought and must have a school of Negro art, a local and a racially representative tradition. ("Legacy" 266)

In "The Legacy of the Ancestral Arts" and his later *Negro Art: Past and Present*, Locke found a solution for the problem he saw in American art. African plastic arts had become an inspiration for European modernists and could, he argued, become a source for African American artists. Locke wrote, "if African art is capable of producing the ferment in modern art that it has, surely this is not too much to expect of its influence upon the culturally awakened Negro artist of the present generation" ("Legacy" 267). Locke found in the "new artistic respect for the African idiom and the natural ambition of Negro artists for a racial idiom in their art expression" the most viable means of combating the "timid conventionalism" engendered by "racial disparagement" (262). In other words, the respect commanded by African art among modern artists and those who admired it would translate into respect for African American artists engaging with African forms. Moreover, African American visual artists could assert simultaneously the modernity and the modernism of the New Negro.

Locke's comments are a useful frame for classroom discussions about the development of modern, New Negro aesthetics. Instructors could invite students to juxtapose Locke's ideas with the material aspects of *The New Negro*, asking them to pay attention to the way in which illustrations, including African art, abstract designs by Reiss, and drawings by Riess and Douglas, appear and form a visual discourse to complement the textual discourse (see Nadell and Carroll). Students could also apply the ideas of a modern, African-inspired African American art to the works of a variety of artists. Possible works include Hayden's *Fétiche et Fleurs* (1926) and Barthé's *Fera Benga* (1935), which thematically refer to African art. The sculpture of Savage and Barthé is also particularly useful as it thematically refers to African art. Students could also use Sargent Johnson's folk-inspired sculpture *Forever Free* (1935) (Patton 132) and William H. Johnson's *Going to Church* (1940-41) (Patton 153) to complicate Locke's understanding of African art as the primary source material for an African American modernism.

Question 7: What was the institutional context of New Negro art?

African American graphic arts are closely aligned with the publishing history of African American letters; African American painting and sculpture has a different history. The production of such art was intimately tied to schools, guilds, government programs, patrons, and prizes.

Locke assiduously courted wealthy patrons, including Albert C. Barnes, who collected African art and contributed an essay, "Negro Art and America," to *The New Negro*. As a patron, Barnes articulated his own, limiting ideas about the so-called primitivism of African American arts. Students may wish to explore the role of Barnes and other patrons, including Charlotte Osgood Mason, who believed that African Americans had a special, spiritual nature, and A'Lelia Walker, the daughter of the first African American female millionaire, whose Dark Tower Salon served as a gathering place for Harlem Renaissance notables and showcased the work of Douglas (see Patton 126).

The Harmon Foundation, founded by a philanthropist and real estate mogul, began making awards in 1926. Among those who received the awards were Woodruff, Hayden, and Motley. In addition, the Harmon Foundation sponsored its first "Exhibit of Fine Arts, Production of American Negro Artists" in 1929, and then others in 1930 and 1931 (Reynolds and Wright 33). While prizes were an important source of funding for African Americans and exhibits a valuable form of exposure, the Harmon Foundation's involvement in African American art raises questions about the dynamic between patron and artist. Romare Bearden claimed, "Its attitude from the beginning has been of a coddling and patronizing nature … . By its choice of the type of work it favors, it has allowed the Negro artist to accept standards that are both artificial and corrupt" (Reynolds and Wright 41). Bearden points to the way in which the Harmon Foundation judged, and hence influenced or limited, the visual arts. Students may ask questions about the role of patrons and foundations in the development of African American fine arts, the role of non-African Americans in crafting New Negro visual aesthetics, and the financial constraints on the development of the fine arts.

The 1930s saw the development of a number of venues that supported the development of up-and-coming African American artists. In 1932, Savage opened the Savage Studio of Arts and Crafts at 63 West 143rd Street, which enabled her to train young African American artists. The Harlem Artists Guild served as a forum for artists to discuss their work and the social and political issues that interested them. In 1937, the Works Progress Administration sponsored the Harlem Community Art Center, directed by Savage (see Patton 145-47). Students may discuss the difference between organizations such as these and those that operated toward the end of the 1920s.

Question 8: How do the visual arts help us to rethink the Harlem Renaissance in time and space?

Following Locke and later scholars, we can argue that Harlem Renaissance visual arts were belated. Many painters and sculptors did not begin to flourish until the end of the 1920s and 1930s. Moreover, many neither lived nor studied in Harlem. Their artistic homes were San Francisco, Chicago, and especially Paris. Yet they wrestled with many of the same questions that preoccupied writers and critics: the nature of racial representation; the position of African American art in the culture of the United States and in the larger field of modern art; and the development of viable visual aesthetics that draw on a wide variety of sources, including the plastic art of Africa and Egypt, the folk art of the South, and the modernist art of Europe. Studies of the visual arts of Douglas, Motley, Hayden, Savage, Lawrence, and others thus allow us to view the Harlem Renaissance as a multi-media, transnational phenomenon that pushed the boundaries of upper Manhattan and of the 1920s.

WORKS CITED

Carroll, Anne. *Word, Image, and the New Negro: Representation and Identity in the Harlem Renaissance.* Bloomington: Indiana UP, 2005.

Collins, Lisa Gail. *The Art of History.* New Brunswick: Rutgers UP, 2002.

Du Bois, W.E.B. "A Questionnaire." 1926. *The Critics and the Harlem Renaissance*. Ed. Cary D. Wintz. New York: Garland, 1996.

Gates, Henry Louis Jr. "The Trope of a New Negro and the Reconstruction of the Image of the Black." *Representations* 24 (1988): 129–55.

Locke, Alain, ed. *The New Negro*. 1925. New York: Touchstone, 1992.

———. "Negro Youth Speaks." *The New Negro*. 47–53.

———. "The Legacy of the Ancestral Arts." *The New Negro*. 254–67.

———. "To Certain of Our Philistines." *Opportunity* 3 (May 1925): 155–56.

Nadell, Martha Jane. *Enter the New Negroes: Images of Race in American Culture*. Cambridge: Harvard UP, 2004.

Patton, Sharon F. *African-American Art*. Oxford: Oxford UP, 1998.

Powell, Richard J. et al. *Rhapsodies in Black: Art of the Harlem Renaissance*. Berkeley: U of California P, 1997.

Reynolds, Gary A. and Beryl J. Wright. *Against the Odds: African-American Artists and the Harmon Foundation*. Newark: Newark Museum of Art, 1989.

Sherrard-Johnson, Cherene. *Portraits of the New Negro Woman: Visual and Literary Culture of the Harlem Renaissance*. New Brunswick: Rutgers UP, 2007.

Wallace, Michele. "Modernism, Postmodernism and the Problem of the Visual in Afro-American Culture." *Out There: Marginalization and Contemporary Cultures*. Eds. Russell Ferguson et al. Cambridge: M.I.T. P, 1990. 39–50.

Williams, Adriana. *Covarrubias*. Ed. Doris Ober. Austin: U of Texas P, 1994.

Wintz, Cary D. *Harlem Speaks: A Living History of the Harlem Renaissance*. Naperville, Illinois: Sourcebooks, 2007.

CHAPTER FIVE

Harlem and the New Woman

AMBER HARRIS LEICHNER

There is, however, an advantage in focusing upon the women of Harlem—modern city in the world's metropolis. Here, more than anywhere else, the Negro woman is free from the cruder handicaps of primitive household hardships and the grosser forms of sex and race subjugation. Here, she has considerable opportunity to measure her powers in the intellectual industrial fields of the great city. The questions naturally arise: "What are her difficulties?" and, "How is she solving them?"

ELISE JOHNSON McDOUGALD,
"THE TASK OF NEGRO WOMANHOOD"

In her touchstone essay, one of the few pieces by women included in Alain Locke's 1925 anthology *The New Negro*, essayist, teacher, and supporter of the causes of both African Americans and women, Elise Johnson McDougald points to the rapidly changing social position of the Negro woman as one of the most important cultural issues of the period, having implications at all levels of African American society. But she urges her readers to recognize New Negro Womanhood not as homogenous but as a "colorful pageant of individuals, each differently endowed," and cautions that "their problems cannot be thought of in mass" (369).

Keeping McDougald's theory of New Negro Womanhood in mind helps us to understand the complexity and depth of women's critical and literary contributions to the Harlem Renaissance. It is important to understand that during this period, African American women sought to define their roles as New Women within

New Negro discourse. They occupied a tense space, unable to embrace fully either of the period's two prevailing political movements: the decidedly *masculine* New Negro of the Harlem Renaissance and the effectively *white* New Woman of postsuffarage feminism. As a result, the New Negro Woman was obligated to create her own modernist literary aesthetic. Though New Negro Women's literature cannot be categorized into one uniform genre, style, form, message, or geographical setting, it is united by a particularly powerful link between gender issues and racial identity, a link that is characteristic of the era and a crucial stepping-stone to African American women writers today.

Framing our understanding of this literature is the sudden increase in magazine circulation between the wars, and the emergence of the New Woman as a popular "go-to" heroine in mainstream periodical fiction. This heroine, in all of her youthful determination and vigor, represents a turn from the motherly, submissive, and sacrificing "angel of the hearth" figure idealized in nineteenth-century literature. The New Woman's roots reach back to the suffrage movement, but by the 1920s, she no longer need actively carry a banner for the feminist cause. The New Woman has dreams that extend beyond the private realms of marriage and family to reach the public sphere, where she might find occupations that offer her a sense of relevance and fulfillment within culture and society. Perhaps most important, the career-minded New Woman is willing to strike out on her own to achieve her dreams of success, even if it means leaving her small home town and family for the relative anonymity of an urban center.

The New Woman was forged from a racist suffrage movement, led by white women, many of them from the South, who consistently sacrificed black women for Southern political support. Hardball politics complicated the model of modern feminism for black women, who did not enjoy equal footing with their white sisters. Activist white women often ignored black women's issues (such as antilynching legislation) or barred black women outright from participating in women's suffrage organizations. As Paula Giddings asserts, "White women simply were willing to let Black women go down the proverbial drain to get the vote for themselves" (162-63). New Negro Women's literature often subtly or explicitly draws attention to this dual oppression. For example, Angela Murray, the heroine of Jessie Redmon Fauset's *Plum Bun* (1928), chooses to pass for white after moving to New York City to enroll in art school. Though she imagines everything that had always stood in her way to success will disappear once the world sees her as "white," the reality of her new life as Angèle Mory is just as complicated as her previous one. Still hindered by the limitations that society places on women, white or black, Angela's altered position places her conspicuously outside both the white bohemian and Harlem black communities she inhabits. She escapes racial oppression only to experience more fully gender discrimination. For Angela, an aspiring artist, dreams of creative independence and a meaningful identity are fulfilled only once she decides to become a New Negro Woman, and she does this by dropping her white persona to come out as a proud African American with essential roots in the black community that she initially abandons.

The intersection of the New Woman and the New Negro meant for black women writers being torn between allegiance to race on one side and gender on the other, and blending the two seamlessly proved difficult. The New Negro, as this figure came to be defined by Locke and others, was portrayed as the antithesis of the "Old Negro" myth, embodied in the Uncle Tom figure of plantation lore. The New Negro had the courage and gusto of a male soldier returning victorious from the Great War, a man able to rise up and fight racism directly. The era's rhetoric portrayed the New Negro in militaristic terms and using masculine imagery, as illustrated by the cover of the May 1923 issue of *The Messenger*, which imagines "The New Negro" of its title as a version of Auguste Rodin's *The Thinker* (1880).

Women were not overlooked entirely by the New Negro paradigm. The frontispiece of *The New Negro* featured Winold Reiss's iconic image, *The Brown Madonna*—a tribute to the essential role of women as mothers, caregivers, and educators to generations of African American families. In this manner black women were valued for the influence they could wield upon domestic space in a legacy of slavery and destruction of the black family. Alice Dunbar-Nelson describes this concept in "Woman's Most Serious Problem" (1927): "the training of human souls needs to begin at home in the old-fashioned family life, augmented later, if necessary, in the expensive schools and settlements of great cities" (114). Dunbar-Nelson spent much of her life in a matriarchal household and never had children of her own, suggesting that the messages and pressures felt by black women writers were immensely complicated. Maternal occupations are important in any culture, but there are, at the same time, obvious limitations to a strictly maternal social role for women writers.

The lives and literature of Harlem Renaissance women help us understand what it meant to be a New Negro Woman in an age of great contradictions for them. It was a time when there were more avenues than ever available to aspiring women writers, and many of them took advantage of emerging opportunities to see their words in print, but their words often say just enough to hint at the many voices that were not being heard, from the teeming streets of Jazz Age Harlem to the industrial cities of the north to the rural enclaves of the South. The majority of women writing and publishing in the newly established African American periodicals of the day were from the black middle class. They were themselves New Women—educated and often self-supporting, many of them single or childless. Often these women had fulltime jobs as teachers, nurses, librarians, social workers, or secretaries that demanded most of their time and attention. The fact that, without a lot of free time, extensive support networks in the white male publishing industry, or the financial assistance that writers such as Langston Hughes and Claude McKay received from wealthy white patrons, so many women could publish their works is a testimony to both the receptive literary environment of the time and their intense desire to be heard.[1]

The message these women writers were imparting in their works was as multifaceted and complex as McDougald suggests. Through the use of characters and storylines drawn from contemporary African American culture and communities across the United States, they sought to eradicate stereotyped, racist images of black female identity, characterized by the Southern mammy or (to quote McDougald) the "grotesque Aunt Jemimas of the street-car advertisements," and to replace them with authentic modern images of black womanhood reflective of the optimistic and motivated generation flocking to Harlem and other northern cities. Writers such as Fauset and Nella Larsen used their fiction to explore the internal and external struggles of young, middle-class New Negro Women seeking their places in a society not always ready for their talents. Zora Neale Hurston put her New Negro Women characters in Southern rural settings and black folk traditions, giving them the strength and desire necessary to forge thoroughly modern autonomous paths, much as she did in her own well-traveled life. And, perhaps most important of all, women poets dominated the pages of Harlem periodicals *Opportunity*, *The Crisis*, *The Messenger*, and *Negro World*. Writers such as Georgia Douglas Johnson, Angelina Weld Grimké, and Alice Dunbar-Nelson covered the full span of African American experience in their poetry—from lost love to lynching to an African ancestral heritage. Their poetic portraits of women were as varied as their themes: wives, mothers, lovers, washerwomen, teachers, nature worshippers, and dreamers. Likewise, short story writers such as Dorothy West and lesser-known figures such as Florida Ruffin Ridley, Edythe Mae Gordon, Anita Scott Coleman, and Marita Bonner took their readers into settings from small New England communities to Harlem tenement houses and jazz clubs to Southern plantations.

Whatever the genre or genres New Negro Women chose as the vehicles to express their ideas, much of their work has been neglected for a variety of reasons: the long tradition of the American literary canon privileging white male writers; difficulty in accessing and recovering forgotten literature after the decline of the New Negro movement in the 1930s; disintegration of the outlets and platforms that had given women writers a voice; and later critical exclusion of women from the dominant Harlem Renaissance paradigm of New Negro militancy, since their work was judged to be outdated and bourgeois.

Within the last decade, revisionist and feminist scholarship have helped to recover women's voices from this era and place them alongside the works of their contemporaries, an effort that is quickly extending and deepening our under-standing of the Harlem Renaissance as a whole. One example of such an effort is *The Harlem Renaissance and Beyond* (1990), a groundbreaking collection of biogra-phies and selected bibliographies of 100 black women writers from 1900 to 1945 edited by Lorraine Elena Roses and Ruth Elizabeth Randolph. The previous lack of information on most of the writers in the volume underscores how swiftly New Negro Women writers exited the literary and cultural scene; it was not uncom-mon for a writer to publish a handful of stories or poems and never be heard from again. Gloria Hull and Cheryl Wall have undertaken more extensive explo-rations of the New Negro Woman experience while widening the geographical boundaries of the Harlem Renaissance with their treatments of individual writers and their immensely complex, modern lives. Hull's influential study of Angelina Weld Grimké, Alice Dunbar-Nelson, and Georgia Douglas Johnson, *Color, Sex, and Poetry* (1987), describes three central writers who resided not in Harlem, but in Boston, Delaware, and Washington, D.C., respectively. Likewise, Wall's *Women of the Harlem Renaissance* (1995), with its in-depth portraits of Fauset, Larsen, and Hurston, is an excellent starting point for an inquiry into the cultural and biographical contexts of New Negro Womanhood.

The most famous women writers of the Harlem Renaissance—Fauset, Larsen, and Hurston—have each been recovered from obscurity by these and other scholars in recent decades and given rightful credit for being among the most influential of Harlem Renaissance figures. Now we recognize Fauset—the "midwife" of the New Negro Movement—as a novelist and poet in her own right and as the literary gatekeeper of *The Crisis*, as important as Charles S. Johnson (of *Opportunity* magazine) or Alain Locke. *The Crisis*, edited by W.E.B. Du Bois and published by the National Association for the Advancement of Colored People, was the most widely circulated African American magazine of its time, and Fauset, as its literary editor from 1919 to 1926, helped to bring many new writers into the New Negro fold, among them Hughes and Jean Toomer. Indeed, it was in honor of the publication of *There is Confusion* (1924), Fauset's first of four novels, that the Civic Club held the now famous 1924 dinner we know today as the era's kick-off point for Harlem's literary elite. Ironically, the dinner is representative of the inadequate New Negro response to women writers, for Fauset's novel was quickly forgotten in the fervor to introduce to influential white publishers and patrons the new generation of young (male) writers.[2]

It is instructive to take a closer look at Jessie Fauset, who was born in New Jersey in 1882, raised in Philadelphia, and educated at Cornell and the University of Pennsylvania, where she was often the only African American student. A well-traveled New Negro Woman who had been to Europe as well as northern Africa, Fauset thought of herself as a writer first and foremost, even as she gained prominence in her editorial position at *The Crisis*. In addition to her work as a fiction writer, Fauset was also an accomplished poet and essayist who was fluent in French. She did not marry until the age of 47, and she did not have children. Sadly, Fauset's career fit into the mold of most New Negro Women writers. When the era went into decline, she was forced to abandon her writing in favor of teaching. In addition, her reputation as a writer suffered considerable damage as a result of disparaging labels such as "Rear Guard," as literary scholar Robert Bone described her in *The Negro Novel in America* (1958).[3] Because her novels were primarily concerned with the experiences of middle-class women and utilized romantic conventions, they were dismissed as bourgeois and generally irrelevant. But to study Fauset's works today is to see a writer critically engaged with the multiple layers of oppression experienced by New Negro Women and the ways in which that oppression might be subverted.[4]

Much like Fauset, Larsen's literary reputation tumbled into premature obscurity, though her fall was hastened by accusations of plagiarism. Recent biographies by Thadious Davis and George Hutchinson have helped to shed light on the mysterious, complex story of Larsen's life. Married to a prominent Harlem physician, Larsen was a professional woman herself, first training to be a nurse and then working as a librarian before becoming a full-time writer. She never had children and later divorced. After publishing two acclaimed novels, *Quicksand* (1928) and *Passing* (1929), and being the first black woman to win a Guggenheim Fellowship, Larsen disappeared from the Harlem literary scene, living out her days in seclusion while working the night shift as a nurse in a Manhattan hospital. Larsen used her fictional characters to "explor[e] strategies of concealment, self-invention, and passing" (Wall 88). Whether that exploration is manifested in the passing scheme undertaken with disastrous results by Clare Kendry in *Passing*, or in the thwarted New Negro Woman aspirations experienced by Helga Crane in *Quicksand*, Larsen is preoccupied with the pressures that racism and sexism exert on a modern black woman who desires autonomous development of her talents and her free expression of sexuality. Helga Crane's story is representative of the New Negro Woman's wish to enter the professional realm, only to be defeated by modern urban racism and sexism. This is the case when Helga attempts to find employment in Chicago, armed with a college degree and teaching experience at one of the "finest schools for Negroes anywhere in the country." Helga is turned away because she does not have the proper "references" for domestic service (2–3, 33). Helga's story reflects the limitations of the New Negro Movement's aim of using literature and art as weapons against the economic and social oppression of racism. Helga's cultivated artistic taste and exceptional education are no defense against a society that continues to view her as either an exotic sexual object or an unskilled servant. Unfortunately,

Larsen's success at achieving the lasting goals of New Negro Womanhood was as limited as Helga's.

Among the most positive portrayals of New Negro Womanhood as it pertains to Southern working-class or rural women are the heroines of Zora Neale Huston's fiction. From Janie Crawford in *Their Eyes Were Watching God* (1937) to the washerwoman Delia Jones in the short story "Sweat" (1926), Hurston's women characters do not hesitate to follow their hearts or defend their lives, even when it casts them out of accepted women's roles. As Cheryl Wall puts it, Hurston shows that "material poverty is not tantamount to spiritual poverty or experiential deprivation" (140). For Janie, the opportunity to find happiness occurs only when she decides to leave her first husband and embark on an adventure that includes two more marriages, ownership of a business and property, labor as a migrant worker, and surviving a hurricane. For Delia, strength is channeled into the purchase of her own home and disposal of an abusive husband.

Even as Hurston used female characters to explore the possibilities of the New Negro Woman in literature, her own life reflected a similarly driven, determined, and uninhibited spunk. Her theories of African American language and art were shaped by her upbringing in the small black community of Eatonville in rural Florida and in her research and collection of black folklore in the rural communities of Florida, Louisiana, and Haiti. She was the first black woman to graduate from Barnard, and she studied with anthropologist Franz Boas while working on an M.A. at Columbia University. Although briefly married at one point, Hurston was self-supporting her entire life and never had children. In writing everything from novels and short fiction to plays and essays, Hurston experimented with form and dialect in innovative ways, believing that "Negro folklore is not a thing of the past. It is still in the making" ("Characteristics" 65). Despite her impressive literary output and its nearly exclusive focus on African American culture, Hurston disappeared as a real presence on the literary scene by mid-century, when she was forced to find work as a maid. She died in poverty and was buried in an unmarked grave. It was not until the 1970s that attention was brought back to this iconic Harlem Renaissance writer by Alice Walker and Hurston biographer Robert Hemenway, who petitioned the Modern Language Association to bring *Their Eyes Were Watching God* back into print.

Like the period's women novelists, short fiction writers took advantage of the nearly insatiable public appetite for literature by African American writers. The majority of aspiring women writers did not have the time or financial security to publish novels; therefore, the short story became one of the chosen genres for expression. Though women's short fiction represented a large portion of stories published in black periodicals, the lives of the women who wrote them are still shrouded in a long shadow of neglect. With little biographical information to convey their New

Negro Woman experiences to us today, we must look for clues in their fiction, most of which has been recovered relatively recently. In these narratives, we can find the New Woman theme that dominated magazine short fiction by white women writers of the time, but black women writers revised the theme to fit their own frame of reference. In their stories are some of the first depictions of realistic black family life and urban domestic communities. No longer constrained by social mores of the nineteenth century, these writers felt freer to explore subjects such as prostitution, female sexuality, and racial oppression in open or semivisible ways. Yet, whereas white women writers often allowed their New Woman heroines to "have it all" at the end of the story, black women writers were often less optimistic about society's acceptance of a true New Negro Woman. Their thwarted heroines, therefore, serve to interrogate racist and sexist social frameworks.

To study a group of active New Negro Women who wrote short stories, one has only to look to Boston, home of the *Saturday Evening Quill*, which had a brief run from 1928 to 1930 and published several stories by women whose names have now dropped into obscurity: Florida Ruffin Ridley, born in Boston in 1861; Edythe Mae Gordon, born in Washington, D.C. in 1896; and Gertrude Schalk, born in Boston in 1906. These women did not fit the typical image of the young Negro artist, and all three resided outside of Harlem. But their stories—depicting everyone from financially unsuccessful and physically depleted husbands to young women driven to "hostessing" in dark jazz clubs to New England mixed-blood matriarchs—offer insight into the hopes and fears of average middle-class women of the New Negro era who did not have a Harlem address or connections to powerful publishers and patrons. If not for the existence of periodicals such as the *Saturday Evening Quill*, which offered additional venues for the New Negro Woman aesthetic and voice, the Harlem Renaissance might have been limited culturally by its geographical boundaries. Selected stories of these New England writers and others can be found in Roses and Randolph's *Harlem's Glory* (1996). Stories written by other lesser-known writers, as well as more familiar names such as Gwendolyn Bennett and Dorothy West, are included in Marcy Knopf's *The Sleeper Wakes* (1993), Patton and Honey's *Double-Take* (2001), and Craig Gable's *Ebony Rising* (2004).

Surpassing even the short story for sheer volume in the pages of African American periodicals was poetry. Women poets of the Harlem Renaissance, many of whom also wrote prose, reached a wide, middle-class audience with their verse. The New Woman and New Negro were prominent themes in this poetry, though often they appeared as subtext, and the connections between the two were not always pronounced. As Roses and Randolph assert, these women writers were "expected to identify themselves as either black or female, but never both" (203). Perhaps this explains why Harlem Renaissance scholarship was slow to bring the many women poets who participated in the movement into the forefront of critical assessment. Women writers who achieved unparalleled success in the 1920s and 1930s were dismissed almost completely when the male New Negro aesthetic was solidified by the canonization of its male luminaries—Hughes, Countee Cullen, Sterling Brown, and Claude McKay. Even Georgia Douglas Johnson, who published three volumes of verse between 1918 and 1928 (along with a fourth collection in 1962), essentially disappeared from discussions of African American poetry. The first anthology recovering women's poetry from this period did not appear until Erlene Stetson's *Black Sister* in 1981, followed by Maureen Honey's more inclusive *Shadowed Dreams* in 1989, now expanded and revised in 2006.

The work of a handful of New Negro Women poets found its way into post-Harlem Renaissance publications. Among the most famous of these was Angelina Weld Grimké. Grimké's case, though defined in part by her reclusive personality, poetics, and context, is representative of many other black women writers of her time in its trajectory. A dramatist and short fiction writer as well as a poet, Grimké's verse echoes that of Imagists such as H.D. and Amy Lowell. Gloria Hull, the scholar most responsible for recovering Grimké's works and life, categorizes her poetry as elegies, love lyrics, nature lyrics, racial poems, and poems about life and universal human experience (137). Hull adds that the dominant feeling of Grimké's work is sadness. Often, Grimké's voice is one of longing, of unfulfilled desire and expectation. Although highly respected in her era, Grimké stopped publishing in the early 1930s and lived out her days reclusively in New York City, alone and childless.

In the classroom, students can use the lessons of New Negro Women's literature to talk about the role gender played in the shaping of the Harlem Renaissance as we now know it. At the same time, students can also consider how the element of race affected the New Woman ideal of the early twentieth century. The study of women's writing also offers an opportunity to discuss the importance of literary recovery work in defining this period. Projects might be designed around finding, collecting, and comparing various writers, literary forms, or themes in the several African American periodicals published during the Harlem Renaissance. There are myriad possibilities for further exploration of the ways in which American literary modernism is complicated and enriched by the contributions of women writers of the Harlem Renaissance.

My admiration for the writings and lives of New Negro Women has only grown as I have come to know them better, for their works speak to us today in subtle and urgent ways about what it meant to be "young, a woman, and colored" (to use Hurston's phrase) in the early decades of the twentieth century. But the New Negro Woman can also offer insight into our own time, our longings, our hopes, our fears, and our strength. The fact that the words of black women writers of the Harlem Renaissance are still relevant and accessible to us despite decades of obscurity and imposed silence is proof of their literary accomplishment. We can now look forward with relish to becoming familiar with more recovered New Negro Woman voices and stories as they are brought back into the light for new generations of readers.

NOTES

1. Zora Neale Hurston was an exception in the patronage system, and her patron, Charlotte Osgood Mason, also supported Hughes.
2. For two different perspectives on this dinner, see Lewis (93-94) and Wall (69–70).
3. Bone places Fauset in the company of Walter White and W.E.B. Du Bois, "a group of novelists who sought a middle ground between the established traditions of the Negro novel and the radical innovations of the Harlem School" (97). For Bone, the Harlem School, in which he includes writers such as Hughes, Countee Cullen, and Toomer, represents those "Negro writers of the 1920's who did not shrink from the implications of cultural dualism" and "turned to the folk for their major characters and a low-life milieu for their principle setting" (65). Despite this critical dichotomy of the Harlem Renaissance literary scene, Bone notes that in "all her primness, Miss Fauset presents something of a paradox, for in her editorial work on the *Crisis* she often championed the young rebels of the Harlem School" (101).
4. As Fauset's novels receive more critical attention, her significance as a fiction writer continues to be debated. For example, Marxist feminist scholar Hazel V. Carby argues that "ultimately the conservatism of Fauset's ideology dominates her texts" (167).

WORKS CITED

Bone, Robert A. *The Negro Novel in America*. New Haven: Yale UP, 1958.

Carby, Hazel V. *Reconstructing Womanhood: The Emergence of the Afro-American Woman Novelist*. New York: Oxford UP, 1987.

Davis, Thadious. *Nella Larsen: Novelist of the Harlem Renaissance*. Baton Rouge: Louisiana State UP, 1994.

Dunbar-Nelson, Alice. *The Goodness of St. Rocque and Other Stories*. New York: Dodd, Mead, 1899.

———. *Violets and Other Tales*. Boston: Privately printed, 1895.

———. "Woman's Most Serious Problem." *The Messenger*. Mar. 1927. Rpt. *Double-Take: A Revisionist Harlem Renaissance Anthology*. Ed. Venetria K. Patton and Maureen Honey. New Brunswick: Rutgers UP, 2001. 113–15.

Fauset, Jessie Redmon. *Plum Bun*. 1929. Ed. Deborah E. McDowell. New Brunswick: Rutgers UP, 1990.

Gable, Craig, ed. *Ebony Rising: Short Fiction of the Greater Harlem Renaissance Era*. Bloomington: Indiana UP, 2004.

Giddings, Paula. *When and Where I Enter: The Impact of Black Women on Race and Sex in America*. New York: William Morrow, 1984.

Honey, Maureen. *Breaking the Ties that Bind: Popular Stories of the New Woman, 1915–1930*. Norman: Oklahoma UP, 1992.

————, ed. *Shadowed Dreams: Women's Poetry of the Harlem Renaissance* rev. edition. New Brunswick: Rutgers UP, 2006.

Hull, Gloria T. *Color Sex and Poetry: Three Women Writers of the Harlem Renaissance*. Bloomington: Indiana UP, 1987.

————. ed. *Give Us Each Day: The Diary of Alice Dunbar-Nelson*. New York: Norton, 1984.

Hurston, Zora Neale. *Their Eyes Were Watching God*. Philadelphia: Lippincott, 1937.

————. "Characteristics of Negro Expression." *Negro: Anthology*. Ed. Nancy Cunard. London: Wishart. 1935. Rpt. Patton and Honey 61–73.

————. "Sweat." *Fire!!*. Nov. 1926. Rpt. Patton and Honey. 329–38.

Hutchinson, George. *In Search of Nella Larsen: A Biography of the Color Line*. Cambridge: Harvard UP, 2006.

Knopf, Marcy, ed. *The Sleeper Wakes: Harlem Renaissance Stories by Women*. New Brunswick: Rutgers UP, 1993.

Larsen, Nella. *Quicksand* and *Passing*. Ed. Deborah E. McDowell. New Brunswick: Rutgers UP, 1993.

Lewis, David Levering. *When Harlem Was in Vogue*. New York: Knopf, 1981.

Locke, Alain. "The New Negro." 1925. *The New Negro: An Interpretation*. Ed. William Loren Katz. New York: Arno, 1968. 3–16.

McDougald, Elise Johnson. "The Task of Negro Womanhood." 1925. *The New Negro: An Interpretation*. Ed. William Loren Katz. New York: Arno, 1968. 369–82.

Patton, Venetria K., and Maureen Honey, eds. *Double-Take: A Revisionist Harlem Renaissance Anthology*. New Brunswick: Rutgers UP, 2001.

Roses, Lorraine Elena, and Ruth Elizabeth Randolph, eds. *Harlem Renaissance and Beyond: Literary Biographies of 100 Black Women Writers, 1900–1945*. Boston: G.K. Hall, 1990.

Stetson, Erlene, ed. *Black Sister: Poetry by Black American Women, 1746–1980*. Bloomington: Indiana UP, 1981.

Wall, Cheryl A. *Women of the Harlem Renaissance*. Bloomington: Indiana UP, 1995.

CHAPTER SIX

On Teaching a Black Queer Harlem Renaissance

LAURA HARRIS

That sexuality is a taboo subject within African American culture is theoretically central to much analysis on black sexuality: Books in the field argue it; colleagues at conferences claim it; students in classes already know it. In addition to this commonly asserted black reticence on sex, a collective, persistent black homophobia is also assigned to African American discourses that suggest representational traditions of black queer sexuality are scarce, deviant, and sub-cultural. I argue for a counterintuitive understanding of the Harlem Renaissance as one moment that ruptures this common knowledge of black silence on sexuality and its subsequent entrenched homophobia; the Renaissance offers one context through which to examine how African American literary representations offer a rich discourse on sexuality, one crosscut by gender, class, geography, and queerness. The Renaissance marks a singular theoretical space for the articulation of black queer identities in great part because Harlem itself already marked a non-normative queer race and class subjectivity, a black dissonance in the white space of modernity. Instead of being intellectually content with blanket assertions about black sexual silence and homophobia, I ask when, where, what, and how black queer sexuality is articulated in the body of Harlem Renaissance work. In doing so, I hope to contribute to an ongoing critical revision of black queer sexuality and the Harlem Renaissance, in particular as regards the philosophical framework for the teaching of race and sexuality studies, arguably one of the more community activist labors that academics are now performing daily.

In his foreword to *Gay Rebel of the Harlem Renaissance: Selections from the work of Richard Bruce Nugent* (2002), Henry Louis Gates Jr. writes that:

> The homosexuality of several of the Harlem Renaissance writers is now generally known and is even occasionally mentioned in scholarly studies, but rarely has it been examined in depth. In fact, it is astonishing that so many prominent participants in the Renaissance were reportedly gay, lesbian, or bisexual. The movement that enabled outsider Negro artists to emerge as a group for the first time was also the movement that enabled gay and lesbian artists to express their sexuality with a greater degree of freedom than at any other period in American history. For those both black and homosexual, who knows what it meant to emerge from behind more than one veil for the very first time? (xi)

Gates's queer postivity is succinctly established as he recognizes black queer sexuality as one of the formative cultural influences at work in the Harlem Renaissance and points towards the rich theoretical opportunities such a recognition presents. Further in his brief appraisal of a queer Renaissance, Gates recognizes the contradictory nature of queer black sexuality; he writes, "Harlem ... could be ... remarkably tolerant of a variety of sexualities, even though homophobia remained a fundamental aspect of black culture" (xii). Gates is not responsible for the notion that black sexual shame or homophobia suppressed black queer sexuality or only tolerated it during the Harlem Renaissance; rather, this is an oft repeated refrain, one for which the question "Ashamed to discuss queer sexuality with whom?" seems theoretically crucial. Even if there are cultural seeds of "truth" to this prevailing discourse about black sexual shame and homophobia, there are equally its contradictions in great abundance in black cultural production, especially that of the Harlem Renaissance.

In calling for its queer recognition, Gates posits the Harlem Renaissance as central to both black and sexuality studies by situating its black cultural production as tantamount to the cultural and literary production articulating sexual marginality in North America. While Gates does lend his living-large academic blessings to Thomas Wirth's independent scholarship on Nugent as queer bohemian writer of the Renaissance, I disagree with Gates's theoretical approach to such recognition, or rather lack of it. Gates's foreword is wholeheartedly humanitarian in tone; it seeks a liberal inclusiveness, one that may well be useful for canonically sanctioned teaching, but an approach that works only at the cost of recognizing what is historically and theoretically valuable about queer cultural production by black artists in the 1920s via a *passing* of them into the canon of respectable black American gay writers. This, without examining thoroughly what it is their work creates may call into question such canonical formations or black and queer aesthetic resistance to canons. A critical teaching of the Harlem Renaissance requires locating it as a civil rights movement of black urban modernity not only imbued with expressions of lived sexual difference but with sexuality as a formative politics and aesthetic. It is urgent to recognize that the Harlem Renaissance offers a historical opportunity not only to recognize the queer lives and production of black artists and intellectuals but also to draw out the theoretical amd aesthetic implications that this cultural moment offers as it contributes further insights into North American histories of race, class, geography, sexuality and cultural production.

Rather than rely solely on inclusivity or visibility as signs of progress, it is a complex, contradictory understanding of black queer sexuality that must become central to understandings of the period overall, that must be made "visible" overall. From feminist readings of blues women's sexualities in both their personal lives and performances (Davis) to current recuperations of the daily queer visibility of Harlem Renaissance artists such as Richard Bruce Nugent, sexuality studies for this period have a strong foundation from which to build. Not only during its heyday did the black urban 1920s of the Harlem Renaissance signify a not-so-subcultural queer iconography, a claim I return to in a moment, but from queer subject matter in then popular novels such as Wallace Thurman's *Infants of the Spring* (1932) to urban studies such as Kevin Mumsford's *Interzones* (1997) to contemporary black queer expressive reclamation such as found in Rodney Evans's film *Brother to Brother* (2004), the Harlem Renaissance was and remains a site of queer black cultural production, both in its historical materiality and in its current theoretical examinations and artistic invocations. The weight of such evidence reminds us that Gates accurately reports the disturbing dearth of scholarly research in this area, and for the purposes of my discussion here, in the teaching of this subject.

Gates is indeed progressive in relation to some scholars still theorizing Harlem Renaissance studies as if sexuality in that period existed in a vacuum without relation to or being contextualized within the social structures and intellectual, artistic, or political alliances of the moment. For example, in his assiduously researched and culturally crossreferenced *The Harlem Renaissance in Black and White* (1995), George Hutchinson writes on male intellectual networks across race and social spheres during the period without a discussion of queer male sexualities as a formative context. In her expertly compiled archive of letters, *Remember Me to Harlem: The Letters of Langston Hughes and Carl Van Vechten* (2002), Emily Bernard claims (much like Arnold Rampersad once did) that there is not any "evidence" of Langston Hughes having same sex relations (Bernard xxiii). Putting aside the problematic juridical implications of seeking for hard evidence of black queer sexual practices (whatever such practices are imagined to be!) in both cases of scholarship, a theoretical consideration of queer male intellectual bonds interracially or analysis of the queer cultural camaraderie exhibited socially is a disturbing critical lacuna, a heterocentric intellectual faux-pas that mars otherwise excellent work. For example, while "evidence" that Hughes and Van Vechten were lovers may be absent, often the discussion in their letters centers on a queer social milieu of male dancers, female impersonators, and other "eccentric" types (Bernard 124–25). Instead of using social science and often homophobic frameworks of genital contact as evidence of lived queerness and identification, theoretically it is far more interesting for black cultural scholars to inquire why Hughes and Van Vechten spent so much time hanging out in and gossiping about the queer culture of the period. What do they have to say about it? How does their dialogue impact an understanding of cultural ties and production across race and sexuality boundaries back then? In short, I argue that at this particular point in Harlem Renaissance studies and its teaching, only a willful, reactionary (mis)reading of sexuality during the Harlem Renaissance could begin yet again with presumptions of black heterosexuality. Such a (mis)reading vehemently presumes heteronormativity against an abundance of queer narrative and cultural codes to the contrary, both historical and contemporary.

Taking as a critical starting point the coexistence of black homophobia and the tolerance for black sexual diversity in Harlem to which Gates alludes, the Harlem Renaissance was indeed a period that witnessed the presence, survival, and growth of a thriving black queer community in urban America. While history demonstrates the yearning of African Americans to find financial and physical security in the promised land of the north when it was brutally denied to them in the South, a less emphasized historical narrative suggests that an escape to urban anonymity and a diverse milieu also motivated black queers. For example, infamous blues singer Gladys Bentley escaped to Harlem as a teenage runaway when her family placed too much scrutiny on her masculine desires and traits. However, despite the relative tolerance of homosexuality in black communities of the north, African Americans had the same difficulties as their white counterparts: Mable Hampton, a renowned lesbian and then newcomer to Harlem from North Carolina, was arrested on prostitution charges in 1920; and the career of Augustus Granvill Dill, the business editor of the *Crisis* and a protégé of W.E.B. Du Bois, was destroyed when he was arrested for soliciting homosexual sex in a public restroom. Despite these difficulties, Lesbian, Gay, Bisexual, and Transgendered (LGBT) African Americans were able to forge a thriving community in Harlem.

The success of the Harlem Renaissance as a cultural movement seeking civil rights was predicated upon the coming together of a collection of presumably unlikely social acquaintances: a camaraderie of elite black male intellectuals and writers with an elite cadre of white male and female intellectuals, writers, and philanthropists; a black female artistic and intellectual network that resisted traditional gender roles and often encouraged a small but flamboyant group of black artists whose public personas, genders, and sexualities were always under scrutiny in gossip columns or other forms of social observation. One highly visible example of this unprecedented type of alliance can be found in the otherwise socially implausible friendship that the Harlem Renaissance produced between Carl Van Vechten, the wealthy, sophisticated gay white critic, and Gladys Bentley, the transgendered, dispossessed, lesbian blues performer. Their casual yet impactful friendship, which arose out of social mixing across class and race boundaries in a modern urban milieu, was founded in great part on their recognition of a queer camaraderie. In this remarkable, brief, yet spectacular eruption of black cosmo-politan urbanity, the coming together in a mutually productive and pleasurable relationship of such apparently unrelated figures as Van Vechten and Bentley exemplifies some of the central dynamics of the queer Harlem Renaissance. From Nugent, who published what may be the first openly gay black male piece of short fiction in the twentieth century; to buffet flats; to Hamilton Lodge drag balls; to the widely acknowledged relationship between Countee Cullen and Harold Jackman; to millionaire heiress A'Lelia Walker, who showered what may be characterized as "fag hag" affections on black male social circles through extravagant parties and literary salon fundraisers—to name but a few of its *passing* spectacles—the Harlem Renaissance was profoundly queer.

In understanding this queer sexuality in the Harlem Renaissance, a useful rubric is that of invisibility, the utility of a private Harlem black queer space simultaneous to Harlem's public representation of middleclass heterosexuality. This space—constituted in great part by the negotiation of passing through social borders, especially those of class—that separates race and sexuality can be seen in many places, from novels containing representations of ambivalent sexual alterity; to cultural insider narratives of queerness such as those acknowledging Cullen and Jackman as a couple (see Schwarz); to the performances of Bentley, who like her famous counterparts Ma Rainey and Bessie Smith was a pioneer in the rise of the black female blues singer during the 1920s. However, unlike Rainey and Smith, Bentley built her career as a notorious Harlem performer, a well-known queer "secret" of the in-crowd of Harlemites and white patrons, such as Van Vechten, who attended her show. Bentley's success as a blues singer was linked with her overtly classed public lesbian persona—one that proudly displayed the "bulldagger" image. Eric Garber writes that this image was "the one identifiable black lesbian stereotype of this period: the tough-talking, masculine acting, cross-dressing, and sexually worldly 'bull dagger'"(56). Bentley's blues artistry entailed a gender perfor-mance that was strongly connected to the active LGBT subculture of the Harlem Renaissance period and to a black working-class social milieu.

I read the spectacle of Bentley's "open secret," her *passing* performance, as it importantly served both to transgress and to produce the class and sexual identity dictates of the Harlem Renaissance, namely that of black middleclass heterosexuality. Bentley-as-open-secret-of-Harlem trangresses and produces this public space of the Harlem Renaissance because of the private space that exists over, within, and between public space, that is constitutive of that public space and the different modes of cultural production and subjectivity circulating within it. Namely, just as the domain of the subject requires the domain of abject beings, public heteronormative space is defined in opposition to an open secret of queer private space in public (see Butler; Chauncey). In the case of Bentley's persona or a buffet flat in relation to Harlem's image and its civil rights agenda, what made Harlem and its subjects nominally "straight" and "middleclass" was opposition to a publicly circulating private narrative: the "open secret" of black queerness and workingclass identity as embodied in Bentley's *passing* of her own queerly sexual, classed black subjectivity as a spectacle of blues performance. Garber notes that while Bessie Smith sang about "mannish acting women," and Ma Rainey enjoyed "wearing a collar and a tie" in "Prove It On Me Blues," Bentley made the black bulldagger role that Lucille Bogan sang about in her "B.D. Women Blues" (1935) the center of her performance. Bentley performed in tuxedos and top hats, sang to women in the audience, exulted in being the object of sexually suggestive queer gossip, and married her white female lover in a highly gossiped about wedding.

Willful (mis)readings of the Harlem Renaissance which fail to recognize or continue to dispute the tremendous influence of its queer cultural milieu contribute, knowingly or otherwise, to contemporary racist and homophobic reactions to queerly sexual, classed black subjectivities; we might at least agree the past is urgent to understanding the present and future. Further, claims about black sexual shame and homophobia should not be circulated like the common sense truth of an old wives' tale; rather, such claims require indepth examination and cultural unpacking.

Let's return to my disagreement with Gates's foreword to *Gay Rebel of the Harlem Renaissance*. Clearly, Gates's queer-positive intellectual stance and iconic visibility are useful to Wirth's black, queer, independent scholarship, an area of study founded in great part by indie scholars such as Wirth and Garber as opposed to a predominately black middleclass academic sphere. As I stated earlier, it is the theoretical assumption of this foreword that I argue against in studying and teaching the Harlem Renaissance. Very brief in form, a page and a half, and utterly humanist in tone by verifying the "truth" of Wirth's work, within the African American literary tradition it bears a jarring resemblance to slave narrative forewords by notable white abolitionists. However, beyond formal concerns, by seeming liberally to release black queers from their Harlem Renaissance closet, critically it participates in a post-Harlem Renaissance "closeting" through a reliance on a historical and theoretical inaccuracy: that black queer life was marginal as opposed to central to Harlem Renaissance culture and politics.

Finally, as queer (mis)readings of the Harlem Renaissance go, it is intriguing to note two dissonant yet useful teaching moments of queer presence: First, so compelling was Bentley's performance that decades later artist Romare Bearden mistook her for a cross-dressing male when he identified her as a male-to-female impersonator called Gladys Bentley who sang at the Clam House (Braithwaite-Willis 110); and second, of interest is the footnote to the Harold Jackman dedication of Countee Cullen's poem *Heritage* in the first and second edition of *The Norton Anthology of African American Literature* (1997 and 2004) identifying Jackman as "probably Cullen's closest friend" (1347). Both the contemporary canonical closeting of Cullen and Jackman as lovers and Bearden's quirky, historically prescient (trans)gender (mis)read of Bentley as a drag queen point towards the complex narratives yet to be fully unpacked in the teaching of Harlem Renaissance and queer sexuality studies.

WORKS CITED

Bernard, Emily, ed. *Remember Me To Harlem: The Letters of Langston Hughes and Carl Van Vechten.* New York: Vintage, 2002.

Braithwaite-Willis, Deborah, ed. *Van Der Zee, Photographer: 1886–1983.* New York: Harry N. Abrams, 1993.

Brother to Brother. Dir. Rodney Evans. DVD. Wolfe Video, 2005.

Butler, Judith. *Bodies That Matter: On the Discursive Limits of Sex.* New York: Routledge, 1993.

Chauncey, George. *Gay New York: Gender, Urban Culture, and the Making of the Gay Male World, 1890–1940.* New York: Basic, 1995.

Davis, Angela Y. *Blues Legacies and Black Feminism.* New York: Vintage, 1999.

Garber, Eric. "Gladys Bentley: The Bulldagger Who Sang the Blues." *Outlook* 1 (1988): 52–61.

———. "A Spectacle in Color: The Lesbian and Gay Subculture of Jazz Age Harlem." *Hidden from History: Reclaiming the Gay and Lesbian Past.* Eds. Martin Duberman et al. New York: Meridian, 1989. 318–31.

Gates, Henry Louis, Jr. and Nellie Y. McKay, eds. *The Norton Anthology of African American Literature.* New York: Norton, 2004.

Hull, Gloria T. *Color, Sex, and Poetry: Three Women Writers of the Harlem Renaissance.* Bloomington: Indiana UP, 1987.

Hutchinson, George. *The Harlem Renaissance in Black and White.* Cambridge: Harvard UP, 1995.

McDowell, Deborah E. "Introduction." *Quicksand* and *Passing.* New Brunswick: Rutgers UP, 1986.

Mumsford, Kevin J. *Interzones: Black/White Sex Districts in Chicago and New York in the Early Twentieth Century.* New York: Columbia UP, 1997.

Schwarz, Christa, A.B. *Gay Voices of the Harlem Renaissance.* Bloomington: Indiana UP, 2003.

Thurman, Wallace. *Infants of the Spring.* 1932. New York: Modern Library, 1999.

——— et al., eds. *Fire!!* 1926. Elizabeth, NJ: Fire!! Press, 1992.

Watson, Steven. *The Harlem Renaissance: Hub of African-American Culture, 1920–1930.* New York: Pantheon, 1995.

Wirth, Thomas, ed. *Gay Rebel of the Harlem Renaissance: Selections from the Work of Richard Bruce Nugent.* Durham: Duke UP, 2002.

CHAPTER SEVEN

Teaching Women Poets of the Harlem Renaissance

MAUREEN HONEY

Although male poets of the Harlem Renaissance enjoy plenty of name recognition by contemporary scholars, when I ask people to name a woman poet from the era, I am generally met with silence. We know that poetry was the preferred genre for Harlem Renaissance writers and that women contributed substantially to poetic production, but we are yet to become familiar enough with their work to have a sense of what they added to the African American or modernist literary canons. Langston Hughes, Sterling Brown, and others are known for their innovative use of jazz, blues, and work songs in poetry, elevating these folk and urban vernacular formats to new ways of expressing cultural pride and identity. Hughes's "The Negro Speaks of Rivers" (1921) is legendary, while Brown's "Southern Road" (1932) famously conveys the back-breaking, soul-destroying work of chain gangs in the South. Claude McKay is credited with striking a new militant note of New Negro resistance with his 1919 poem "If We Must Die." Countee Cullen's "Heritage" (1925) and "Yet Do I Marvel" (1925) are iconic poems emblematizing the era's reclaiming of Africa as a cultural center and emphasis on artistic awakening. But where are the female-authored poetic texts that symbolize this period of race pride and modernist innovation?

One reason for this puzzling divide, I think, is that women writers in general have had to be recovered for a late twentieth-century critical establishment that could not hear their voices or see the ways they centrally shaped the literary canon—but black women writers, in particular, have faced the double barriers of race and gender, making their voices even harder to hear. We have had to reconstruct the historical context for New Negro female writers in order to grasp the particular metaphors, cadences, and concerns that animate their verse as black women in an era of segregation, violence, political disenfranchisement, and racist caricatures. These poetic characteristics include a reliance on traditional verse forms that hark back to nineteenth-century Romantic poets, such as Browning, Tennyson, and Keats, but with a distinctive emphasis on night, trees, pregnancy, veils, and other images that point to their identities as modern black women resisting dominant culture stereotypes and erasure. When teaching this poetry, it is important to draw attention to these race- and gender-coded references, so that students understand the direct relationship between writer and poem.

Angelina Weld Grimké's poem "The Black Finger," which appeared originally in *Opportunity* in 1923 and then in Alain Locke's touchstone text *The New Negro* (1925), offers a useful example. The central image of the tree is a trope signifying the resilience, strength, and strong roots of black people, and it is one that extends over much of the period's poetry: "I have just seen a most beautiful thing: / Slim and still, / Against a gold, gold sky, / A straight, black cypress / Sensitive / Exquisite / A black finger / Pointing upwards. / Why, beautiful still finger, are you black? / And why are you pointing upwards?" Trees are stationary and partly symbolic of women's immobility, but they also stand for quiet endurance, pride, dignity, and aspiration, as well as hardy survival of harsh conditions.

Another example is the use of night, as in Gwendolyn Bennett's "Street Lamps in Early Spring," which also appeared in *Opportunity* in 1926: "Night wears a garment / All velvet soft, all violet blue ... / And over her face she draws a veil / As shimmering fine as floating dew ... / And here and there / In the black of her hair / The subtle hands of Night / Move slowly with their gem-starred light." The preference for nighttime over daylight expressed in this poem and in much women's poetry of the Harlem Renaissance served a variety of functions. One was to assert the primacy of blackness in a world favoring white things. Quieter, calmer, less dramatic than the day, night is in these poems an essential force in life, the contemplation of which brings serenity to a restless, discontented spirit. Bennett's poem captures another aspect of night's usefulness as a metaphor for black women poets. Night here draws over her face a veil and is cast as a goddess whose features are hidden. In this way, night stands for the masked self, one that escapes the distorted negative images of those who fail to see a black woman clearly. Not only a vibrant female force who rules her domain wisely, night offers as well respite from the daily struggle to survive, for in a dark world, blackness cannot be used as a marker of difference or become an object of attack.

Nature metaphors such as these point to the indirect coded quality of much women's verse in the 1920s and beyond. Although much of it is wrung free of overt anger or protest, it yet traces a theme of regeneration through retreat and disguise that echoes the writer's search for a way to make herself heard without facing annihilation. In an era when black women had very little political or economic power, such coded allusions to strategies for surviving racism and sexism within accepted literary forms made sense. As well, the Harlem Renaissance was all about fighting racism through achievement in the arts, the primary route at the time for defining the New Negro man or woman. This was a modern figure at odds with plantation images of blacks inherited from slavery, and women as well as men fashioned themselves as literary spokespeople for the race by appropriating classic poetic forms.

At the same time, women poets had to deal with editors, publishers, and critics who favored young male writers. The image of the New Negro was largely male, given its association with black soldiers in World War I, vagabond travel throughout Europe or the Caribbean, and migration to factories in the urban north. As Alain Locke expresses it in his essay "The New Negro" in the 1925 anthology of the same name,

> For generations the Negro has been the peasant matrix of that section of America [the South] which has most undervalued him. ... He now becomes a conscious contributor and lays aside the status of a beneficiary and ward for that of a collaborator and participant in American civilization. The great social gain in this is the releasing of our talented group from the arid fields of controversy and debate to the productive fields of creative expression. (15)

The New Negro is a "he" in the period's conversations about a renaissance in African American artistic production, and women poets responded to this by centering their verse on female imagery, especially fecundity and birth. A good example is Mae Cowdery's "After the Japanese," published in her collection *We Lift Our Voices* (1936): "Night turned over / In her sleep / And a star fell / Into the sea. / Earth was a beautiful / Snow woman / Until the rain / Washed her face one day. / I am the rain / Throbbing futilely / On the cold roof / Of your heart. / The moon / Is a Madonna / Cradling in the crescent curve / Of her breast / A newborn star" (12). As in this poem, nature is often personified as female and brought to life as a woman, for it was a way for poets to find mirrors in a literary landscape dominated by men.

It is also important for teachers to emphasize that women poets saw themselves as modernists and, as such, experimented with new verse forms, such as Imagism and blank verse, as well as with daring forays into erotic or sensual material. Angelina Weld Grimké was especially adept at creating crystallized images in a few lines meant to convey heightened sensory attention to one's surroundings, as in "Dusk," published in Countee Cullen's influential collection of New Negro poetry, *Caroling Dusk* (1927): "Twin Stars through my purpling pane, / The shriveling husk / Of a yellowing moon on the wane, / And the dusk" (46). She was also capable of evoking sweeping emotional transport, as in "El Beso," published originally in 1909 and in the ground-breaking *Negro Poets and Their Poems* (1923):

> Twilight—and you
> Quiet—the stars;
> Snare of the shine of your teeth,
> Your provocative laughter,
> The gloom of your hair;
> Lure of you, eye and lip;
> Yearning, yearning,
> Languor, surrender;
> Your mouth,
> And madness, madness,
> Tremulous, breathless, flaming,
> The space of a sigh;
> Then awakening—remembrance,
> Pain, regret—your sobbing;
> And again, quiet—the stars,
> Twilight—and you. (154)

Emotional and erotic frankness such as this characterizes women's poetry of the 1920s, which brought a sensual quality to verse that had been absent from previous African American poetry and signaled the poets' identities as modern women with passionate drives.

Both heterosexual and lesbian longing for erotic and passionate connection is central to women's verse and provides students with an accessible reference point for the modernity of this early writing. Another example of this erotic verse is Mae Cowdery's "Insatiate" (also published in *We Lift Our Voices*), which makes direct reference to a female lover:

> If my love were meat and bread
> And sweet cool wine to drink,
> They would not be enough,
> For I must have a finer table spread
> To sate my entity.
> If her lips were rubies red,
> Her eyes two sapphires blue,
> Her fingers ten sticks of white jade,

Coral tipped ... and her hair of purple hue
Hung down in a silken shawl ...
They would not be enough to fill the coffers of my needs. (57)

Renewed attention to the Harlem Renaissance as a site of gay and lesbian activity
is revealing that it was very much a part of Harlem artistic circles. Lesbian blues
singers Bessie Smith, Ma Rainey, and Gladys Bentley, for instance, were star performers during the 1920s, and their sexual preferences for women were known to
those who frequented jazz clubs. Two primary organizers of Harlem social life,
A'Lelia Walker and Carl Van Vechten, routinely sought the company of lesbians
and gay men. Writers Countee Cullen, Bruce Nugent, Langston Hughes, and
Wallace Thurman are now thought to have been gay or bisexual, as was intellectual leader Alain Locke. The lesbian poetry produced by women such as Cowdery
provides an important marker of this aspect of the Renaissance and is the earliest
African American literature to contain lesbian themes. It is a ground-breaking
link to lesbian and gay poetry of today, one that students quickly appreciate.

Another aspect of experimental modernism running through women's poetry
is the use of urban street vernacular punctuated by jazz and blues rhythms. Helene
Johnson arguably produced the best of this poetry and is strikingly bold in her use
of slang, foreshadowing today's hip-hop artists. In "Poem," for example, which
appeared in *Caroling Dusk*, she rhapsodizes over a sexy Harlem street youth hanging out at the Lafayette Theater:

Little brown boy,
Slim, dark, big-eyed,
Crooning love songs to your banjo
Down at the Lafayette—
Gee, boy, I love the way you hold your head,
High sort of and a bit to one side,
Like a prince, a jazz prince. And I love
Your eyes flashing, and your hands,
And your patent-leathered feet,
And your shoulders jerking the jig-wa.
And I love your teeth flashing,
And the way your hair shines in the spotlight
Like it was the real stuff.
Gee, brown boy, I loves you all over. (218)

Reminiscent of Langston Hughes and Sterling Brown, Johnson was able to break
through traditional verse forms to create a particularly African American modern

voice that is urban, sassy, and sparkling with musical cadences. Reading this poetry aloud to students is among the most exciting and riveting pedagogical tools a teacher can use to make the Harlem Renaissance come alive.

Above all, it is important for students to know that women were among the prime movers and shakers of the New Negro movement, with Jessie Fauset serving as literary editor of *The Crisis* under W.E.B. Du Bois and Gwendolyn Bennett as a key editor at *Opportunity* under Charles S. Johnson; Georgia Douglas Johnson's Saturday night salons in Washington D.C. were a central meeting point for the young literary lions garnering publishing contracts at Harper and Row and other major houses. Fauset published four novels during the Harlem Renaissance and Johnson published three volumes of poetry. Nella Larsen's two novels were critically acclaimed and won her a Guggenheim Fellowship while Zora Neale Hurston was a major star even at the time. They should also be made aware that most of the women publishing during the Renaissance were poets who made substantial contributions to the central journals and anthologies of their day. Yet by World War II, their poetry had already been largely forgotten and erased from postwar anthologies.

To teach these poets, then, is to participate in a larger recovery project of women writers begun in the 1970s with the reprinting of Kate Chopin's *The Awakening* (1899), Zora Neale Hurston's *Their Eyes Were Watching God* (1937), and other fine novels that had been left behind by a largely white, largely male critical establishment formed in the conservative aftermath of World War II. Although white female poets, such as Sylvia Plath, Elizabeth Bishop, and others enjoyed a resurgence of interest at this time, it was not until Erlene Stetson's ground-breaking *Black Sister: Poetry by Black American Women, 1746–1980* (1981) that women's poetry from the 1920s was brought back into print in a substantial way. With Ann Allen Shockley's *Afro-American Women Writers, 1746–1933* (1988), we began to see that black women poets from the early twentieth century produced an important link between Phillis Wheatley and contemporary poets of the postmodern period. *Shadowed Dreams: Women's Poetry of the Harlem Renaissance* (1989; revised and expanded edition 2006) followed these anthologies, and for the first time this poetry was reprinted in anything like the volume that had characterized its explosion onto the literary scene in the Harlem Renaissance itself. Around that time, major critical work started to appear by Gloria Hull (*Color, Sex, and Poetry* [1987] and *The Works of Alice Dunbar Nelson* [1988]), Cheryl Wall (*Women of the Harlem Renaissance* [1995]), and Lorraine Elena Roses and Ruth Randolph (*The Harlem Renaissance and Beyond* [1990] and *Harlem's Glory* [1996]) that provided biographical and historical information highlighting the importance of these writers to the African American canon.

These are still among the most central reference works on women poets and were joined by reprints of period collections published as part of the G.K. Hall series edited by Henry Louis Gates Jr., African-American Women Writers, 1910–1940. Verner D. Mitchell's reprint anthology, *Helene Johnson: Poet of the Harlem Renaissance* (2000), is the most recent of these and followed Claudia Tate's *The Selected Works of Georgia Douglas Johnson* (1997) and Carolivia Herron's *Selected Works of Angelina Weld Grimké* (1991). Reprint anthologies of minor writers have also started to appear in the G.K. Hall series: *Voices in the Poetic Tradition* (1996) by Clara Ann Thompson, J. Pauline Smith, and Mazie Earhart Clark; *Hope's Highway; Clouds and Sunshine* (1995) by Sarah Lee Brown Fleming; and *Selected Works of Edythe Mae Gordon* (1996). Contemporary anthologies are also paying greater attention to women poets of the period: *The Norton Anthology of African American Literature* (1997), *The Portable Harlem Renaissance Reader* (1994), *Voices from the Harlem Renaissance* (1976), *The Crisis Reader* and *The Opportunity Reader* (1999), *Double-Take: A Revisionist Harlem Renaissance Anthology* (2001), *The New Cavalcade: African American Writing from 1760 to the Present* (1991–1992), and *Cornerstones: An Anthology of African American Literature* (1996). Such anthologies attempt to redress the gender imbalance of poetry reprinted in the past by including more selections by women.

For teaching purposes, the best anthologies to use for teaching Harlem Renaissance women poets in a general or an umbrella course on African American literature are *The Norton Anthology of African American Literature* (if a course is broader than the Harlem Renaissance) and *The Portable Harlem Renaissance Reader*, *Voices From the Harlem Renaissance*, and *Double-Take* (if the course covers men and women, multiple genres, and a large unit on the Renaissance). *The Norton Anthology* provides a useful, though brief, historical context for the Harlem Renaissance, which it defines as 1919–1940. Although more women poets are included than in previous anthologies, there are still only five of them represented in a total of twenty-four female-authored poems. The five women poets selected, however, stand at the core of the most important writers: Angelina Weld Grimké, Anne Spencer, Georgia Douglas Johnson, Gwendolyn Bennett, and Helene Johnson. If one had to choose only five women poets to teach, this would not be a bad group. On the other hand, many who give us a much better picture of the period's diversity are left out, and no lesbian poetry is included.

On par with the *Norton* are *The Portable Harlem Renaissance Reader* and *Voices From the Harlem Renaissance*, which also provide a variety of genres while covering both men and women but include only a limited number of poems by women. Just fifteen poems by six women are in *The Portable* and nine poems by seven women in *Voices*. Again, the women are well chosen with the notable omission of Angelina Weld Grimké, who should be on any list of poets to teach (included are Bennett, Spencer, Helene and Georgia Douglas Johnson, Mae Cowdery, and Jessie Fauset), but the offerings are somewhat minimal. David Levering Lewis's and Nathan Huggins's introductions respectively are comprehensive descriptions of the historical and cultural context for literature of the period, albeit incomplete on the subject of gender.

Better coverage of women writers, including the poets, in the broad anthologies is provided by *Double-Take*, which is the first Harlem Renaissance anthology that includes equal numbers of selections by men and women; it also includes lesbian and gay writers. A multigenre anthology that presents male and female writers in order of their birth dates, it provides a lengthy introduction highlighting gender issues while introducing each writer with biographical information. Altogether, fifty-six poems by eleven women are included, a hefty number that allows for coverage of some important issues left out of many Renaissance anthologies. It does not, however, go in depth on the themes and poetic forms that make this period such a central one for studying African American poetry because it covers a vast amount of literature by so many writers. At the same time, the introduction provides a comprehensive look at major issues of the period, including a substantial commentary on the centrality of gender.

For teachers who wish to focus more inclusively or more in-depth on women writers, either as a course or as a unit in a course, the best anthologies are *Black Sister*, *Harlem's Glory*, and *Shadowed Dreams*. *Black Sister* covers the broadest period of time, 1746–1980, which means its section on the Harlem Renaissance is somewhat shortened, but nevertheless it contains a solid selection of core Renaissance poets with thirty-eight of their poems: Georgia and Helene Johnson, Grimké, Fauset, Spencer, Bennett, Cowdery, and Alice Dunbar-Nelson. Erlene Stetson's introductions for the historically divided sections emphasize poetic form and theme rather than historical framework, a drawback for teachers looking to frame the Renaissance as a literary period. *Harlem's Glory* focuses only on women and also covers a wide period of time—1900–1950—a considerable broadening of the definition of the Harlem Renaissance, but this liberal time frame results in the representation of a large number of writers as well as selections by them. Altogether, there are fifty-four poems by fourteen poets. The volume is arranged thematically and poetry is mixed in with essays and short fiction. Many of the minor writers are represented in this collection, adding diverse voices to our knowledge of African American literature from the early twentieth century. Drawing on their 1990 collection of literary biographies of one hundred black women writers from 1900 to 1945, *Harlem Renaissance and Beyond*, editors Lorraine Elena Roses and Ruth Randolph provide valuable biographical and literary reference material at the back of *Harlem's Glory* on the writers covered, including several photos. Each of the ten sections is introduced with a thematic description and the biographical notes are wonderfully comprehensive, but for teachers needing historical context on the Harlem Renaissance per se, this anthology will need to be supplemented by another text that provides such a frame.

My anthology, *Shadowed Dreams*, is the only collection devoted exclusively to women poets of the Harlem Renaissance. As such, it is too narrow for use as a general anthology, but as a supplement to other texts, it provides an in-depth look at black women's poetry between the wars, with an emphasis on the 1920s, when the Renaissance was at its peak. As well, the lengthy critical introduction frames this poetry and its significance well by calling attention to women's use of race-inflected nature metaphors in their pastoral verse, feminist themes, erotic tropes (including same-sex love), use of the vernacular, and New Negro militancy. The revised edition of *Shadowed Dreams* (2006) substantially expands the offerings of the first edition and changes the arrangement from a thematic one to a collection organized by author for easier reference and clearer understanding of each poet's voice. In addition, biographical sections have been added as an introduction to each poet, further strengthening each one's poetic identity.

Whichever text(s) a teacher selects, women's poetry of the Harlem Renaissance lends itself to bridging the gap between today's cultural/historical framework and yesterday's in terms of educating students about this crucial African American artistic movement. Because poems are aural and oral as well as visual, it is possible to bring sound and motion to the printed page by asking students to read and even perform their favorite pieces. Women's poetry from this era is highly accessible to contemporary readers, for it was originally designed to be accessible to a diverse African American audience. Because art was viewed as a political weapon breaking down racist segregation in pre–Civil Rights America, literature of the Harlem Renaissance is unusually populist in its form and content. The poetry is arguably the most populist genre of the period because of its directness, brevity, and familiar imagery. It was designed for the masses, which makes it easier for contemporary teachers to present.

Having taught women's poetry from the Renaissance era thematically, I believe it is more useful to present poets as individual writers with distinctive voices and specific biographical descriptions. The interplay between a woman's poetry and her biography illuminates the poems while bringing the poet more vividly to life. I think it is best, therefore, to focus units on poets to whom students find themselves drawn and to discuss them as individual artists who nevertheless share a historical moment and a literary community. The most prominent women poets who have produced the most important work and should, therefore, be included in any course on the Harlem Renaissance include Gwendolyn Bennett, Mae Cowdery, Alice Dunbar-Nelson, Jessie Fauset, Angelina Weld Grimké, Georgia Douglas Johnson, Helene Johnson, and Anne Spencer. Most of them were feminists as well as race activists and most of them were at the center of the New Negro movement in Harlem and Washington D.C. Other poets who produced a solid body of very fine work and who would make a course even more vibrant are newly emerging writers gaining critical attention: Carrie Williams Clifford, Anita Scott Coleman, Blanche Taylor Dickinson, Edythe Mae Gordon, Gladys Casely Hayford (a.k.a. Aquah Laluah), Virginia Houston, Effie Lee Newsome, Esther Popel, and Lucy Mae Turner (granddaughter of iconic slave rebel Nat Turner). There are undoubtedly others who will emerge in the future.

As we become more familiar with the work of women poets of the Harlem Renaissance, we will begin to identify touchstone texts as we have done with the male poets, poems that symbolize the militant spirit, pride, and cultural sensibility of the era. Potential candidates, in my mind, are Gwendolyn Bennett's "Song" (1925), Mae Cowdery's "Goal" (1927), Jessie Fauset's ode to Sojourner Truth, "Oriflamme" (1920), Angelina Weld Grimké's "The Black Finger" (1923), Georgia Douglas Johnson's "The Heart of a Woman" (1918), Helene Johnson's "Bottled" (1927), Anne Spencer's "White Things" (1923), and Lucy Ariel Williams's "Northboun'" (1926). (All of these titles can be found in *Shadowed Dreams*.) Only when that happens will we be able to speak a woman's name when asked which poets of the Harlem Renaissance immediately come to mind as immortalized voices in the literary canon.

WORKS CITED

Chopin, Kate. *The Awakening*. 1899. Ed. Margaret Culley. New York: Norton, 1976.

Cowdery, Mae. *We Lift Our Voices, and Other Poems*. Ed. William Stanley Braithwaite. Philadelphia: Alpress, 1936.

Davis, Arthur Paul et al., eds. *The New Cavalcade: African American Writing from 1760 to the Present*. 2 vols. Washington, D.C.: Howard UP, 1991–1992.

Donalson, Melvin Burke, ed. *Cornerstones: An Anthology of African American Literature*. New York: St. Martin's, 1996.

Dunbar-Nelson, Alice. *The Works of Alice Dunbar-Nelson*. 3 vols. Ed. Gloria T. Hull. New York: Oxford UP, 1988.

Fleming, Sarah Lee Brown. *Hope's Highway; Clouds and Sunshine*. New York: G.K. Hall, 1995.

Gates, Henry Louis Jr., and Nellie Y. McKay, eds. *The Norton Anthology of African American Literature*. New York: Norton, 1997.

Grimké, Angelina Weld. *Selected Works of Angelina Weld Grimké*. Ed. Carolivia Herron. New York: Oxford UP, 1991.

Honey, Maureen, ed. *Shadowed Dreams: Women's Poetry of the Harlem Renaissance*, rev. edition. New Brunswick: Rutgers UP, 2006.

Huggins, Nathan Irvin, ed. *Voices from the Harlem Renaissance*. New York: Oxford UP, 1976.

Hull, Gloria T. *Color, Sex, and Poetry: Three Women Writers of the Harlem Renaissance*. Bloomington: Indiana UP, 1987.

Hurston, Zora Neale. *Their Eyes Were Watching God.* 1937. New York: Harper, 1998.

Johnson, Georgia Douglas. *The Selected Works of Georgia Douglas Johnson.* Ed. Claudia Tate. New York: G.K. Hall, 1997.

Lewis, David Levering, ed. *The Portable Harlem Renaissance Reader.* New York: Viking, 1994.

Locke, Alain, ed. *The New Negro.* 1925. New York: Atheneum, 1992.

Mitchell, Verner D., ed. *This Waiting for Love: Helene Johnson, Poet of the Harlem Renaissance.* Amherst: U of Massachusetts P, 2000.

Patton, Venetria K., and Maureen Honey, eds. *Double-Take: A Revisionist Harlem Renaissance Anthology.* New Brunswick: Rutgers UP, 2001.

Roses, Lorraine Elena, and Ruth Elizabeth Randolph. *Harlem Renaissance and Beyond: Literary Biographies of 100 Black Women Writers, 1900–1945.* Boston: G.K. Hall, 1990.

———, eds. *Harlem's Glory: Black Women Writing, 1900–1950.* Cambridge: Harvard UP, 1996.

Shockley, Ann Allen, ed. *Afro-American Women Writers, 1746–1933: An Anthology and Critical Guide.* Boston: G.K. Hall, 1988.

Stetson, Erlene, ed. *Black Sister: Poetry by Black Women, 1746–1980.* Bloomington: Indiana UP, 1981.

Thompson, Clara Ann. *Voices in the Poetic Tradition: Clara Ann Thompson, J. Pauline Smith, Mazie Earhart Clark.* Introduction Mary Anne Stewart Boelcskevy. New York: G.K. Hall, 1996.

Wall, Cheryl A. *Women of the Harlem Renaissance.* Bloomington: Indiana UP, 1995.

Wilson, Sondra Kathryn, ed. *The Crisis Reader: Stories, Poetry, and Essays from the N.A.A.C.P.'s Crisis Magazine.* New York: Modern, 1999.

———, ed. *The Opportunity Reader: Stories, Poetry, and Essays from the Urban League's Opportunity Magazine.* New York: Modern, 1999.

Part II. Harlem Renaissance Writers and Texts

CHAPTER EIGHT

Teaching Sterling Brown's Poetry

JAMES SMETHURST

Sterling Brown was among the founders of the discipline of African American studies, promoting particularly, as his former student Amiri Baraka recalls, the idea that African American vernacular culture could be the subject of serious academic study in disciplines other than ethnography (Baraka 109–10). In addition, looking at Brown's work as a literary critic and historian, reviewer, editor, teacher, and Negro Affairs editor of the Federal Writers Project during his fantastically productive period from the late 1920s to the early 1940s, one could make the plausible claim that he was the first real academic scholar of black literature and of the representation of African Americans in the literatures of the United States—indeed, arguably the most important African American literary figure of those fifteen or so years. I have found his poetry, especially that in the 1932 collection *Southern Road* (his only published poetry collection until Broadside Press's *The Last Ride of Wild Bill* in 1975), extremely useful in getting students to think about various notions of the relation of the African American artist to the black community circulating during the Harlem Renaissance as well as about the end of the Renaissance era and the beginning of a new sort of cultural moment in the 1930s.

I have taught Brown's poetry in a variety of institutional and disciplinary contexts: at an Ivy League university, a public urban commuter university, and a large state university; in English departments and African American studies departments; to graduate and undergraduate students; and in large survey courses, somewhat less large courses on the Harlem Renaissance and the 1930s, and more specialized seminars in African American poetry. My current institutional location has had a big impact on my understanding of Brown and his importance. Many of the founding members of the Department of Afro-American Studies at the University of Massachusetts-Amherst had a close personal and intellectual relationship to Brown. Indeed, much of the original core group that established Afro-American Studies in 1969 was comprised of graduate students in the Department of English, including Bernard Bell, Esther Terry, and Michael Thelwell, whom Brown had encouraged to go to the University of Massachusetts to work with Jules Chametzky and Sidney Kaplan. This connection was further strengthened a few years later with the arrival of John Bracey Jr., whose mother had taught in the Howard University English Department and for whom Brown was a familiar figure of childhood. A number of these scholars are still extremely active in my department and in the larger university community.

Conversations about Brown with my colleagues, especially Michael Thelwell, have greatly strengthened my sense of Brown's continuing role in African American letters and politics long after the heyday of his publishing activities in the 1930s and early 1940s, a sense further increased by my research into the Black Arts Movement of the 1960s and 1970s. I have gotten from these conversations, and from interviews with such former students of Brown as Baraka and A.B. Spellman, a much more immediate feel for how Brown's classes and his informal seminars on black music and culture at Howard University were vital to the development of several generations of African American intellectuals, artists, and activists, including Baraka, Toni Morrison, Kwame Turé (Stokeley Carmichael), and the other leaders of Howard's Nonviolent Action Group (an affiliate of the Student Nonviolent Coordinating Committee). The informal gatherings, generally featuring storytelling and bourbon, were particularly crucial not only in positing black vernacular culture as a worthy subject of serious study, but also in proposing culture (and its rhetorical style) as an arena for serious thought and analysis, and as a viable mode of intellectual discourse for a black scholar and activist.[1]

Obviously, such an immediate, living connection to Brown's work is not available in many places today. But I raise it to recall how much of Brown's poetry in the 1930s presents models for the relationship of the black artist to an African American audience and for a new scholarship about African American culture in ways that continued not only to be relevant, but also to be influential long after the poetry was initially published (and long after it had gone out of print before the new editions of Brown's verse in the 1970s and 1980s). It is important, I think, for the teacher of Brown's work to recall and to impart to her or his students that if in some senses the significance of Brown and his poetry began (like the Harlem Renaissance itself) to be reclaimed in the 1970s and 1980s, in other important ways it never really was unclaimed.

Despite Brown's continuing presence in what would become African American studies from its earliest genesis to the present, accessibility to his poetry still remains an issue. As of this writing, the most useful collection of Brown's poetry, Michael Harper's edition of *The Collected Poems of Sterling A. Brown*, is in print but has been available only erratically since its initial publication by Harper & Row in 1980. It has the great value of including not only *Southern Road*, but also Brown's second, unpublished collection, *No Hiding Place*, rejected by Harcourt, Brace (the initial publisher of *Southern Road*) in 1936 or 1937, allegedly on account of the manuscript's pronounced leftwing cast.[2] Unfortunately, *Collected Poems* lacks the E. Simms Campbell illustrations that appeared at the beginning of each section of the original edition of *Southern Road*. These illustrations are reproduced in the 1974 Beacon Press reissue of *Southern Road* now generally unavailable except in some libraries and through rare book dealers.

If possible, I would recommend that teachers of *Southern Road*, as well as Brown's later poetry, try to get copies of the illustrations for their classes. One thing that these illustrations do is reinforce how much *Southern Road* is a story of the alienated black intellectual-artist's return to and reengagement with the culture and struggles of the African American folk in the South. The first two sections lay out a vision of the South, a vision of racial and class oppression and a culture of resistance; the third migration, alienation, and cultural appropriation in the urban North; and the final section a sort of return—as indicated by the Campbell illustration depicting a younger man being greeted by an older couple in front of a cabin. As the critic Robert Stepto noted some time ago in *From Behind the Veil*, the story of the alienated black intellectual/artist's descent South to the black folk and their culture and the resulting "shock of recognition" (to quote Edmund Wilson), what Stepto called the "immersion ritual," was an archetypal story of post-Reconstruction African American literature (Stepto 66–71).

However, for Brown, this culture was not, as it was for some of his black and whiter peers, simply one of a close connection to the soil, nature, and a sort of spirituality lost in the migration to the metropolis, but also one of continuous individual and group resistance to racial and class oppression, resistance that could be stoically passive, as in the remarkable fusion of the blues and the gang labor song lyric genres in "Southern Road"; trickily oblique, as is often the case in the Slim Greer poems; or shockingly direct, as in *No Hiding Place*'s "Old Lem,"— or, remarkably all three, as in the famous poem "Strong Men." This emphasis on the southern folk culture as one of struggle, in fact, as the ultimate underpinning for the struggle against racism and Jim Crow segregation, distinguished Brown's poetry from the literature of other Harlem Renaissance era writers, even Langston Hughes, whose vernacular work was far more likely to emphasize urban black culture. This return to and reunion with the folk is not any kind of simple, sentimental fantasy since the final "Vestiges" section of *Southern Road* is from a certain perspective the most formally conservative of the volume, employing, for example, various sorts of sonnets. Brown does not condescend to the folk but puts them on a par with so-called standard literary English works and forms—a parity that is even more emphasized in the concluding section of *No Hiding Place* in which such "standard" literary poems appear alongside blues lyrics and other verse in a folk voice.

It is this sense of parity, of taking vernacular artists and what might be thought of as the folk audience seriously as thinkers, as artists, and as critics that has been useful to me in using Brown's poetry to reflect on the Harlem Renaissance in general. One still finds in Brown the idea that the artist provides a necessary self-consciousness to the folk, even as the folk provide cultural materials to the artist—an idea common among some strands of the Harlem Renaissance, and even before in the work of writers such as James Weldon Johnson. However, Brown goes farther in this respect than nearly all Harlem Renaissance writers—except perhaps Langston Hughes in a somewhat different manner. Brown puts forward a vision of the folk artist, who is quite often not (to quote Johnson) "a black and unknown bard," but a named and well-known blues singer such as Ma Rainey, as a role model for other sorts of artists. In the poem, "Ma Rainey," the successful artist addresses a plebian (though in many ways diverse) black crowd, taking the struggles of their lives, the "hard road" they "must go," and putting them into a form that is both familiar and a spectacle, that clarifies and transforms their experiences into something that gives them strength and allows them to go on. Following this recognition and transformation of their lives, the audience in turn recognizes and honors the artist, and so the symbiotic cultural wheel turns. This, Brown suggests, is the role and goal of the black artist (and the black audience).

This vision can be usefully placed against, say, Langston Hughes's seminal "The Weary Blues," which also takes up the role of the black artist and his or her relation to an African American audience (and tradition of expressive culture) in a way that mirrors some of Brown's model, but in a much more individualistic modality. It can also be read with Wallace Thurman's roman à clef *Infants of the Spring*, which appeared the same year as *Southern Road* and suggested that one of the Harlem Renaissance's chief shortcomings was a provincial and paradoxically insecure and self-satisfied failure to grapple with the cutting edge of international (though chiefly European) modernist literature.

Brown's implicit assessment of the Harlem Renaissance (a judgment made explicit in his critical writing) as often insufficiently engaged with the black masses and their culture, along with Thurman's charge of self-satisfied provincialism, long remained one of the dominant critiques of the movement, particularly during the Black Arts Movement, which did much to revive interest in the

Harlem Renaissance and yet severely criticized it for much the same reasons as Brown's. Brown's poetry can also be extremely useful as an example of a transitional moment between the Harlem Renaissance and Left-influenced black literature of the 1930s and 1940s, proposing not only a critique (and perhaps a post-mortem), but also a sort of argument and augury of how artistically rigorous and socially engaged African American literature might proceed. It is not hard to see how Brown's critique and engaged proposal of a literature of struggle intimately linked to an African American people's culture rooted in the South made him a favorite of Left cultural circles during the 1930s, 1940s, and 1950s, as well as the Black Arts Movement (and Black Studies movement) of the 1960s and 1970s.

Of course, the realities of what students are willing to read and of the amount of money they can afford to spend on textbooks limit the use of Brown's *Collected Poems* for undergraduate classes, especially lower-level surveys where a single anthology will likely serve as the primary, and perhaps exclusive, text of the class. The *Norton Anthology of African American Literature* has the best selection of Brown's work of any of the major anthologies—though I have to admit that I have often used Riverside's *Call and Response* in broad surveys of modern African American literature because of its strengths in other areas. For Harlem Renaissance courses, I have generally used Maureen Honey and Venetria Patton's *Double-Take*, though not so much for its coverage of Brown's work, as for its wide assortment of writing by women. Not surprisingly, Michael Harper and Anthony Walton's *The Vintage Book of African American Poetry* has a good collection of Brown's verse—including examples of Brown's "standard literary" poems that are often excluded from anthologies. However, while some of these texts lack such key Brown poems as "Southern Road" and "Cabaret," all contain "Ma Rainey," allowing discussion of the ways Brown's visions of high, popular, and folk culture, of artist and audience, of individual and community intersected with and diverged from other Harlem Renaissance writers.

I find that a broadly historicist approach works best for me in giving my undergraduates a handle on Brown's work. Any teacher reading this essay knows the problems endemic to the discussion of literature dealing with the South, especially African Americans in the rural South during the 1920s, in undergraduate classes. Beyond the wide undergraduate and secondary school student terror of any sort of formal analysis of poetry, a lack of understanding of the historical moment of the fairly recently installed Jim Crow system is a persistent problem. Frequently, that poems about lynchings, chain gangs, plantations, sharecropping, and so on are not set in the past of the slave era, but in the present of the 1920s and the 1930s (a present that is several decades after the passage of the Thirteenth, Fourteenth, and Fifteenth Amendments) is surprising to many students. The idea that the intense urban residential segregation of the modern ghetto was a recent occurrence for Hughes, Cullen, and Brown, and that the blues as a musical genre was probably no older in the 1920s than rap is today, is also often news. Yet if Brown's work, and that of the Harlem Renaissance as a whole, is not successfully historicized, it becomes hard to understand not only its political charge, but also the skillful manner in which Brown invokes several varieties of literary and cultural tradition even as he proposes a new sort of African American modernity in both art and scholarship.

NOTES

1. For a sense of how Brown mentored Turé and the Howard SNCC activists, see Carmichael and Thelwell (133–35) and Thelwell.
2. For a consideration of Brown's poetry and its relation to the literary Left of the 1930s, see Smethurst (60–92). The best book-length study of Brown's poetry is Mark Sanders's *Afro-Modernist Aesthetics and the Poetry of Sterling A. Brown*—though Joanne V. Gabbins's *Sterling A. Brown* is also useful.

WORKS CITED

Baraka, Amiri. *The Autobiography of LeRoi Jones*. New York: Lawrence, Hill, 1997.

Carmichael, Stokeley, and Ekwueme Michael Thelwell. *Ready for Revolution: The Life and Struggles of Stokeley Carmichael (Kwame Turé)*. New York: Scribner, 2003.

Gabbins, Joanne V. *Sterling A. Brown: Building the Black Aesthetic Tradition*. Westport, CT: Greenwood, 1985.

Sanders, Mark A. *Afro-Modernist Aesthetics and the Poetry of Sterling A. Brown*. Athens: U of Georgia P, 1999.

Smethurst, James Edward. *The New Red Negro: The Literary Left and African-American Poetry, 1930–1946*. New York: Oxford UP, 1999.

Stepto, Robert. *From Behind the Veil: A Study of Afro-American Narrative*. Urbana: U of Illinois P, 1991.

Thelwell, Ekwueme Michael. "The Professor and the Activists: A Memoir of Sterling Brown." *Massachusetts Review* 40.4 (1999–2000): 617–38.

CHAPTER NINE

Teaching Countee Cullen's Poetry

PATRICK S. BERNARD

I approach Countee Cullen by posing this central question: How does his poetry join in a conversation with the politics and aesthetics of the Harlem Renaissance? One simple answer is with specific reference to his preference for the first person singular and plural pronouns, *I* and *we*. Both pronouns demonstrate the centrality of the self in Cullen's poetry. Moreover, an analysis of the pronouns reveals another underlying dialogue in his poetry: the conversation between the individual and the collective self.

Two opening poems effectively dramatize and thematize this conversation. Cullen's first book of poems, *Color*, foregrounds in its very first poem "Yet Do I Marvel" the individual voice (I), whereas his second book of poems, *Copper Sun*, introduces the collective voice (we) in its first poem, "From the Dark Tower." Did Cullen do so to signal the dual voices that dominate his poetry? Or was he intimating at the impossibility of limiting issues of selfhood to one category of articulation?

To further highlight this dialogue, I teach Cullen's poetry alongside his prose writings by introducing my students to the magazine pieces that he wrote under the title "Dark Tower," from 1926 to 1929, for *Opportunity*. The articles are Cullen's discussion of various issues (arts, literature, aesthetics, race, history, heritage, identity) central to the movement. He speaks in the plural voice (*we, our, us*) throughout the essays, starting with the first one of December 1926, in which he recognizes the collective ethos of racial identity and Renaissance aesthetics. With regards to the former, he boldly asserts in the first article, "we belong to a race" (389). For the latter, he defines the Renaissance thus: "the things that we are against [are] the attempt of old uncompromising patterns to rule in a world needing the robust and the new, not because they are novel, but because they fit into the shifting grooves of our times" (388). By claiming the Renaissance as *we*, Cullen establishes himself as part of the conversation about change, innovation, and experimentation. (By the time we finish discussing Cullen, my students mostly fail to acknowledge Cullen's poetry as "robust and new.")

The pronouns provide grammatical and rhetorical instruments as well as ideological and cultural contexts to engage his poetry. In terms of grammar, both pronouns are in the subjective case, in which subjects speak. My students understandably distinguish this from pronouns in the objective case, in which objects are spoken for. For this reason, *I* and *we* have implications for self-representation as well as interpretation. Rhetorically, both pronouns dramatize the conflicts of Cullen's views of the identity of the poet as a writer shaped by *we* versus that of the poet as a universal, transcendental *I*. In Cullen's poetry, therefore, *I* and *we* intersect rhetorical cum autobiographical voices contemplating ideological questions about selfhood, subjectivity, and agency. By the time my students read Cullen's poetry, they are acquainted with the conversation Renaissance writers were having about objectification, self-representation, and the speaking subject.

With reference to Cullen, W.E.B. Du Bois states: "In a time when it is the vogue to make much of the Negro's aptitude for clownishness or to depict him *objectively* as a serio-comic figure, it is a fine and praiseworthy act for Mr. Cullen to show through the interpretation of his own *subjectivity* the inner workings of the Negro soul and mind" (239, my emphasis). Du Bois makes assumptions here about the grammatical, rhetorical, and ideological meaning of the subject and the object in Cullen's poetry. I use Du Bois's distinction of the representation of the "Negro" "objectively as a serio-comic figure" and Cullen's "interpretation of his own subjectivity" to examine the theme of selfhood and subjectivity in the poetry. In fact, Cullen comes close to agreeing with Du Bois when he (Cullen) states that "the New Negro [is] becoming less and less the fanciful creation of a few dreamers, and more and more of a flesh and blood entity" ("Dark Tower," April 1927, 118).

Cullen's view of the New Negro not as a "fanciful creation" but as a "flesh and blood entity" reflects the purposes of his poetry and by extension the agenda of the Renaissance. As my students grapple to understand what Cullen means by "flesh and blood entity," they revisit the "Foreword" and "The New Negro" sections to *The New Negro* that they had read early in the course. In both sections, Alain Locke posits that one of the aims of the Renaissance was to redeem the "external view ... *about* the Negro" (xxv) as a "stock figure ... [who] has been more of a formula than a human being" (5). He continues: "Self-expression [drives] the forces and motives of self-determination. So far as he is culturally articulate, let the Negro speak for himself" (xxv). "Self-expression" and "self-determination" have one common denominator: "self", which for Locke can be realized through "speak[ing]." The "speak[ing]" self, or what Cullen refers to as "a flesh and blood entity," emerges via *I* and *we*. The pronouns then have implications for the auto-biographical voice(s) in Cullen's poetry.

The pronouns are useful devices I use to introduce my students to these voices. (In my course, I focus more on Cullen's autobiography rather than his biography. This is not to suggest that Cullen's biography is not pertinent to a consideration of his poetry.) I use two autobiographical sketches to acquaint my students with the aesthetic as well cultural forces that animated Cullen's life and poetry. The first sketch my students discuss is Cullen the speaking *I* in the following:

> If *I* am to be a poet at all, *I* am going to be POET and not NEGRO POET. That is what has hindered the development of artists among us. Their one note has been the concern with their race. That is all very well, none of us can get away from it. *I* cannot at times. You will see it in my verse. The consciousness of this is too poignant at times. *I* cannot escape it. But what *I* mean is this: *I* shall not write negro subjects for the purpose of propaganda. This is not what a poet is concerned with. Of course, when the emotion rising out of the fact that *I* am a negro is strong, *I* express it. But that is another matter. (qtd. in Early 23; my emphasis)

His well-known passage defined the centrality of the vision of the universal and transcendental *I* in Cullen's imagination and the dialectical and rhetorical challenge it produced in his conceptions of "poet" and "Negro poet." In the passage, *I* claims the individual, personal self articulating aesthetic and racial self-definition outside of race. Cullen provides an insight into the conversations about race and literature in the Renaissance and his (shifting) positions in that dialogue. Before my students relate the implications of the passage to the poetry, they first must answer this crucial question: What does Cullen mean by a poet and a Negro?

Although Cullen never wrote a poem titled "The Negro Poet," he did write one titled "The Poet" (*Copper Sun*), which my students read alongside the passage. In the poem, Cullen describes the poet (the kind he wants to be) as a transcendental being who writes about universal and abstract matters as opposed to realistic material conditions. My students generally agree that "The Poet" is autobiographical because it complements Cullen's sentiments in the passage. But as my students reflect on the passage and the poem, I give them two other poems, "Yet Do I Marvel" and "Incident," to consider. Both poems use the first person singular pronoun to portray a voice speaking as "Negro poet." The autobiographical experiences both poems deal with allow my students to reevaluate the view, contrary to the claim Cullen makes in the passage and "The Poet," that his poetry deals not only with abstract notions or a transcendental *I* but also with his contrasting, contradictory, and ironic views on prevailing conceptions of race and literature.

The second autobiographical sketch my students consider is Cullen the speaking *we* in this excerpt from one of the columns from "Dark Tower," in which he describes his trip to the South:

> We journeyed late last month for the first time to the far South. [...] As our train whirled deeper and deeper into what we could help considering the fastness of a benighted country, we felt that the hand of the rioter had dug its nails deeper into the soil of this land leaving it red and raw with welts of oppression. [...] We were in an untutored land among a proud folk who would not be taught. Strange incredible stories stirred to remembrance within us, and we shuddered at the sight of a charred bit of stick stretched like a slumbering snake along the road; we knew not of what insane rites it might have been part, what human torches it once might have served to light. [...] When leaving next morning, we had to ride a little way in the Jim Crow section. (April 1928, 120)

In this passage, Cullen claims the collective voice speaking about racism, Jim Crow, and segregation. In contrast to the first autobiographical sketch and its insistent *I*, here Cullen uses the communal *we*. I ask my students to consider the following questions: What are the differences between this passage and the first autobiographical sketch? Why would Cullen speak about his individual experience in the plural voice? What does Cullen mean by "strange incredible stories" that stir "remembrance within us"? What is the significance of the "charred bit of stick stretched like a slumbering snake along the road" to the meaning of (1) the stories and (2) the remembrances Cullen is referencing? What "insane rites" is Cullen speaking about? And what is the connection between the rites and the "light" of "human torches"? Student responses (lynching, racial violence, communal memory) to these questions provide transitional moments to consider *we* in some of his poems—for example, "From the Dark Tower," "The Litany of the Dark People," and "The Shroud of Color"—that talk about the collective experience of race. The purpose here is to let my students discover that Cullen's use of *I* and *we* in his poetry is complex. As "Yet Do I Marvel" and "From the Dark Tower" show, he deploys *I* to ponder the meaning of race for his individual sensibilities and *we* to contemplate the collective heritage of race.

I and *we*, therefore, represent double-voiced narrative spaces in Cullen's poetry. He states in his famous poem "Heritage" that he plays a "double part." In the introduction to *Caroling Dusk*, Cullen writes about the "*double obligation* of being both Negro and American" (xii, my emphasis). But for him, this "double" also has to do with how the "Negro poet's" "[i]ndividual diversifying ego [I] transcends the synthesizing hue [we]" (xii). Are Cullen's "double obligations" and "double part" inflections of W.E.B. Du Bois's "double-consciousness"? How does Cullen's poetry engage this double-consciousness? (See Baker, Shucard, Early, Jarraway, and Powers for an extended treatment of this subject in Cullen.) For the purposes of my course, I explore this "double" via the dual poetic voices of Cullen: first, Cullen the Romantic poet (of the "individual diversifying ego") who claimed English Romantic poets and their sensibilities for his inspiration; second, Cullen the Renaissance poet (of the "synthesizing hue") who contemplated the movement's preoccupation with race, literature, identity, and Africa (and its related subjects of memory, history, and heritage).

After this distinction, I then focus on Cullen the Renaissance poet, with emphasis on his most famous poem, "Heritage" (1925). The poem brings out the multiple contexts of Cullen's conversational voices in the movement. To capture this dialogue, I use call and response or antiphony to teach "Heritage." I do so because call and response is the quintessential communicative idiom that allows for the individual voice (*I*) within the collective voice (*we*). Moreover, I have found call and response an effective, productive, and participatory pedagogical strategy to teach the poem. The embedded and interlocking voices in antiphony allow for an analysis that brings out the interface between *I* and *we* and the themes of individuality and community, self and other, memory and history, past and present in "Heritage." When my students analyze "Heritage" as a call and response of voices, they discover the rhetorical richness and contextual echoes of the poem. Because call and response offers speaking positions that facilitate dissent, disagreement, consent, and disapproval, its application to the explication of the poem allows my students to read Cullen's "Heritage" as one of the speaking positions on the subject of Africa in the Renaissance.

Prior to our discussion of the poem in class, I give my students two definitions of "antiphony." First, I offer Geneva Smitherman's definition of call and response as "spontaneous verbal and non-verbal interaction between speaker and listener in which all of the statements ('calls') are punctuated by expressions ('responses') from the listener" (104). Second, I offer Gayl Jones's definition of the idiom: "In a literary text both dialogue and plot structure may demonstrate this call-and-response pattern: one scene may serve as a commentary on a previous scene while a later scene becomes a commentary to that one" (197). (I use these definitions because Smitherman's highlights the oral dimension of the collective voices of antiphony, whereas Jones's points out the literary uses to which the idiom can be put.) I ask my students to use the key words (verbal, non-verbal, interaction, speaker, listener, punctuated, scenes, episodes, plot structure, and dialogue) in both definitions to identify the call and response in "Heritage."

Two views summarize my students' responses: First, they identify a "speaker" (Cullen, the persona) responding to a "listener" (the Harlem Renaissance, Marcus

Garvey, etc.) who might have made the call in the first place. Second, they say that they "hear" an inner monologue, a stream of consciousness that reveals the thought processes of the persona. In this sense, they agree that the poem is a response to an external voice that activated an interior monologue. We read the poem aloud in a call-and-response mode, an approach that lets the students "hear" the voices calling and responding in the poem. By so doing, students discover that the poem reads better than it appears on the page. Reading "Heritage" aloud enables students to "hear" its conversational rhythms.

In general, I use my students' responses as the foundation to embark on an in-depth analysis of the poem's dual call and response. The first call and response examines the poem as one of the voices conversing about the idea of Africa in the Renaissance. The second explores the poem as a network of internal voices calling and responding to each other as the persona engages in what Du Bois calls, with reference to Cullen, an "interpretation of his own subjectivity." Perhaps it is this interior monologue Gerald Early refers to when he calls "Heritage" a "very interiorized speech-act, speech-event" (60).

With regards to the first call and response, I am not surprised that my students identified the call the poem responds to as that of Marcus Garvey's short speech "African Fundamentalism," which many of them previously characterized as hyperbolic and romantic. Chronologically, Garvey's piece (1924) can enter into this call and response conversation with Cullen's "Heritage" (1925). Other voices that may serve as the call to Cullen's "Heritage" are some poems espousing a Garveyite, romantic affirmation of Africa published in *Negro World*, such as John Edward Bruce's "Africa" (1921), George Wells Parker's "When Africa Awakes!" (1923), Arnold J. Ford's "O Africa, My Native Land!" (1920), Ethel Trew Dunlap's "Sweet Afric Maid" (1922), and Ernest E. Mair's "O Afric Maid" (1922). But other poems outside the Garveyite frame—for example, Claude McKay's "Africa" (1921), Langston Hughes's "Danse Africaine" (1922), and Gwendolyn Bennett's "Heritage" (1923)—could serve this purpose as well.

Furthermore, I have found the overlapping voices (between poems and essays, essays and art, short stories and poems) of Locke's *The New Negro* useful in reading Cullen's poem as call and response. The structure of the text makes the poem both a call and a response to other Renaissance voices present in the anthology. I use Arthur A. Schomburg's essay "The Negro Digs Up His Past," which talks about Africa, history, and heritage, as the call to Cullen's poem. Locke's essay "The Legacy of the Ancestral Arts," which in the anthology comes immediately after the poem, serves as the response to Cullen's call in "Heritage."

These texts—poems, essays, speeches—not only expose my students to the divergent and convergent voices about Africa in the movement but also show them the diverse cognates—history, heritage, art, aesthetics, culture, politics,

Utopian idyll—Africa occupied in the Renaissance as a narrative territory of mediation, signification, and representation. These texts are the collective voices (*we*) behind Cullen's poem, and the *I* (and its interior monologue) in "Heritage" can be engaged only when the contextual echoes of *we* are taken into consideration in the first place.

The second call and response leads to the examination of the poem's interior monologue, which, paradoxically, is a dialogue of internal voices. And what are these voices? There are eleven voices. The first voice, the call, "what's Africa to me," triggers the interior monologue of voices responding to it. The call is repeated twice as a refrain in lines 7–10 and 59–62 for pause and transition. The lines are italicized for emphasis. The remaining ten voices respond to this overarching call.

The second voice (lines 2–5) responds by identifying Africa as a distant landscape of "copper sun" and "scarlet sea" and "jungle star" and "Jungle," a bodyscape of "strong bronzed men" or "regal black women" from "whose loins" the persona doubts he sprung. These physical and concrete images launch the genealogical imagination that animates the poem. This voice also introduces two related mobile images, "scarlet sea" and "jungle track," that the persona establishes as the imaginary routes or figurative umbilical cord linking him to Africa.

The third voice (lines 11–18) identifies Africa as "sound," which has been transformed into a "song" the persona wants to hear. This sound is metaphoric and discursive; the song it produces is "sung by wild barbaric birds." Although he loads the song with wildness and primitivism, its sound is irresistible and indestructible. There is an elemental presence to this song that moves flora and fauna and appeals to the young lovers. In contrast to the physical and concrete images in the second voice, Cullen introduces sound as an abstract, ubiquitous image that connects him to Africa; this sound image, and the subsequent ones he uses later in the poem, defies boundaries. In the poem then this "savage" and "primitive" African sound is transgeographical and tropological. Africa comes to him embedded in sound, and only in this way can the genealogical imagination (heritage) the poem takes on can be engaged.

The fourth voice (lines 19–30) responds by stating that Africa is the "Great drums" (the African drums, the tom-tom) throbbing through the air. (See my article "Langston Hughes, the Tom-Tom and the Discursive Place of Memory in Culture," for an explanation of the meaning of the drum in a Harlem Renaissance poet.) He cannot escape the sound of the drums, although he tries to "cram against" his ear their throbbing. Intriguingly, the persona's body, his "somber flesh and skin," becomes an extension of the drums. (Some African drums are made from the skin of animals. The persona's drum is made both from his skin and flesh, suggesting the living drum he sees himself as. To that end, his "dark blood

[is] damned within.") In this sense, his body-as-drum represents his "fount of pride, distress, and joy allied," contradictory impulses that make him the metaphoric drum with gloomy tones. This results in the "surge and foam and fret" that he equates with his living drum. The link between the "dark blood" and "tides of wine" refers to another sinister drum—the barrels of wine that were used as articles to purchase slaves in Africa.

The fifth voice (lines 31–45) engages Africa as a "a book" the persona "thumbs listlessly till slumber comes." This "book" generates unremembering: It cannot make the persona remember Africa, which is mostly reduced to its animals—bats, cats, silver snakes, and birds. The book reproduces the dominant Western script of Africa as a domain of animals. Does Cullen's poem reinforce this script? How do contemporary media—film and television, for example—continue to reproduce this script?

The sixth voice (lines 46–58) speaks of a "here," presumably America, which the persona differentiates from Africa. "Here" differs both in space and time from Africa. Time-wise, "here" is "last year," which contrasts with the refrain's insistence of Africa as "three centuries removed." Unlike Africa, "here" contains "last year's snow," "last year's anything," and the "yearly budding" of trees. In terms of space, the "snow" of "here" differs from the tropical scenery of Africa, where lovers lie in the grass presented in the preceding voices. In this section, the persona compares himself to a "tree" that, paradoxically, has "bough and blossom, flower, fruit" but no roots. He says, "the tree must forget how its past [roots] arose." By extension, the persona is a tree that was "uprooted" from Africa and planted "here."

What caused this uprooting? Slavery, of course. Not surprisingly, the seventh voice (lines 63–69) introduces another sound image, the "unremittant beat / Made by cruel padded feet," a metaphor the persona uses to link Africa, slavery, and his body. The cruel padded feet are an interlocutor cryptically referring to the feet of slave hunters whose act led to the uprooting of the persona. The sound ("beat") of their feet brings memory of slavery and suffering for the protagonist. Moreover, the "beat" of their "feet" brings him no peace and release because they walk through his body's street. His body becomes the "street" that the "feet" go up and down and "back," meaning the past, history, Africa. It is for this reason that the persona states that his "body" connects the "street" and the "jungle track," the metaphorical route that links him to Africa.

The eighth voice (lines 70–92) speaks of Africa as the metaphoric "rain at night" whose rhythms make this voice another sound image that brings the persona restlessness and pain. The rain's "primal measures" "drip through" his being. Paradoxically, the "drip" of the rain results in the "strip" of the persona's being. He says that when "the rain begins to fall," his body and soul must in pain twist, squirm, and writhe (words that were used during this period to describe African dance) to what he refers to as its "weird refrain." Rain becomes a system in which several codes are at work. The "drip" of the rain transforms into and invites the persona to what Cullen describes as "the Lover's Dance." The call and response here is not only between the rhythm of the rain and the dance that responds to it, but intertextual as well. Cullen encloses in quotes lines 88–90 to directly and indirectly refer to other texts—for example, his own poem "The Dance of Love." My students skim the poem to get at its allusive textuality. The crucial intertextual echo is in the poem's epitaph, "After reading Rene Maran's '*Batouala*.'" (Maran's *Batouala: A True Black Novel* was published in 1921; its publication coincided with the Renaissance's complicated and ambiguous interests in Africa. The novel is set in Africa, and one of its central scenes is the dance of love.) Thus, when Cullen states in "Heritage," "Come and Dance the Lover's Dance," is he suggesting an embrace of Africa? Or is he questioning his own "exuberance" over Maran's novel? The rain's rhythm (which now simultaneously becomes the rhythm of dance) prods the persona's memory: "In an old remembered way / Rain works on me night and day." Does he contradict himself here after he had said in the fifth voice that Africa is a "book" that generates unremembering?

The ninth voice (lines 93–100) associates Africa with the "outlandish heathen gods" black men construct out of "rods, clay, and brittle bits of stone." These gods "are naught" to the persona because they have become alien and foreign. He has been "converted" to an equally alien God, Jesus.

The tenth voice (lines 101–24) contemplates the call of this alien God, whose "glowing altar" contrasts sharply with the "rods, clay and brittle bits of stone of the heathen gods" of Africa. He accepts Christ but he plays a "double part," highlighting the themes of Christianity and paganism that dominate the ninth and tenth voices of the poem. His "heart grows sick and falter[s]" because the God he serves is not "black." To that end, he dares "even to give" this God "Dark despairing features" such as "dark rebellious hair." This religion is dehumanizing because it fails to "guarantee and shape a human creed."

The eleventh and final voice (lines 125–37) combines the preceding voices. In this sense, the eleventh voice of the poem is the chorus, which, in call and response, is the point where all voices join together to round off a performance. (Cullen italicizes the lines to suggest its amen-like chorus quality. My students read the lines in unison.) The first word in the eleventh voice is "all," a subtle cue by Cullen inviting all—reader, audience, caller, respondent, and others—to join in saying the final lines of the poem. But "all" may also be referring to the preceding voices, bringing them together. In this respect, the chorus poses this central question: Confronted with and surrounded by "all" these voices, both the external and his own the internal ones, what must the persona do? He acknowledges that he cannot escape the voices because he is condemned, so to speak, to live with them "[a]ll day long and all night through." The cumulative effect of the voices simultaneously enervates and inspires him. They encircle his being. In essence, the voices become his life force, his metaphoric DNA. For this reason, the protagonist realizes that the consequences of failing to live with the voices are dire: perish in the flood, burn in the fire, or die and be entombed in the grave. The voices simultaneously animate and paralyze his existence and paradoxically ensure his survival.

These voices join together to tell interpolated stories calling and responding to each other in the poem. Each voice is an individual unit within the whole. Cullen joins these stories together through repetition, one of the features of call and response. Repetition functions in antiphony for structural, semantic, and musical (rhythmic and improvisational) effects. The repeated refrains, phrases ("I lie", "all day/all night"), body and sound images, and numerous alliterations and assonances act as connective and thematic devices in the poem. The subject of the body, and its variants, occupies the majority of the repetition in the poem. From one angle, Africa is a body observed in its "nakedness," from another the persona's body is subject to physical pain and dehumanization. However configured, the body has entities that not only respond but also call to the indignities it has been put under.

Although heavily embodied, the poem is also a deep ontological reflection by the persona on questions of uncertainty and unknowability, history and memory, the past and the present. The poem's title reinforces the persona's recognition of the centrality of Africa as heritage and memory. Africa's voices, mostly its sound images—the song, the great drums, the rain, the cruel padded feet—are mnemonic devices that the persona translates to contemplate individual and collective memory. Call and response (itself a memory act) makes the performance of memory in the poem an individual as well as a communal experience where the *I* of "Heritage" participates in the collective *we* of Africa as memory in the Renaissance.

I close the discussion of the poem, and by extension Cullen's poetry, by relating it to the subject of memory in the Renaissance. Dorothea Löbbermann observes, "the Harlem Renaissance's concept of cultural renewal through the remembrances and reconstruction of influential past is situated," among other sites, in "Africa as a culturally and spiritually significant place of the past" (210). Seen this way, "Heritage" provides one of the conversational pieces that problematizes Africa as (following Löbbermann) a site of memory (213).

I and *we* make Cullen's poetry teachable. The pronouns represent Cullen's struggles to locate his speaking positions, articulate his resistance to objectification, and engage in the emancipatory possibilities of speaking in one's voice. His self-conscious approach to speak in two voices in his poetry reflects his essential view that identities are shaped along fissures and boundaries of *I* and *we*. Moreover, the pronouns provide locations to discuss the core issues, such as authorial independence, racial identity as individual and collective, the dialectics of the past and the present in self-constitution, selfhood, and subjectivity, in Cullen's poetry and in the wider Harlem Renaissance.

WORKS CITED

Baker, Houston Jr. *A Many-Colored Coat of Dreams: The Poetry of Countee Cullen*. Detroit: Broadside, 1974.

Cullen, Countee. *Color*. New York: Harper, 1925.

———. "The Dark Tower." *Opportunity* 4 (December 1926): 388–90.

———. *Copper Sun*. New York: Harper, 1927.

———, ed. *Caroling Dusk*. New York: Harper, 1927.

———. "The Dark Tower." *Opportunity* 5 (April 1927): 118–19.

———. "The Dark Tower." *Opportunity* 6 (1928): 120.

Du Bois, W.E.B. "Our Book Shelf." *Crisis* 31 (1926).

Early, Gerald. *My Soul's High Song: The Collected Writings of Countee Cullen, Voice of the Harlem Renaissance*. New York: Doubleday, 1991.

Jarraway, David. "No Heaven in Harlem: Countee Cullen and His Diasporic Doubles." *New Voices on the Harlem Renaissance: Essays on Race, Gender, and Literary Discourse*. Eds. Australia Tarver and Paula C. Barnes. Madison: Fairleigh Dickinson UP, 2006. 214–37.

Jones, Gayl. *Liberating Voices: Oral Tradition in African American Literature*. Cambridge: Harvard UP, 1991.

Löbbermann, Dorothea. "Harlem as a Memory Place: Reconstructing the Harlem Renaissance in Space." *Temples for Tomorrow: Looking Back at the Harlem Renaissance*. Eds. Geneviève Fabre and Michel Feith. Bloomington: Indiana UP, 2001. 210–21.

Locke, Alain, ed. *The New Negro*. 1925. New York: Simon & Schuster, 1992.

Powers, Peter. "'The Singing Man Who Must Be Reckoned With': Private Desire and Public Responsibility in the Poetry of Countee Cullen." *African American Review* 34 (2000): 661–78.

Shucard, Alan. *Countee Cullen*. Boston: Twayne, 1984.

Smitherman, Geneva. *Talkin and Testifyin: The Language of Black America*. 1977. Detroit: Wayne State UP, 1986.

CHAPTER TEN

Teaching Jessie Fauset's *Plum Bun*

SUSAN TOMLINSON

I first became aware of Jessie Fauset and her second novel, *Plum Bun* (1929), during a presentation on Nella Larsen's *Passing* (1929) in a graduate seminar. Most of my fellow students and I laughed sympathetically at our colleague's attempt to explain the novel's plot and keep track of its characters. I wanted to learn more about the novel Susan Goodman describes as a "baggy, splay-footed monster" (42). I am still learning more, which is why I teach it whenever possible. *Plum Bun* offers many opportunities for exploring major themes of the Harlem Renaissance, feminist literature, African American literature, and modernism, as well as for examining literary genre and form in twentieth-century American literature. Fauset manipulates-and, as I have argued elsewhere, reinscribes—genres such as the *Bildungsroman*, the *Künstlerroman*, and the romance, and conventions such as sentimentalism and irony; her work invites us to examine the aesthetic and social functions of literary representation.

What follows are some of the approaches I have found useful in teaching *Plum Bun* in American and African American literature survey courses and advanced undergraduate seminars in the Harlem Renaissance, gender and modernism, and twentieth-century American literature. *Plum Bun* is a seductive novel about, among other things, racial seduction, betrayal, and redemption; its protagonist's artistic, cultural, and personal rebirth mirrors the theme of much New Negro movement art: the shedding of objectified stasis and self-denigration and the emergence of a visionary subject. Until the very end *Plum Bun* remains a novel of *becoming*, a text that questions, unravels, and remakes the very terms it assumes—about self-definition and its limits, race pride and its ironies, progressive activism and its blind spots. As a conflicted text, it embodies the conflicts and contradictions of the Harlem Renaissance and the melodrama of cultural representation.

I usually begin the first class devoted to *Plum Bun* with a short biographical lecture about Fauset, stressing what many undergraduates consider the contradiction between her academic achievement and the financial struggles that made her writing career difficult. Because *Plum Bun*, unlike Larsen's *Quicksand* (1928) and James Weldon Johnson's *The Autobiography of an Ex-Colored Man* (1912), doesn't invite autobiographical readings, the obstacles Fauset faced as an African American female artist provide a useful—and conveniently limited—lens through which to read the novel as a *Künstlerroman*. The biographical information in Deborah E. McDowell's comprehensive introduction to the Beacon Press edition highlights experiences that inform Fauset's representations of racism and sexism. Fauset overcame racial exclusion in higher education and graduated Phi Beta Kappa from Cornell University in 1905, completed an M.A. in French at the University of Pennsylvania, and pursued further graduate studies at the Sorbonne, yet neither these academic accomplishments nor her extensive professional experience protected her from the financial insecurity that stalled and eventually ended her writing career.

In order to demonstrate how financially insecure Fauset was in spite of her education and experience, McDowell quotes from the poignant letter Fauset wrote in 1926—one of the Harlem Renaissance's peak years—to the National Association for the Advancement of Colored People (NAACP) vice president Joel Spingarn, requesting his assistance in finding work after she left her editorial position at the *Crisis*. I like to circulate a copy of the entire letter (rpt. in Sylvander [776–77]) because it illustrates not only the racial and sexual barriers Fauset confronted but also the strategies she used to negotiate them. Students often find Fauset's desperation (and what they often interpret as her "servile" tone) very distressing and struggle to reconcile the Ivy League-educated author, editor, and "race woman" with the soon-to-be-unemployed woman describing her clerical skills and offering to work from home if a potential employer maintains a whites-only workplace. I invite the students to read the letter closely as a text, analyzing its rhetorical tensions, its author's self-representation, and its construction of its audience; from that textual analysis we move to considering what we can infer from the letter about the cultural context in which it was written. The letter foreshadows some of the conflicts Fauset goes on to depict in *Plum Bun*, particularly how individuals respond—publicly and privately—to racism and its dehumanization and, crucially, the authorial decisions that go into those representations.

THE MULATTO/PASSING QUESTION

Plum Bun's mulatto/passing theme poses potential challenges, particularly for readers unfamiliar with that theme and its significance in African American literary history. Students in my survey course will have read William Wells Brown's *Clotel* (1853), Frances E.W. Harper's *Iola Leroy* (1893), and Johnson's *Autobiography of an Ex-Colored Man*, while Harlem Renaissance seminar members will have studied Johnson and will be reading Larsen's *Quicksand* and *Passing* immediately after *Plum Bun*. In these classes, therefore, students consider Fauset's novel along this thematic continuum, particularly whether we can read Fauset's manipulation of this literary convention as a modernist act. The novel's subtitle, "A Novel without a Moral," suggests one useful direction; if Harper's and Johnson's novels depict passing as moral passivity, as racial dishonesty and betrayal, how does Fauset reframe the moral question? Does Fauset's treatment of a racially ambiguous protagonist resist or reaffirm dominant constructions of race and community? How seriously should we take the subtitle's multiple meanings?

Students for whom *Plum Bun* is their first exposure to the mulatto/passing theme need a bit more background and much more time to tease passing's textual function out from its social reality, implications, and consequences. In these classes I describe the "tragic mulatto" stereotype and briefly outline the changing role of passing in African American literary history. It's useful to supplement this discussion with examples; a few particularly melodramatic pages from William Dean Howells's *An Imperative Duty* (1891) illustrate the idea of "black blood" as a contaminant, while *Iola Leroy* offers usefully contrasting depictions of its eponymous heroine's refusal *not* to pass as proof of her racial pride and solidarity. In these contexts passing emerges as a literary means of negotiating a theme central to American literature and politics—the conflict between individual and collective identity.

Passing prompts ethical questions, and students are always keen to put literary negotiations and the politics of representation to one side and argue the ethics and psychology of passing: whether Angela rejects and betrays her race, whether her passing is a sign of racial self-loathing and racial complicity, or whether, in a society where being black poses an obstacle to full-fledged participation in the "American dream," Angela has every right to exploit her ostensible whiteness. Debating the ethics of passing is compelling but can also take the discussion too far away from the novel and the thematic role passing plays in it. One way to keep the discussion focused on the novel's representation of passing is to spend time examining how that representation addresses—and at times reframes—ethical questions.

Hazel V. Carby's analysis of Harper's treatment of passing and the mulatto figure in *Iola Leroy* is an indispensable model for weaning students off the politics of passing and redirecting their analysis to its textual function. Responding to critical dismissals of the mulatto figure always as a rehearsal of the "tragic mulatto" stereotype and as a further marginalization of darker-skinned blacks, Carby argues that "historically the mulatto, as narrative figure, has two primary functions: as a vehicle for an exploration of the relationship between the races and, at the same time, an expression of the relationship between the races. The figure of the mulatto should be understood and analyzed as a narrative device of mediation" (89). I extend this reading to characters who are not technically mulatto (biracial) but whose phenotypical whiteness enables them to play a similar role. Focusing on passing itself as a "device of mediation" allows us to think about how Angela's physical appearance and resultant ability to pass blurs and challenges the color line and, more significantly, the themes this character's passing allows the novel to explore. In terms of the novel's psychological realism, particularly regarding how Angela gathers, interprets, and applies her empirical knowledge of race difference, I ask students to examine the race evidence she gathers and the logic she uses to interpret her data. How does Fauset position the narrative logic in relation to the protagonist's logic, and how does that shape a readerly logic? How does Fauset's strategy constitute a cultural critique, and how effective is it?

Discussion questions may also include the following: How does Fauset construct a history and logic behind Angela's decision to pass, and how does that construction engage concepts such as identity, race, and freedom? How does a passing protagonist allow Fauset to examine and critique social constructions of white womanhood? What insights does Angela's white "visitor" perspective offer into Harlem and the New Negro; what role do glimpses of the Harlem Renaissance play in this ostensibly "white" character's life? How does Angela's depiction represent and critique white privilege? And, ultimately, what does race become in *Plum Bun*?

PLUM BUN AS BILDUNGSROMAN AND KÜNSTLERROMAN

Approaching *Plum Bun* as a *Bildungsroman* and a *Künstlerroman* opens a rich discussion of how genre functions and how questions of race and gender revise formal literary convention. In my classes I offer definitions of *Bildungsroman*, stressing its character-formation aspect over what I consider the less nuanced but more popular coming-of-age focus, and *Künstlerroman*, paying close attention to its implications of "becoming." Although it's a somewhat false distinction, at the beginning of our discussion I find it useful to introduce these two approaches separately so that students get a stronger sense of the novel's different projects in which each form participates.

Our *Bildungsroman* analysis focuses on Angela's childhood and family history and the cultural education (or miseducation) she receives at home. We pay close attention to Angela's relationship with her mother, their shared white appearance, and how Angela learns to interpret that whiteness. What Mattie considers a "game of play-acting" (19)—spending Saturdays passing in posh, de facto segregated department stores and hotel restaurants—forms Angela's definition of whiteness, specifically white womanhood, and its black converse. *Plum Bun* genders and racializes the *Bildungsroman*; it depicts how a young woman grows from accepting and complying with ideological definitions of her body's appearance and meaning to forming her own self-definition and subjective occupation of that body.

Angela Murray passes through "Angèle Mory" in order to come out as Angela Murray, and her painting plays a crucial role in this process. Although I consider Fauset's first three novels—*There Is Confusion* (1924), *Plum Bun*, and *The Chinaberry Tree* (1931)—*Künstlerromane*, Fauset uses the genre here to develop Angela's character (a means of her *Bildung*) and to locate the novel and its central characters in specific cultural moments. Passing as a white artist, Angela lives in Greenwich Village, where she befriends Paulette and Martha, who embody the New Woman ideal popular in the 1920s. By this point in the semester, my students are quite familiar with New Negro/Harlem Renaissance visual artists as well as writers, so I focus our discussion of *Plum Bun* as a *Künstlerroman* on how Fauset models Angela's work on the Ashcan and Fourteenth Street Schools' emotional ethos of "art for life's sake" and uses the New Woman figure as a construction of white womanhood against which Angela struggles to remake herself.

Because it is easy for us to underestimate the significance of Angela's painting in the novel—as Angela herself does while she is husband hunting—I find it useful to encourage students to visualize Angela's paintings, literally to describe them based on the details in the novel. We spend considerable time tracing scenes in the novel when Angela is working or thinking about her work, and we consider how her subject matter changes and how those changes mirror other changes in her life, especially her attitude toward race. I circulate reproductions of paintings by Kenneth Hayes Miller, Raphael and Moses Soyer, and Isabel Bishop, and we compare Angela's fictional paintings to real Fourteenth Street School paintings in appearance, subject matter, and social implications. (Ellen Wiley Todd's *The "New Woman" Revised: Painting and Gender Politics on Fourteenth Street* is an excellent source for these images; it also includes a 1928 photograph of Union Square [93], where Angela sketches her "Fourteenth Street Types" series [*Plum Bun* 111, 239–40, 279].) Finally, we compare the Fourteenth Street School's progressive ideals with those of the New Negro movement.

PLUM BUN AND THE "EDUCATION OF FEELINGS"

Plum Bun speaks emotionally even to ordinarily detached students. I have yet to teach the novel to a class that remains unmoved by Angela's relationship with Roger, whose extreme racial bigotry Fauset depicts graphically and harrowingly. Some readers cannot believe that Angela would consider marrying such a cruel and ignorant man. That repulsed disbelief sparks deeper questions about how the relationship develops Angela as a character (the psychological implications of her sleeping with racism—and misogyny and class dominance—personified) while it develops Angela's character (what she learns and how she changes).

Like her nineteenth-century predecessors such as Frances E.W. Harper and Harriet Jacobs, Fauset uses sentimentalism to demonstrate racism's dehumanizing effects. None depicts more intricately this dehumanization or appeals more effectively to readers' sympathies than the scene in which Roger has a black party thrown out of a restaurant. This scene not only showcases Fauset's technique but also exposes the mechanics of sentimentalism by casting Angela as the object of its suasion. The reader witnesses with Angela the spectacle of Roger's cruelty and the patrons' humiliation and then watches the scene *move* Angela. The spectacle shifts from Roger's act to Angela's feeling, which in the Tolstoyan sense is educated by her empathy with Roger's victims. Angela imagines her father, sister, and high school boyfriend (but not, tellingly, herself) suffering like the ejected patrons and suffers on their behalf. Likewise, the reader identifies with Angela's feeling and experiences with and through her racism's psychic assault. Angela's sentimental reading of Roger's behavior becomes a sentimental set piece that moves the novel's reader.

My Harlem Renaissance class spends the first several weeks of the semester analyzing and comparing the arguments in W.E.B. Du Bois's "Criteria for Negro Art," Fauset's "Some Notes on Color," Alain Locke's eponymous essay in *The New Negro*, Langston Hughes's "The Negro Artist and the Racial Mountain," George Schuyler's "The Negro-Art Hokum," and Zora Neale Hurston's "What White Publishers Won't Print." As we conclude our work on each novel, we return to one of those essays to think about how that work of "Negro art" challenges, affirms, or otherwise engages the argument. While Fauset's work functions as both a call for and a response to the debates that shaped the Harlem Renaissance and continue to shape how we participate in defining the movement, I like to return to Du Bois (thinly veiled in *Plum Bun* as Van Meier) as we finish this novel. How would Angela respond to his assertion that "all art is propaganda and ever shall be" (22)? What propaganda does her painting espouse, and can we reconcile her work's politics with the novel's? *Plum Bun* confounds genre, movement, and meaning; its aesthetics and politics are its excess. Like its protagonist, the novel behaves very badly. Unlike Angela, however, it refuses to reform and conform to our questions; rather, it continues to ask its own.

WORKS CITED

Brown, William Wells. *Clotel, or The President's Daughter: A Narrative of Slave Life in the United States.* 1853. Ed. Robert Levine. New York: St. Martin's, 1999.

Carby, Hazel V. *Reconstructing Womanhood: The Emergence of the Afro-American Woman Novelist.* New York: Oxford UP, 1987.

Du Bois, W.E.B. "Criteria of Negro Art." 1926. *African American Literary Theory: A Reader.* Ed. Winston Napier. New York: New York UP, 2000. 17–23.

Fauset, Jessie Redmon. *Plum Bun: A Novel Without a Moral.* 1929. Ed. Deborah E. McDowell. Boston: Beacon, 1990.

———. "Some Notes on Color." *The World Tomorrow* (March 1922): 76–77.

Goodman, Susan. *Civil Wars: American Novelists and Manners, 1880–1940.* Baltimore: Johns Hopkins UP, 2003.

Harper, Frances E.W. *Iola Leroy; or Shadows Uplifted.* 1892. Ed. Hazel V. Carby. Boston: Beacon, 1987.

Howells, William Dean. *An Imperative Duty.* 1893. Whitefish, MT: Kessinger, 2004.

Hughes, Langston. "The Negro Artist and the Racial Mountain." 1926. *Within the Circle: An Anthology of African American Literary Criticism from the Harlem Renaissance to the Present.* Ed. Angelyn Mitchell. Durham: Duke UP, 1994. 55–59.

Hurston, Zora Neale. "What White Publishers Won't Print." 1950. *Within the Circle.* 117–21.

Jacobs, Harriet. *Incidents in the Life of a Slave Girl, Written by Herself.* 1861. Ed. Jean Fagan Yellin. Cambridge: Harvard UP, 1987.

Johnson, James Weldon. *The Autobiography of an Ex-Colored Man.* 1912. Ed. William L. Andrews. New York: Penguin, 1990.

Locke, Alain. "The New Negro." *The New Negro: Voices of the Harlem Renaissance.* Ed. Alain Locke. 1925. New York: Touchstone, 1997. 3–16.

McDowell, Deborah E. "Introduction." *Plum Bun: A Novel without a Moral.* By Jessie Redmon Fauset. Boston: Beacon, 1990. ix–xxxiii.

Schuyler, George S. "The Negro-Art Hokum." 1926. *Double Talk: A Revisionist Harlem Renaissance Anthology.* Ed. Venetria K. Patton and Maureen Honey. New Brunswick: Rutgers UP, 2001. 36–39.

Sylvander, Carolyn Wedin. "Jessie Redmon Fauset." *Afro-American Writers from the Harlem Renaissance to 1940.* Ed. Trudier Harris and Thadious M. Davis. Detroit: Gale, 1987. 76–88.

Todd, Ellen Wiley. *The "New Woman" Revised: Painting and Gender Politics on Fourteenth Street.* Berkeley: U of California P, 1993.

Tomlinson, Susan. "Vision to Visionary: The New Negro Woman as Cultural Worker in Jessie Redmon Fauset's *Plum Bun.*" *Legacy: A Journal of American Women Writers* 19 (2002): 90–97.

CHAPTER ELEVEN

Teaching Waldo Frank's *Holiday*

KATHLEEN PFEIFFER

"Waldo Frank has had the courage of the artist in treating such an episode," Walter White writes in his 1924 review of *Holiday*, a fictional account of—and political protest against—lynching. White commends Frank for "courageously handling (lynching) without sob-stuff, melodrama or the desire to prove anything." Today, the only readily available edition of Waldo Frank's *Holiday* (1923) is the 2003 paperback reissue published by the University of Illinois Press; this inexpensive version reproduces the text from the novel's hardcover first edition, so that students are able to read the book in its original font, to view and discuss its layout, and to question its atypical structure. To give but a few examples of its odd format: *Holiday* employs italicization seemingly at random, a dream sequence appears unexpectedly, nontraditional ellipses and blocks of space separate passages, and Frank eschews conventional punctuation. Walter White may have praised Waldo Frank's courage, but he had little patience for such experimental strategies, noting that "one is vaguely annoyed by the symbolic phrasing, the apparent irrelevancies."

After several years of lonely scholarly engagement with Waldo Frank's *Holiday* as I wrote the introduction to the University of Illinois Press reissue, I had the opportunity to share it with students in two successive semesters. Both classes focused on the Harlem Renaissance: during the fall of 2004, in an American Studies course of undergraduates ranging from sophomore to postbaccalaureate; and then during the winter of 2005 in a graduate seminar of advanced Master's students in literature. In both classes, numerous students cited *Holiday* as one of their favorite books (though admittedly, some found it a book they loved to hate) and in both classes, I felt it to be an exceptionally successful text. Specifically, *Holiday* allowed me to teach a range of topics involving literature, culture, society, and history: We discussed shifting attitudes toward racial identity, the relationship between an author's race and publishing success during the Harlem Renaissance, lynching, protest literature, literary style, the evolution of American literary modernism, relationships between white mentors and black writers, Christian themes and iconography, and the lyric novel. Several students in the Master's seminar are high school teachers of English and history, and they went on to adapt portions of our discussion of *Holiday* to their own classroom use. In my experience, it is wholly appropriate for undergraduate and graduate courses; and while it is a structurally challenging text, I believe that it can usefully inform advanced high school classrooms as well.

Holiday depicts the events of a single day in a Southern town called Nazareth, and it is structured cyclically, tracing the day according to the earth's movement. The novel thus aligns narrative structure with the passage of time (note that the sections are Part One: Dusk; Part Two: Dawn; Part Three: Noon; Interlude; Part Four: Dusk) and, ultimately, with history. Nazareth is segregated, a fact underscored by the frequent appearance of the word "nigger" on the first page. Frank employs this term self-consciously and deliberately, however, and one useful strategy for introducing the class to this language comes from the novel's second page, where John Cloud is described. "He is tall and slender," Frank writes, "His slenderness is lithe. He is the color of dusk on the shadowed road he walks. White folk call him 'Lank.' They do not see how his height sings, they do not see how hungry and frail he is beside the pine. 'Big nigger' they see" (10). When I ask students to comment on this passage, they point to its depiction of the blindness of white people and note the eloquent compassion with which John Cloud is described. This eloquence extends to the description of "Niggertown" as well—an area defined by song, laughter, greenery, and trees. John Cloud lives with his mammy, and she fears for his safety and well-being because she sees the look in his eyes. Students may view this depiction of African Americans as romanticized and as drawing on cultural stereotypes, yet Waldo Frank also makes it very clear that John is choking in this "Niggertown."

By contrast, the white man's world, an urban downtown area, is defined by commerce and longing. Ask students to note how many times that word "longing" appears in relation to Nazareth; they will be amazed. Students who are attuned to color imagery can't fail to note the heavy-handedness with which Frank underscores the uniquely American character of his fictional town as well: "Red earth, blue bay, whitening sky round to the monochrome of dusk" (33). From the start, relations between whites and blacks in Nazareth are tense at best and downright dangerous at worst. The opening section depicts this racial divide in a brutal scene that describes the death of a Negro worker who slips on the pier and falls into the water. He might have been saved; the white men who are able to swim don't want to get their clothes wet, however, so the man is crushed by a docking ship named the *Psyche*. Here we meet Virginia Hade, the wealthy white woman who is John Cloud's boss, and her brother Bob, one of the excellent swimmers who watches the black man drown.

Both white and black Nazareth are in the throes of spiritual revivals, and *Holiday* underscores the differences between the two communities. We see John Cloud, his mother, and his putative fiancée Mary Cartier walk to church in the "perfect night" where "shadowed secrets" surround them (38). Main Street, by contrast, "fights night" with blazing, jagged, ugly electric lights (40). The black preacher is meeting a great deal more success than his white counterpart, and we see this contrast through John Cloud and Virginia Hade: John, soothed by the music that has spilled out into the night from his church, falls asleep, while Virginia, having sunk in "the dry human sea" of an "acid shrill" revival meeting, lies in her bed, awake and frightened (44). Virginia's insomnia leads to a fragmented stream of consciousness that reveals her own racial self-hatred; when she tells herself that she has a black soul, she is able to sleep and thus concludes Part One: Dusk.

In Part Two: Dawn and Part Three: Noon, the novel follows John Cloud to work, where he is the overseer of the orchard owned by the Hade family; Virginia is its manager. The fall day's blazing heat leads him to recommend that the company call off work for the afternoon and give the workers a holiday. The workers go home, and John and Virginia each leave work to seek the cool—separately—at the same quiet, heavily shaded, remote spot on the bay. John is swimming naked when Virginia arrives. Virginia wanders through Niggertown and has an odd, elliptical and curiously erotic conversation with Mary Cartier before arriving at the bay. This odd eroticism also informs John and Virginia's conversation, a halting and peculiar interaction that concludes with Virginia insisting that the two exchange knives. John obeys, gives Virginia his pocketknife and leaves; Virginia then stabs herself at the waist. The "Interlude" section takes us inside Virginia's mind, in another troubling and nuanced stream of consciousness passage. She walks back to town, bleeding and holding John Cloud's knife, and she pauses outside the white revival tent. It has been an impotent revival in white Nazareth, and Virginia arrives at the tent in the very moment that the failed and frustrated unsaved white men emerge en masse. Bob Hade instantly recognizes the knife his sister carries as belonging to John Cloud and immediately organizes his lynching. The novel ends: John Cloud is burned to death as Virginia lies quietly in her bed.

The chief difficulty of teaching *Holiday* in a course on the Harlem Renaissance lies in the question of whether it belongs in the course at all; this, however, is also its greatest advantage. To include *Holiday* in a Harlem Renaissance course is to challenge and problematize the Renaissance itself. For the instructor who has assigned the *Survey Graphic* special edition on the New Negro, an introduction to *Holiday's* place in Harlem literature can begin by discussing the Boni & Liveright advertisement on page 707, in which Waldo Frank's novel is positioned between Jean Toomer's *Cane* and Jessie Fauset's *There is Confusion*. Students will note that the photographs of Jean Toomer and Jessie Fauset appearing alongside their books visually evince their racial identity and thereby suggest the importance of each author's own racial experience in establishing each text's authenticity. But students should note too that Waldo Frank is listed in the *Survey Graphic's* recommended reading, "A Select List of Magazines and Books By and About Negroes." Thus, while Harlem Renaissance studies today have made Fauset and Toomer familiar names to many students and scholars, this *Survey Graphic* juxtaposition gives instructors the opportunity to identify the contrast between the three writers in 1925, and to emphasize the fact that Waldo Frank was by far the more recognizable and prominent writer at the time. Indeed, a full understanding of Frank's literary stature and cultural power in 1920s America is absolutely central to a student's full appreciation of *Holiday's* import.

Biographical information about Frank underscores his prominence and serves the additional purpose of providing students with valuable context about the evolution, principles, and goals of American literary modernism. A brief biographical overview is provided in my introduction, but instructors who want more material about Frank's career beyond *Holiday* will find helpful details in the biographical essays by Wilton Eckley and Casey Blake. A brief lecture about Frank's life and accomplishments prior to 1923, when *Holiday* appeared in print, could emphasize some significant trends in American literary history. The youngest child of intellectual and ambitious nonobservant Jewish parents, Frank's own aptitude was evident in his having completed Yale in three years, earning both the B.A. and the M.A. His artistic and intellectual versatility is evident in a number of his activities: his close involvement with Greenwich Village avant-garde writers; his political activism (Frank registered as the first conscientious objector to the first World War); his participation in the founding of the *seven arts* little magazine; his tremendous artistic debt to Walt Whitman's *Democratic Vistas*; and especially, the aesthetically and politically significant *Our America* (1919), the nonfiction work of cultural criticism Frank published just prior to *Holiday*. *Our America* called on American writers to develop a "lyric novel," a new form evolving out of the lyric poem, and a form that Frank envisioned as rejecting the structural constraints of the traditional novel. Like other modernist texts, the lyric novel would employ stream of consciousness and nontraditional narrative mechanisms, but its focus was ultimately somewhat mystical in its desire to achieve a sort of spiritual wholeness through literature. As Frank imagined this new form, the lyric novel would invite readers to share its characters' consciousness as the characters themselves experience their own thoughts and insights; the lyric novel would provide access to spiritual truth. *Holiday* is a lyric novel in this tradition.

Information about *Our America* and Frank's vision of the lyric novel is valuable to students of the Harlem Renaissance because not only did Frank influence a whole generation of young Americans, but also his writing motivated the ambitious Jean Toomer to seek him out as a mentor. Both *Our America* and Toomer serve as important influences on *Holiday's* evolution because the novel first began as Waldo Frank's intention to "add a Negro chapter" to *Our America* but then evolved into a more complex project as a result of his correspondence with Toomer. Indeed, any full appreciation of *Holiday's* evolution, composition, and reception (or of Toomer's *Cane* [1923] for that matter) must consider the complicated, intense, and often misunderstood relationship between Toomer and Frank. The introduction to *Holiday* covers this material in sufficient detail for students to understand the tensions at work, but Daniel Terris's essay "Waldo Frank, Jean Toomer, and the Critique of Racial Voyeurism" also gives an excellent and detailed account of their relationship. Students will be interested to learn about Waldo Frank's "research" trip to the Spartanburg, South Carolina area, during which Toomer helped him to pass as black in order to better understand the Southern racial landscape. For the instructor who is able to obtain a copy of Waldo Frank's *Memoirs*, the pages recounting that trip could be a helpful handout to the class; but even a briefer, selected passage such as the one below might prove useful:

> Wherever we went, to welcome and honor us, turkeys and hogs were slaughtered, and the richest yams were smothered in brown sugar. The farther away from town, the more complete the Negro plasm, the more free the sweetness of this people. Of course, the two young guests were entertained by those economically placed to bring them the most comfort. But humbler neighbors dropped in, and I soon got a sense of the community. Those that worked at home or on the farm, the least touched by the white world, were the happiest; those who went to Spartanburg each day to make their living—lifters of heavy loads, barbers, servants, et cetera—were the most confused, resentful, and neurotic. I felt shame, as if I must confess the sins of my own fathers; I felt with the Negro. This empathy was startling. Lying in dark sleep I would dream I was a Negro, would spring from sleep reaching for my clothes on the chair beside the bed, to finger them, to smell them … in proof I was white and myself. (105)

A close reading of this passage reveals much about Frank's attitudes and assumptions, and my students have been very interested in discussing these comments in relation to the novel. (For the course that is also reading and discussing Carl Van Vechten's *Nigger Heaven* [1926], it may be worth considering that Van Vechten also recorded dreams that he was black in his own daybooks.

On Saturday, September 4, 1926, in the midst of receiving reviews of the newly published novel, Van Vechten writes, "Edna Kenton comes to dine with me. We talk about *Nigger Heaven* all the evening. She leaves at midnight. I go to bed about one & dream I am a Negro being chased in riots" [132]).

As Frank's interest in the development of a distinctly American "lyric novel" might suggest, *Holiday* is a very literary text, and it responds very well to strategies of close reading that trace the development of central metaphors, as the Terris essay illustrates in helpful detail. Repeated imagery connecting rope to snake to phallus begs discussion; likewise, references to color—note where one finds red, white, and blue—appear particularly pointed. Asking students to trace biblical themes and images can uncover a particularly compelling subtextual design, as my graduate class learned when led in discussion by a student who is a Catholic priest and biblical scholar. For instance, to see John Cloud as a Christ figure ("J.C.") is also to note how the town of Nazareth evokes the Garden of Eden (after all, Nazareth's primary business is the production of exotic fruit). While this imagery might seem to paradoxically conflate Old and New Testament mythology, the biblical relationship between Eden and crucifixion is quite direct: Original sin is paid for by Christ's death. Yet in *Holiday*, the most "sinful" behavior, students agree, is committed by wealthy whites. Identifying these contradictions allows students to question Frank's use of irony. Are his depictions of African Americans to be taken as romanticized or ironic? Do his depictions of whites reflect the racial shame he admits to in his *Memoirs*?

Reading *Holiday* thematically, one might focus on lynching and compare John Cloud's lynching with other literary or artistic depictions. For instance, an interdisciplinary unit might read *Holiday* alongside Langston Hughes's "Christ in Alabama" (1931); the class could listen to Billie Holiday's "Strange Fruit" (1939) and perhaps examine a William H. Johnson crucifixion portrait such as *Jesus and the Three Marys* (1935), a vibrant painting that can be located easily through a search on Google images. These artistic depictions would be even more powerfully provocative if read in conjunction with historical accounts of lynching, and if viewed alongside photographs of actual lynchings. An instructor could ask students to consider Frank's novel in relation to the Dyer antilynching bill and other political activities supporting antilynching legislation. Frank's commitment to progressive politics was lifelong and deeply felt, and an excellent classroom debate could be structured around the question of how this novel seeks social change.

Finally, my classes were very interested in discussing not only why the novel fell out of favor and out of print, but also why it has come back into print now. I point out to students that a number of my university colleagues teach the novel in relation to American modernism. In addition, as current scholarship on literature and racial identity has, in the past decade, been turning toward the necessarily interconnected role of whiteness in shaping black identity (in such works as George Hutchinson's *The Harlem Renaissance in Black and White* and Ann Douglas's *Terrible Honesty*), literary critics, cultural scholars, and educated general readers have demonstrated interest in the fascinating complexity of interracial literary influence. The successful reissue of Carl Van Vechten's *Nigger Heaven* underscores this; for example, public interest in Van Vechten's novel increased dramatically in the weeks following the publication of *Remember Me to Harlem*, Emily Bernard's excellent and very well-received edition of letters between Van Vechten and Hughes. These observations have led my classes to an insightful discussion about the politics of the book marketplace and the fluctuation of canonical status, a conversation that is, in my view, imperative for any class reading African American literature.

WORKS CITED

Bernard, Emily, ed. *Remember Me to Harlem: The Letters of Langston Hughes and Carl Van Vechten, 1925–1964.* New York: Knopf, 2001.

Blake, Casey. "Waldo Frank." *Modern American Critics, 1920–1955.* DLB 63. Ed. Gregory S. Jay. Detroit: Gale, 1988. 122–30.

Douglas, Ann. *Terrible Honesty: Mongrel Manhattan in the 1920s.* New York: Noonday, 1995.

Eckley, Wilton. "Waldo Frank." *American Novelists, 1910–1945 Part 2: F. Scott Fitzgerald–O. E. Rolvaag.* DLB 9. Ed. James J. Martine. Detroit: Gale, 1981. 28–34.

Fauset, Jessie. *There is Confusion.* 1924. Ed. Thadious Davis. Boston: Northeastern UP, 1989.

Frank, Waldo. *Holiday.* 1923. Ed. Kathleen Pfeiffer. Urbana: U of Illinois P, 2003.

———. *Memoirs of Waldo Frank.* Ed. Alan Trachtenberg. Amherst: U of Massachusetts P, 1973.

———. *Our America.* New York: Boni and Liveright, 1919.

Hutchinson, George. *The Harlem Renaissance in Black and White.* Cambridge: Harvard UP, 1995.

Terris, Daniel. "Waldo Frank, Jean Toomer, and the Critique of Racial Voyeurism." *Race and the Modern Artist.* Ed. Heather Hathaway et al. New York: Oxford UP, 2003. 92–114.

Toomer, Jean. *Cane.* 1923. Ed. Darwin Turner. New York: Norton, 1988.

Van Vechten, Carl. *Nigger Heaven.* 1926. Ed. Kathleen Pfeiffer. Urbana: U of Illinois P, 2000.

———. *The Splendid Drunken Twenties: Selection From the Daybooks 1922–1930.* Ed. Bruce Kellner. Urbana: U of Illinois P, 2003.

White, Walter. "Review of *Holiday* by Waldo Frank." *The Crisis* (February 1924).

CHAPTER TWELVE

Teaching Langston Hughes's Poetry

ANITA PATTERSON

In a 1927 address to the Walt Whitman Foundation in Camden, New Jersey, Langston Hughes remarked that "poetry should be direct, comprehensible and the epitome of simplicity" (qtd. in Rampersad 146). The graceful simplicity of Langston Hughes's poems is, in part, what makes them such a pleasure to teach. Readers are drawn to Hughes because he is memorably easy to read, and easy to love. In contrast to the arduous obliquities of modernist works written by Hughes's contemporaries—poems that look hard even without the footnotes—Hughes's lyrics speak to students with lucid immediacy, giving them renewed confidence in their ability to read, comprehend, and enjoy. The temptation here is to let them read for themselves, without any intervening commentary, contextualization, comparison, or formal analysis.

But Hughes's commitment to lyric simplicity also presents a serious pedagogical challenge. Left entirely to themselves, many students would miss out on his great achievements as a craftsman; assuming a proprietary relation to his work, they would fail to perceive the enigmatic reticence that lies at the heart of his greatest poems. The reason for this is that Hughes's poems, like his public personae, are deliberately crafted to conceal the complexity and range of his technique. Reading Hughes, we encounter an art of deceptive and therefore difficult simplicity.

The concern with reticence and craftsmanship is something Hughes shared with many of his Euro-American modernist contemporaries. Although Ezra Pound's lyric practice is, in many respects, very different from Hughes's, the two poets would agree that literary craftsmanship exacts itself as reticence, that is, in the absence of explicit self-revelation. For Hughes, as for Pound, the craftsman speaks primarily through the implications of form.

It is true that Hughes's poetics derives from a line of development in twentieth-century American poetry that Pound denounced for its "mushy technique" and "general floppiness"—a line that extends from Whitman to Carl Sandburg, Edgar Lee Masters, E.A. Robinson, and Amy Lowell. What's more, Hughes was scrupulously indirect regarding the presence of modernist influences in his own work. All we can be sure of is that the two poets maintained a correspondence over the course of many years, and in 1932 Hughes wrote a letter to Pound saying, "I have known your work for more than ten years and many of your poems insist on remaining in my head" (qtd. in Roessel 214). But as Arnold Rampersad, Faith Berry, and Edward J. Mullen have shown, Hughes not only read Conrad, Joyce, D.H. Lawrence, and other important modernist writers of his day; he was also involved in an extensive transnational literary network including Carson McCullers, Marianne Moore, W.H. Auden, André Malraux, Louis Aragon, Bertholt Brecht, Ernest Hemingway, Diego Rivera, Nicolás Guillén, Alejo Carpentier, Jacques Roumain, Pablo Neruda, Jorge Luis Borges, Léopold Sédar Senghor, and Aimé Césaire.

Teaching Hughes, we should certainly be well aware that he was one of the leading voices of the Harlem Renaissance in the 1920s—a poet who redefined the standards for poetry, laying the foundation for the flourishing of a twentieth-century African American literary tradition; a radical activist who was a devoted supporter of the Scottsboro Boys; a member of the John Reed Club and the Congress of American Revolutionary Writers; president of the League of Struggle for Negro Rights; and a role model, mentor, and friend to young and emerging writers of the Renaissance. We should also understand that even the briefest of poems in Hughes's corpus engage sociohistorical contexts such as slavery, Reconstruction, the Great Migration, and the pernicious threat of racial violence against African Americans. A number of critics have dwelt at length on Hughes's importance to the aesthetic philosophy of the Harlem Renaissance, as well as the cultural distinctiveness of Hughes's sources and idiom. Steven Tracy and James Emmanuel, for instance, have studied the centrality of the blues to Hughes's lyric practice; and scholars such as Richard Barksdale, R. Baxter Miller, and Onwuchekwa Jemie have emphasized how Hughes adapted vernacular forms at a time when folk literature and song were unjustly derided and neglected by a black literary establishment bent on assimilation with the mainstream.

While maintaining a clear sense of Hughes's cultural contexts and distinctiveness, however, it is also instructive to keep his close links to transnational modernism in mind, because this will further enhance how well students grasp the essential hybridity of the Harlem Renaissance, and the volatile interplay of influences and ideas among avant-garde movements in the United States and other parts of the world. Students will be better equipped to draw illuminating comparisons among writers and artists across geographic and cultural divides. Like Carl Sandburg, Marianne Moore, and Aimé Césaire, Hughes searched for verse forms that would transmute the spoken word into well-wrought, written artifacts. Like Pound and Brecht, he often employed personae or masks as literary devices. Like Eliot, he was born in Missouri, led the life of an expatriate in Paris during a formative moment in his coming of age as a poet, and had a lifelong interest in the relationship between the rhythms of poetry and music.

In light of my opening comment about Hughes's craftsmanship, I'd like to suggest ways to highlight aspects of his formal techniques in the classroom. Hughes was dauntingly prolific, so it's best to proceed chronologically, illustrating how his work developed over time. I suggest that you sample selections from each of these three categories: first, the early poetry (written between 1921 and 1930) adapted from vernacular forms such as the spirituals, the blues, ballads, and jazz; then the more politically engaged poetry, from the proletarian free verse of the 1930s to the Freedom and Democracy poems of the World War II era; and, finally, the late poetry shaped by the impact of jazz—from *Montage of a Dream Deferred* (1951) to *Ask Your Mama* (1961).

There is a large body of excellent scholarship on Hughes's poetry. Have a look at the criticism and bibliographies in *Langston Hughes: Critical Perspectives Past and Present* (1993), edited by Henry Louis Gates; *Critical Essays on Langston Hughes* (1986), edited by Edward J. Mullen; and *Langston Hughes: Black Genius, A Critical Evaluation* (1971), edited by Therman B. O'Daniel. Given the instructive value of chronology, it's useful to have Steven Tracy's *A Historical Guide to Langston Hughes* (2004) and especially Arnold Rampersad's edition of *The Collected Poems of Langston Hughes* (1994) on hand, so you can be sure about the dates of publication, where the poem first appeared, and any revisions Hughes may have made. Since the cost of the Rampersad volume may be prohibitively high for many students, you should feel free to assign the 1959 edition of *Selected Poems*, arranged and compiled by Hughes himself, but be aware that this volume is not organized chronologically.

I won't dwell on Hughes's adaptation of vernacular forms in his early poems, since so much has been well said on this subject already. It's been my experience that students are generally familiar with the blues, but it's useful to explain to them that different blues styles emerged in different regions of the United States and in different historical periods. Steven Tracy clearly documents how Hughes drew heavily on the stanzaic forms, themes, and imagery of early blues played by itinerant bluesmen up through the 1920s, as well as the vaudeville-influenced blues Hughes would have first heard in the early 1920s while he was staying in Harlem. Students are often surprised to hear that Hughes's radical experimentation with blues forms and his desire to represent with vivid realism the lives of lower-class African Americans, were harshly criticized by reviewers when *Fine Clothes to the Jew* appeared in 1927. His insistence on artistic freedom is beautifully articulated in the essay "The Negro Artist and the Racial Mountain," published a year earlier in the *Nation*. The essay—which has been reprinted in *The Norton Anthology of African American Literature* and is widely available—inspired many younger Harlem Renaissance writers who wished to draw on the materials of folk literature and song, and it's well worth assigning.

Introducing students to Hughes's poetics, I often trace significant formal developments: when and how he departs from a conventional blues stanza or metaphor, for instance; or the effects of his movement from short lyrics written in perfectly rhymed stanzas to long lyric sequences written in free verse and formally influenced by jazz; or the difference between his early realism, poems of political declamation, and the difficult opacity and indirection of his later works.

But it's equally important to stress continuities in Hughes's corpus, such as his realist method of observation, his lifelong interest in the expressive possibilities of the vernacular, his persistent return to the anchorage of folk materials, and his bold experimentations with poetic form. One way to illustrate both continuity and innovation in Hughes's lyric practice is to focus on selected poems written in rhymed quatrains over the course of his entire career. Not all of these poems are adaptations from the blues. Hughes broke fresh ground in his poetry, partly because he understood that his engagement with canonical texts and his concern with European and American prosody would provide a much-needed, clarifying distance from the rich but potentially formulaic idioms he drew from African American folk culture. Like Eliot and Pound, who praised the craftsmanship and understatement of Théophile Gautier's rhymed quatrains, Hughes worked hard to perfect his use of this device.

How do these rhymed quatrains convey meaning in Hughes's poetry? Sometimes they dramatize a claustrophobic sense of lonely entrapment in poems centering on spatial metaphors (as in "Cross," "Pictures to the Wall," "Walls," "Empty House," "Lonesome Corner," "Final Curve," and "Room"). We should also recall that a great majority of Hughes's poems about lynching are written in rhymed quatrains, intimating a need for the distancing effects of formal convention (as in "Song for a Dark Girl," "Flight," "The Town of Scottsboro," "Sliver," and "Georgia Dusk"). Hughes never dispensed with rhymed poetry altogether, and the centrality of the rhymed quatrain to his poetics is evident in the fact that "Flotsam," published posthumously in the June–July 1968 issue of *Crisis*, was the very last poem Hughes submitted to that magazine before he died.

Teaching Hughes's free verse poems is often hard because there's a temptation to neglect the work's formal aspects altogether. Hughes's free verse is closer to Whitman's or Sandburg's than it is to Eliot's, because he does not always retain what Eliot called the "ghost of meter," the echo of a familiar metrical cadence behind every line. Instead, Hughes borrowed Whitman's methods, creating line breaks that are syntactically organized, and usually end-stopped (i.e., ending in punctuated pauses).

Another point worth emphasizing is the tension between realism and mythic declamation in Hughes's free verse poetry. I'll run through one example of this to give you a sense of Hughes's technique. In the early poem "I, too," Hughes envelopes his poem within a refrain and variation ("I, too, sing America" and "I, too, am America"), achieving a mode of mythic declamation that recalls Whitman and especially Carl Sandburg. But where Whitman's epic stance requires that his mythic speaker "assume" the thoughts and experiences of his readers, Hughes's poem demands that readers relinquish such assumptions about his speaker, their own "darker brother." The place where we witness the extremes of this confrontation between, on the one hand, the contradictory impulses toward mythic transcendence and, on the other, the descent into sociohistorical fact is in the third stanza out of five—the structural keystone to the entire poem:

Tomorrow,
I'll be at the table
When company comes.
Nobody'll dare
Say to me, "Eat in the kitchen,"
Then.

(*Collected* 46)

Hughes made a small but significant revision to this poem in the version he published in *Selected Poems*. In earlier versions, the second line of the stanza was "I'll sit at the table"; he changed the more dramatic, active verb "sit" to the more abstract, mythic, and philosophically charged verb "be." As a result, the stanza is even more wonderfully fraught with the tension between the language of racial hierarchy and the language of myth, between the speaker's social experience of subjugation and his knowing self-description as a mysterious, even typological figure. The "darker brother" of the title, a figure we identify in part with the biblical character Esau, takes on an additional, somewhat ominously ambiguous identification with the figures at the Last Supper.

There's obviously more to be said about this stanza, and much more about Hughes's poetry in general, but I don't have space in this short essay. I'll end by mentioning how important it is to notice the range and complexity of the figures of speech Hughes employs to depict blackness. Try to get students to notice how strikingly difficult Hughes's imagery is when it comes to race. Hughes is great at using imagery that raises haunting questions (e.g., with "darker brother" we are left asking, "Compared to what?"), and some of his figures of speech are so compounded that even Emily Dickinson would have been proud of them (as in the poem "Negro" where Hughes writes "Black like the depths of my Africa" and countless other examples). You might consider assigning the chapter titled "Negro" in Hughes's autobiography, *The Big Sea* (1940), and ask students what Hughes means in his opening line: "You see, unfortunately, I am not black" (11).

I usually end by having students listen to a recording of Hughes reading aloud. There are a number of superb recordings available, such as *The Voice of Langston Hughes* (1994) on the Smithsonian Folkways label, with selections culled from six previously released Folkways albums. After having studied his poems as crafted artifacts, it is a sheer delight to hear them come to life in the poet's own voice.

WORKS CITED

Barksdale, Richard. *Langston Hughes: The Poet and His Critics*. Chicago: American Library Association, 1977.

Berry, Faith. *Langston Hughes: Before and Beyond Harlem*. Westport, CT: Lawrence Hill, 1983.

Emmanuel, James A. *Langston Hughes*. New York: Twayne, 1967.

Gates, Henry Louis, and Appiah, K.A., eds. *Langston Hughes: Critical Perspectives Past and Present*. New York: Amistad, 1993.

Hughes, Langston. *The Collected Poems of Langston Hughes*. Ed. Arnold Rampersad. New York: Knopf, 1994.

———. *Selected Poems*. New York: Vintage, 1990.

———. *The Big Sea*. 1940. New York: Hill and Wang, 1993.

———. "The Negro Artist and the Racial Mountain." *The Norton Anthology of African-American Literature*. Ed. Henry Louis Gates Jr. and Nellie McKay. New York: Norton, 1997. 1267–71.

Jemie, Onwuchekwa. *Langston Hughes: An Introduction to the Poetry*. New York: Columbia UP, 1976.

Miller, R. Baxter. *The Art and Imagination of Langston Hughes*. Lexington: UP of Kentucky, 1989.

Mullen, Edward J. *Critical Essays on Langston Hughes*. Boston: G.K. Hall, 1986.

O'Daniel, Therman B. *Langston Hughes: Black Genius, A Critical Evaluation*. New York: William Morrow, 1971.

Rampersad, Arnold. *The Life of Langston Hughes*. 2nd edition. Vol. 1. Oxford: Oxford UP, 1986. 2 vols.

Roessel, David. "'A Racial Act': The Letters of Langston Hughes and Ezra Pound." *Ezra Pound and African American Modernism*. Ed. Michael Coyle. Orono, Maine: National Poetry Foundation, 2001. 207–42.

Tracy, Steven. *A Historical Guide to Langston Hughes*. New York: Oxford UP, 2004.

———. *Langston Hughes and the Blues*. Chicago: U of Illinois P, 1988.

CHAPTER THIRTEEN

Teaching Langston Hughes's *The Ways of White Folks*

HANS OSTROM

The Ways of White Folks, Langston Hughes's first and most significant collection of short stories, was published by Alfred A. Knopf in 1934 and consequently appeared after the Harlem Renaissance had come and gone; therefore, one way to read and to teach the collection is as a retrospective on that literary and cultural era (Hutchinson; Lewis). Hughes's first autobiography, *The Big Sea* (1940), covers this period of time, too, so it can be useful to anyone teaching the book of stories.

As well as appearing at an important moment in African American literary history, the book materialized at a critical period in Hughes's life and career (Rampersad vol. 1). Hughes was in his thirties and had achieved success as a writer, but he had severed ties with his patron, Mrs. Charlotte Osgood Mason, after a bitter disagreement about his writing. He had finished a college degree at Lincoln University (Pennsylvania) and traveled extensively, experiencing intellectual and social freedom, but he had witnessed the demise of the Harlem Renaissance and the erosion of hope that the New Negro movement had inspired. He had also seen how the Great Depression had struck African Americans with particular brutality. He was esteemed by some readers but, after the publication of the poem "Christ in Alabama" in 1931, reviled by others (Ostrom, *Encyclopedia* 74–75; Rampersad 1:224–25).

The Ways of White Folks makes art out of such personal and social turmoil. It also signifies Hughes's growth as a writer, for the collection is Hughes's first sustained foray into short fiction; the foray is bold, authoritative, and unified. I see it as one of the great unified collections of short fiction from its period, equal in stature to James James Joyce's *Dubliners* (1914) and Ernest Hemingway's *In Our Time* (1925) (Ostrom, *Study* 3–8). The fact that mine is an arguable point, and a point that might inflame devotees of "classic" Modernist short fiction, makes it all the more useful pedagogically. Finally, the book appeared after the Modernist short story—developed by writers such as Katherine Mansfield, William Faulkner, and D.H. Lawrence, as well as Joyce and Hemingway—had established itself in its several guises. In fact, according to Rampersad (1:282–93), a reading of stories by Lawrence influenced Hughes's conception of the short story, especially as a genre that might, among other things, convey social critique.

In any event, biographical, literary, and cultural contexts are certainly available to teachers who want to contextualize the book in these ways.

I've taught the *Ways of White Folks* in a variety of undergraduate settings (as well as lectured about it to Swedish graduate students in American literature): creative writing (short fiction); a major-authors course on Hughes and James Baldwin; and a senior-level core-curriculum class specifically on the Harlem Renaissance. It is an extremely versatile collection with regard to the curriculum. The edition I use is the paperback Vintage one, which faithfully reprints the book essentially as it appeared in 1934. It has a marvelous picture of the young, handsome Hughes—probably taken by Carl Van Vechten. Hughes looks like a movie star from the era.

In all the courses but especially the Harlem Renaissance one, I often begin by discussing the biographical, social, and cultural contexts noted above. I do this for several reasons. Because the book itself is so socially alert, it invites such placement in time. Because the book looks at "white folks'" behavior with a sharp, clear, critical eye, it can make white students defensive, and from all students, it can elicit a reaction against what they perceive to be overtly "political" literature. (They often perceive any literature with a clear point of view on issues to be "political.") Put another way, the book creates the same problems and opportunities that all ironic, satiric, and socially alert literature creates, with the bonus of its focus on ethnicity.

Some students take Hughes's social critique personally, even though the book appeared nearly three quarters of a century ago, and even though Hughes takes pains to use a line from the story "Berry" as a cautionary epigraph for the whole book: "The ways of white folks, I mean *some* white folks." The hint: Don't take it personally, (white) reader. Hughes is letting all readers know his stories represent the behavior of certain whites and are not an essentialist condemnation of whites in general.

Other students will argue that the ethnic conflict he describes belongs to a bygone era, even as many readers will notice the persistence of the conflicts he describes.

I'm always aware than many undergraduates have been acclimated to a kind of modernist short story that is more indirect, introspective, and stylish than Hughes's version of the short story, which is at once blunt and sharp, unadorned and pungent. Such students have often been trained chiefly to read literature from a formalist point of view, one that de-emphasizes or ignores biography and history.

For all these reasons, establishing context seems prudent.

I also mention, with intended irony, that some of Hughes's best friends were white, including Nöel Sullivan, to whom the book is dedicated, and Carl Van Vechten, an important figure in the Harlem Renaissance (Ostrom, *Encyclopedia* 382–83, 408–409). Sometimes I ask why an African American writer in the 1930s would bother writing about white folks. The question is meant to focus students' attention on Hughes's *position* with regard to segregationist white America and to invite students to consider the extent to which, for most African Americans, "white America," as a ubiquitous, multifaceted, potentially dangerous institutional presence, was something that required attention. It's a point worth raising, at any rate, because in his famous essay "The Negro Artist and the Racial Mountain" (1926) Hughes encourages "Negro" writers to write about "Negro" experience, in whatever form that experience has taken. Obviously, the experience of Hughes and others included having to negotiate the ways of white folks.

In my opinion and experience, at least seven of the fourteen stories in *The Ways of White Folks* must be taught, partly because these seven are so accomplished and readable, but also because they get to the heart of Hughes's matter: the confluence of sex, social class, and ethnicity (and often gender, too) in the 1920s and early 1930s. These stories are "Cora Unashamed," "Slave on the Block," "Home," "Passing," "The Blues I'm Playing," "Berry," and "Father and Son." When I've had students write about the book, one suggested essay-topic is to trace sexual, class, or ethnic conflict in any two or three of these seven stories. Another suggested essay approach is to analyze the *confluence* of sex (or whites' perceptions of "the black body"), class, gender, and ethnicity in one or two of these seven. Of course, the same topics can be applied to other stories in the book.

Below I'll provide an intentionally quick, condensed commentary on each of the seven.

"Cora Unashamed" exposes hypocrisies: Christian hypocrisy, American small-town hypocrisy, middle-class hypocrisy, and ethnic hypocrisy. The white family presents itself as upstanding, but instead of greeting their daughter's out-of-wedlock pregnancy with Christian love and forgiveness, the family forces her to have an abortion, which kills her. The family treats Cora as if they are better than she is, for they are white and middle class, and she is black and working class. But in the end, Cora rises morally not just above the family but the whole town. From the outside, the family looks like a piece of classic Americana: well-to-do, well established, and redolent of small-town American values. From the inside, they delegate parenting almost entirely to Cora, they would rather endanger their daughter's life than be embarrassed, and they ignore Cora's wisdom when it would be most useful. One interesting, provocative question to ask students about the story is this: "To what extent might we read 'Cora Unashamed' as an anti-abortion story? What is the textual evidence for this claim, and what is the textual evidence against it?" Side note: A cinematic adaptation of "Cora Unashamed" exists (Pratt), starring Regina Taylor.

"Slave on the Block" cuts to the quick of a classic Harlem Renaissance problem: the fact that many whites who suddenly became interested in African American culture became interested for the "wrong" reasons; moreover, the interest was short-lived: a trend, a passing fancy. In this particular story, the white folks see the black folks almost strictly as sexual folks—a wrong reason for being interested in African American culture. The white folks also perceive black folks to be primitive, and the white folks think nothing of creating art (in this case, a sculpture of a "slave on the block") about African American experiences, and they create the art without asking themselves any questions about artistic authority or historical awareness. A side-note: Hughes defended the novel *Nigger Heaven* (1926), written by his white friend Carl Van Vechten, so he was obviously not categorically opposed to a white person making art out of black experience. The very title of Van Vechten's book was and remains potentially offensive and incendiary, of course, but the fact that Hughes defended the novel complicates questions raised in "Slave on the Block." A side-note to the side-note: In the 1920s, African Americans sometimes used "nigger heaven" to refer to the balcony in theaters, so one of Van Vechten's meta-phorical tactics was presumably to compare Harlem (uptown) to the balcony of New-York-as-theater and to imply that Harlem was becoming relatively heavenly to African Americans. But, of course, that reference, with which Van Vechten and Hughes were familiar, is entirely arcane now and, for college students today, leaves only the incendiary aspect of the title intact.

In both of these stories, we can hear echoes if not see the influence of D.H. Lawrence. The stories drip with situational irony, and in both narratives, sex, class, and ethnicity collide. Are they insufficiently subtle for modernist tastes? Maybe. A counterargument would be this: To suggest that white/black relations were "un-subtle" in the 1920s and 1930s is hardly unreasonable. One person's lack of subtlety might be another person's legitimate sense of realism.

An interesting line to pursue in class with regard to these stories is their con-nection to today's American culture. Ask students whether they see any evidence of white hypocrisy with regard to ethnic issues. An easy example is that while many Americans make noise about "stemming the tide" of illegal immigration, the American economy thrives on paying low wages to undocumented workers. This is an issue of ethnic hypocrisy in the sense that, in many instances, white business-persons are profiting from Latin American, chiefly Mexican, workers. Students will come up with more—and probably better—examples. One may also ask students to consider examples of cultural phenomena in which "white folks" seem to be enthralled by the culture of "black folks" in ways that might seem complicated, at least. An easy example is the fact that the primary audience for—or at least the main consumer segment of—rap music is young white males. To what extent might this phenomenon parallel the phenomenon represented in "Slave on the Block"? I've enjoyed getting students' perspective on why young suburban white males might be drawn to the music and lyrics of urban black males (though, of course, there are plenty of women rap musicians). If we discuss how attractive—at least from afar—the "gangsta" life is to white suburban youths, I am always ready to point out America's long love affair with real and fictional gangsters, and this often leads back to a discussion of white hypocrisy, whereby a person who denounces the violence of rap music and hip hop culture might be an aficionado of *The Godfather* and *Scarface* films or the *Sopranos* television series and not see the contradiction.

"Home" is a tough, unflinching story about lynching. To some degree, it teaches itself. I sometimes bring in data to show how extensive the problem of lynching was, far into the twentieth century, not just in the South, but in almost every state in the union (Asante and Mattson 98–101). Parallels to the infamous case of Emmett Till usually arise. The main character in "Home" is very appealing: a talented musician who had thrived in Europe but who had seen Europe's own struggles with economic depression—a kind, smart, talented man murdered because of the horrific pathology of racism.

"Passing" is an epistolary story, "written" by a young black man who is passing for white. Obviously, Harlem Renaissance literature abounds in the literature of passing. Hughes's story, because it's so direct and to the point, is a narrative version of Passing 101. I've found it interesting to explore the connections between form (a letter-story that gives the illusion of a secret document) and topic (passing as a kind of espionage). Sometimes it's nice to point out that the long tradition of Anglo-American fiction begins, in the eighteenth century, with epistolary novels such as Samuel Richardson's *Pamela* (1740) and *Clarissa* (1747–1748). It's good sometimes, I think, to place Hughes on such a big literary map. The story "Berry" draws on another long narrative tradition—the use of a naive main character to expose the hypocrisy of society. ("A Good Job Gone," not among my main seven stories, does the same thing, except with a first-person narrator, a practical black man who just wants to hang on to his job.)

"The Blues I'm Playing" and "Father and Son" are the "big" stories of the collection. They are complex, multilayered narratives concerning powerful themes: patronage, power, sex, and "high" versus "low" art ("The Blues I'm Playing");

and miscegenation, denial, power, myths of the Old South, betrayal, and revenge ("Father and Son"). "The Blues I'm Playing" is probably my favorite Hughes story, with the possible exception of "On the Road," from another collection. I think it's one of the great American short stories. Clearly it came out of Hughes's own troubles with white patronage, but the artistic transformation of the material is complete; the story exists magnificently by itself, even if one may draw parallels to Hughes's biography. It's one of those "reservoir" texts that keeps providing things to talk about in class; it's beautifully constructed; the plot, subplots, scenes, and phrasing are wonderful.

Many regard "Father and Son" as Hughes's best story. Sometimes I think that if Hughes and Faulkner had experienced a brief Vulcan mind-meld, this story would be the result. It is Faulknerian because it's rooted in the Old South, it expresses notions of inescapable tragedy, and it's melodramatic—broadly played, loud, and violent. It's Hughesian in part because "the tragic mulatto" was a topic Hughes returned to repeatedly in poems and plays. Indeed, this story "recycles" the characters and plot of an earlier play, *Mulatto* (1931) (Ostrom, *Encyclopedia* 119–20). These are stories to read especially closely in class, stories with which to take your time.

With regard to "The Blues I'm Playing," students often jump at the chance to talk about "low" (blues, pop music, graphic novels) and "high" (classical music, classic literature, opera) art and to interrogate the assumptions behind the categories.

"Red-Headed Baby," "Little Dog," "Mother and Child," and "One Christmas Eve" are by no means unsuccessful stories, and they certainly present interesting topics and narrative moves to discuss. I simply don't find them as compelling and rich as the main seven stories I teach. "Poor Little Black Fellow" raises wonderful issues about "white folks" actually trying to adopt and rear "black folks"; it brings up issues of social class; and it makes use of contrasts between Europe and the United States.

Really the only difficult story to teach in the collection is "Rejuvenation through Joy," in my opinion. It's a long story (30 pages), and that would be all right if the satire didn't hinge on a kind of quasi-religious, "primitivist scam" that seems very much of the 1930s and not easily transported beyond the period. There are some parallels to certain contemporary scams and other deliberate distortions of New Age religions, I suppose. And the story does touch on questions of exoticism and primitivism that plagued the Harlem Renaissance. But it's the one story in the collection I haven't found a good way to teach, although I'd love to hear from someone who has had success with it.

The Ways of White Folks: a great book. It may, like Lawrence's fiction, seem at first to be something of a blunt ironic, satiric instrument, but on further inspection, its narratives are rich, deceptively complex (just like Hughes's poetry), and abounding in a great variety of topics, problems, themes, issues, and narrative choices. It is also a highly portable book that teachers can carry into a variety of courses. *The Ways of White Folks*: a teachable book because it creates so many teachable moments.

WORKS CITED

Asante, Molefi K., and Mark T. Mattson. *The African-American Atlas: Black History and Culture.* New York: Macmillan, 1988.

Hughes, Langston. *The Big Sea.* New York: Knopf, 1940.

———. "The Negro Artist and the Racial Mountain." June 1926. Lewis 91–95.

Hutchinson, George. *The Harlem Renaissance in Black and White.* Cambridge: Harvard UP, 1995.

———. *The Ways of White Folks.* 1934. New York: Vintage, 1990.

Lewis, David Levering, ed. *The Portable Harlem Renaissance Reader.* New York: Penguin, 1994.

———. *When Harlem Was in Vogue.* New York: Oxford UP, 1981.

Ostrom, Hans. *A Langston Hughes Encyclopedia.* Westport, CT: Greenwood, 2002.

———. *Langston Hughes: A Study of the Short Fiction.* New York: Twayne, 1993.

Pratt, Deborah M., dir. *Cora Unashamed.* Alexandria: PBS Home Video; Burbank: Warner Home Video, 2000.

Rampersad, Arnold. *The Life of Langston Hughes.* 2 vols. New York: Oxford UP, 1986–1988.

Van Vechten, Carl. *Nigger Heaven.* 1926. Ed. Kathleen Pfeiffer. Urbana: U of Illinois P, 2000.

CHAPTER FOURTEEN

Teaching James Weldon Johnson's *The Autobiography of an Ex-Colored Man*

LAWRENCE J. OLIVER

When I teach my undergraduate course in the Harlem Renaissance, I explain to the students that while the "movement" is generally associated with the 1920s and 1930s, the foundation for the flowering of African American arts and letters had been established at the dawn of the twentieth century, as courageous black intellectuals challenged both white supremacy and the accommodationist ideology embodied by Booker T. Washington. Thus I always begin the course with selections from W.E.B. Du Bois's *The Souls of Black Folk* (1903). Setting that work in its historical context, I introduce students to the reform or "progressive" spirit of the era, with due attention to the period's best-known political figure, Theodore Roosevelt, whose "The Negro Problem" (1905) projects the unconscious racism that infected the thinking of many white liberals of the time. I then introduce them to the "Other" side of progressive-era American history: to the segregation, peonage, and lynchings that mark it as the "nadir" of African American history. When discussing *The Souls of Black Folk*, we, of course, explore Du Bois' famous statement on "double consciousness" and how his dual perspective—as American and "Negro"—allowed him to critique the dominant ideology's definitions of "American" culture and "progress."

The exploration and critique continues, I inform my class, in the next assignment: James Weldon Johnson's *The Autobiography of an Ex-Colored Man*, which Johnson began writing in 1905, published anonymously in 1912, and then reissued in 1927. Johnson is indisputably a major figure of the Harlem Renaissance. As

David Levering Lewis asserts, during the Harlem Renaissance Johnson was recognized "within the race and without, as Afro-America's elder statesman" (143). A teacher could devote an entire class period simply to sketching the remarkable life and careers of this multitalented individual.[1] After teaching and practicing law in Florida (he was the first black admitted to the Florida bar, over white protests), he moved to New York City, where he launched successful careers as poet, novelist, songwriter, foreign diplomat, journalist, National Association for the Advancement of Colored People field secretary (the first black to hold that post), literary critic, editor, and college professor. "Lift Every Voice and Sing" (1900), which he coauthored with his brother Rosamond and which is often referred to as the "Negro National Anthem," is still sung in black churches and civil-rights celebrations across the nation. During the 1920s and 1930s, he produced a steady stream of books, articles, and anthologies that had a shaping influence on the Harlem Renaissance and that are assigned in Harlem Renaissance classes today: *The Book of American Negro Poetry* (1922, rev. ed. 1931), *The Book of American Negro Spirituals* (1925), *The Second Book of Negro Spirituals* (1926), *God's Trombones: Seven Negro Sermons in Verse* (1927), and *Black Manhattan* (1930). His essay "Harlem: The Culture Capital," which was included in Alain Locke's landmark collection *The New Negro: An Interpretation* (1925), captures the heady spirit of the movement in its prime. In addition to being a prolific and influential author, he was friend, mentor, and correspondent to many of the younger writers of the period. Even Zora Neale Hurston, who was prone to caustic remarks about the elder generation of black intellectuals, speaks admiringly of him in her autobiography *Dust Tracks on the Road* (1942).

The Autobiography of an Ex-Colored Man is today regarded as a classic work not only of African American but of American literature. Many scholars would agree with Henry Louis Gates Jr. that it had a "greater impact upon the subsequent shape of Afro-American fiction" (vi) than any African American novel published between the Civil War and the Harlem Renaissance. However, the anonymously published "autobiography" had little impact when it was initially published in 1912, despite the efforts of Johnson's mentor and supporter Brander Matthews, an influential critic and professor of dramatic literature at Columbia University (see Oliver 47–62). Johnson, who admired Matthews's literary criticism, introduced himself to the professor after moving to New York City in 1902 and then took a class from him. He later sent Matthews a draft of the novel from Puerto Cabello, Venezuela, where he was serving as consul, and where he began developing a lifelong interest in foreign cultures and international affairs. Matthews, like his lifelong friend Theodore Roosevelt, was not entirely free of the "scientific" racialism espoused by some of his eminent colleagues at Columbia and other prestigious universities. However, he was sufficiently open-minded to recognize and encourage Johnson's literary talent. When the novel was published, he sent copies to Roosevelt, Rudyard Kipling, and his other friends urging them to read it: "It is not exactly fact—but it is truth," he wrote Roosevelt. "And it lets the light into some dark and curious places" (qtd. in Oliver 56).[2] Matthews, of course, knew that the anonymous "autobiography" was actually a novel, but when he reviewed the book in the pages of *Munsey's Magazine* (Aug. 1913), he did not reveal that secret. Echoing his letter to Roosevelt, he asserted that whether novel or autobiography, the narrative was "indisputabl[y] written by a colored man," who "takes us into many circles, the existence of which is unknown to white readers. … It may not be a record of actual fact, but it contains what is higher than actual fact, the essential truth" (798).

An unsigned review attributed to Jessie Fauset in *The Crisis*, the magazine of the NAACP, concurred with the preface—signed by "The Publishers" but drafted by Johnson—that the book is a "composite and proportionate presentation of the entire race," narrated in dispassionate style. Fauset adds that the story is "indeed an epitome of the race situation in the United States" at the time (qtd. in Price and Oliver 21).[3]

Yet, despite the positive reviews and the promotional efforts of the publishers and Professor Matthews, Johnson's novel did not attain a wide readership in 1912 and was soon out of print. But as the Harlem Renaissance gained steam in the 1920s and increasing numbers of white readers took interest in the inner lives of "exotic" Others, the time was ripe for republication of the novel. In 1927, Alfred Knopf released a new edition of the book, identifying Johnson as the author of the novel and, following British usage, changing the spelling of "colored" to "coloured." The new edition bore a flattering introduction by Carl Van Vechten, a New York art critic and culture broker whose parties brought together many notable writers and artists of the Harlem Renaissance. (Friend to Alfred Knopf as well as Johnson, Van Vechten annually hosted a joint birthday party for them, since their birthdays fell on the same day.) Van Vechten declared that this "remarkable" book, which he acknowledges influenced his own novel of Harlem life, *Nigger Heaven* (1926), may be read not so much as the fictionalized autobiography of one black man, but rather as a "composite autobiography of the Negro race in the United States in modern times." Clearly that claim is inflated, especially when one considers that this narrative of an ex-colored *man* virtually ignores the lives of black women (which is why I include one of Nella Larsen's novels of female passing, *Quicksand* [1928] or *Passing* [1929], on my reading list). But Van Vechten was on the mark when he praised Johnson for celebrating what we would now call "black expressive culture" in 1912, "five or six years before the rest of us began to shout about it, singing hosannas to rag-time" (xxxvii).

As critics have noted, Van Vechten's introduction and the publisher's preface to the first edition implicitly connect Johnson's novel to the literary tradition of the slave narrative. Slave narratives generally were introduced by a statement from a respected white individual who testified to the authenticity of the narrative and to the ex-slave's ability to write it. The autobiographies of freed slaves such as Frederick Douglass and Harriet Jacobs are narratives of *empowerment*: The authors not only condemn slavery, they also demonstrate their humanity and project a strong, indeed heroic, personal identity as they narrate their resistance to and eventual escape from bondage. In sharp contrast to a Douglass or Jacobs, Johnson's ex-colored man is deeply flawed: His picaresque travels map the traditional slave escape route from the South to the North (with a sojourn in Europe), but during his journey he is the epitome of vacillation. As he himself realizes, the motives behind his actions are "largely mixed with selfishness" (89). Even when he rejects the millionaire offer of patronship and a hedonistic lifestyle in Europe (chapter 9) and decides instead to return to the South and use his "gifts" (a Du Boisian term) to mine the rich heritage of ragtime and slave spirituals, he admits that his decision is based "on purely selfish grounds" (89). After returning from Europe, he identifies with his black heritage. He alludes to that "remarkable book," *The Souls of Black Folk*; expresses admiration for African Americans' progress in the face of enormous obstacles; and marvels at the profound beauty of the Negro spirituals. Once again, however, his courage and commitment falter, and selfishness guides his decisions. After witnessing the horrible lynching, he decides to pass for white and pursue the "white man's success"—money (117). But, as he realizes in the closing pages of the narrative, his "success" has cost him dearly. Rather than attaining spiritual freedom and dignity, he feels small and selfish. The music manuscripts that represent his African spiritual self—what Du Bois would call his "soul"—lie fading in a box. In one of the book's many ironies, the narrator, who has revealed his secret racial identity to the world, feels compelled to hide it from the two offspring of his marriage to a white woman.

If the narrator's discovery and then denial of the "soul of black folk" looks back to Du Bois' classic work and to the slave narratives, it also anticipates the cultural struggle and a resulting controversy that was at the heart of the Harlem Renaissance of the 1920s and 1930s. Some scholars have contended that the Harlem Renaissance was a failure because it was a cultural event primarily sponsored by and staged for whites who wanted a taste of the "exotic" life behind the Veil. As one critic bluntly puts it, "The grandsons of the human property of slave times remained at risk of becoming the intellectual property of their latter-day 'rescuers'" (Griffiths 337). (Van Vechten, in fact, urged African American artists and writers to be as "black" as possible to appeal to white consumers [Schulz 44].) Other scholars contend that the blacks who shaped the Harlem Renaissance took advantage of white support and created a largely independent cultural movement that anticipated the Black Arts Movement of the 1960s and 1970s. Johnson's literary career can be used to furnish evidence for both sides of this controversy.[4] In my view, however, he exemplifies yet a third critical perspective on the movement—a perspective that was developed by George Hutchinson in his superb study *The Harlem Renaissance in Black and White* (1995). Hutchinson demonstrates that the Harlem Renaissance was the product of numerous intellectual currents and ideologies—nationalism, modernism, internationalism—in conflict over American cultural identity or the "national soul" (11). Thus the Harlem Renaissance was neither "black" nor "white," but a fusion of both, made possible by various "inter-racial modernist networks" (447). Not only as a writer but also in several of his other careers noted above, Johnson took advantage of interracial and international personal networks and cultural traditions in order to help create a richly diverse modern American literature and culture. Indeed, his remarkable life epitomized such diversity of interests, culture, and language (he was fluent in Spanish).

In his essay titled "The Dilemma of the Negro Author," published in 1928 when the Harlem Renaissance was in full swing, Johnson asserted that black writers must stand firmly on their "racial foundation," but then "fashion something that rises above race, and reaches out to the universal truth and beauty. And so when a Negro does write so as to fuse white and black America into one interested and approving audience he has performed no slight feat, and has most likely done a sound piece of literary work" (752). In *The Autobiography of an Ex-Colored Man*—a novel of racial passing that originally passed as an autobiography—Johnson attained such a feat of fusion and most certainly bequeathed American literature a sound piece of literary work.

DISCUSSION TOPICS

I have taught *The Autobiography of an Ex-Colored Man* many times, in several different courses, and most students find the novel readable and engaging, and I have never had difficulty generating good discussion. I usually divide students into small groups and assign each group a discussion question. The group's responsibility is then to lead the class discussion of that particular question. Below are a few of the questions that I assign. The list, of course, is not exhaustive.

1. Explain how Johnson's narrator embodies the concept of "double consciousness" described by Du Bois in *The Souls of Black Folk*. What other themes of Du Bois's book does Johnson dramatize in his novel? As Robert Stepto observed long ago, that Johnson had *Souls* in mind as he composed his novel is "manifest almost to the point of embarrassment" (46), beginning with the reference to drawing the "veil" in the preface to the 1912 edition. Most students will make the connections with other images and motifs in Du Bois' work—for example, the "problem of the

color line" (45); appreciation of slaves' Sorrow Songs and expressive culture; and the central theme: that African Americans have provided the "gift of the Spirit" (193) to a materialistic mainstream culture of "vulgar money-getters" (84). But where Du Bois seeks to create something positive out of his "double consciousness," blending the best qualities of his "African" and "American" selves, Johnson's narrator rejects such cultural amalgamation.

2. Describe the narrative technique of the novel. How reliable is the narrator? Obviously, students need to be cognizant of the narrative point-of-view, which allows for ironic distance between Johnson and his flawed character. It is at times uncertain whether the narrator is presenting his own limited, selfish views or expressing Johnson's, as he occasionally does. Of course, students need to know that Johnson was a dark-skinned man for whom "passing" was not an option. They should also be informed that Johnson originally considered titling the book "The Chameleon" and asked what that title suggests about Johnson's aims in the novel.

In discussing narrative technique and genre, I note that Johnson composed the novel in the first decade of the twentieth century, as literary realism was giving way to modernism. Clearly, the novel is saturated with realistic details as it attempts to lift the "veil" for white audiences and introduce them to black culture in the South and north, and as it explores realities of race (including passing) and racism (including segregation and lynching). However, there are also elements that are commonly associated with literary modernism: a limited narrative point-of-view that creates ambiguity; the generally spare prose and a reliance on images to suggest meaning; and the "inward turn," the exploration of the narrator's conflicted psyche. Moreover, as Donald Goellnicht and others maintain, Johnson is engaged in a "kind of playful and productive transgression of boundaries between fiction and non-fiction" (qtd. in Price and Oliver 128).

3. Johnson deliberately repeats and revises (or "signifies" on) the slave narratives (e.g., Frederick Douglass's) and black autobiographies (including *Up from Slavery* [1901]). What are the parallels with slave narratives and autobiographies? How does Johnson revise the tradition and for what purpose? One of the more interesting aspects of Johnson's novel of racial passing is that it itself offers an example of "generic passing," since it was, as noted above, initially presented as an anonymous autobiography. Donald Goellnicht's article presents the parallels with the slave narratives and also addresses the difficult question of when Johnson is parodying (in the Bakhtinian sense of that term) the tradition. Goellnicht also provides an interesting reading of the "problematic Preface" of the 1912 edition: Is the Preface, which was drafted by Johnson but attributed to "The Publishers," meant to parody the "authenticating" statements that introduce slave narratives and black autobiographies? Or did Johnson in fact allow the publishers to give their stamp of approval in order to increase sales of the book?

4. For most white Americans during the Progressive Era and Harlem Renaissance, "Anglo Saxons" and "Negroes" exhibited fixed biological "race traits." How does this novel of "passing" complicate the notion of ineluctable racial identity? Before engaging this question, students need to become familiar with the history of racial theory and racism in the early twentieth century and, of course, must be aware that race is a social construct. I always devote some lecture time to Franz Boas's challenge to the dominant racial "science" of the day, noting that Boas was a professor and colleague of Brander Matthews at Columbia University. As noted above, some Southern newspapers rejected wholesale the notion that a person with "Negro blood" could pass as white. Among the novel's many ironies is that, before he learns that he is "black," the young narrator calls a black youth "nigger," and he doesn't learn about black people and culture until his move to Atlanta. The narrator's ultimate decision to pass for white offers an excellent opportunity to engage students in discussion of white privilege. David Roediger's introduction to his *Black on White* is a good assignment for students unfamiliar with "critical whiteness," and he cites Johnson several times. If teaching the novel to students who have a grounding in contemporary literary theory, especially Foucaldian, the discussion can move from "black" or "white" identity to more theoretical questions regarding human identity and authorship. Frederick T. Griffiths's exploration of "authorship's disappearance and reappearance within the strong continuities of African American autobiographical practice" (316), including *The Autobiography of an Ex-Colored Man*, is an excellent resource at this level. Catherine Rottenberg's essay is also useful, especially her insights into the "in between" position of the "Jewish-looking man" on the Pullman car (chapter 10).

NOTES

1. Eugene D. Levy's *Black Leader, Black Voice* (1973) provides the fullest account of Johnson's remarkable life.

2. Johnson campaigned for Roosevelt during the 1904 presidential election and even cowrote a campaign song for him, which TR found to be "bully good" (*Along This Way* [1933] in *Writings* 372–75).

3. Southern reviews were predictably hostile: "an insult to Southern womanhood," fumed one. Another dismissed the narrative as pure fiction rather than essential truth because, the reviewer asserted, the difference between "negro" and "Anglo Saxon" was so distinctive and self-evident that it was impossible for anyone with "negro" blood to pass for white (qtd. in Price and Oliver 7). Of course, the narrative *was* a fiction, but one based on real-life cases. See Johnson's essay "Stranger than Fiction" (*Writings* 620–22).

4. The ambivalences and contradictions of Johnson's thought and writings are summarized by Lewis (147–49).

WORKS CITED

Badaracco, Claire Hoertz. "*The Autobiography of an Ex-Coloured Man* by James Weldon Johnson: The 1927 Knopf Edition." *Papers of the Bibliographical Society of America* 96.2 (June 2002): 279–87.

Du Bois, W.E.B. *The Souls of Black Folk*. Ed. David Blight and Robert Gooding-Williams. New York: Bedford, 1997.

Gates, Henry Louis Jr. Introduction to *The Autobiography of an Ex-Coloured Man*. New York: Vintage, 1989. v–xxiii.

Goellnicht, Donald C. "Passing as Autobiography: James Weldon Johnson's *The Autobiography of an Ex-Coloured Man*." In Price and Oliver. 115–35.

Griffiths, Frederick T. "Copy Wright: What Is an (Invisible) Author?" *New Literary History* 33 (2002): 315–41.

Hurston, Zora Neale. *Dust Tracks on a Road*. 1942. New York: Harper, 1990.

Hutchinson, George. *The Harlem Renaissance in Black and White*. Cambridge: Harvard UP, 1995.

Johnson, James Weldon. *James Weldon Johnson: Writings*. Ed. William L. Andrews. New York: Library of America, 2004.

Levy, Eugene D. *James Weldon Johnson: Black Leader, Black Voice*. Chicago: U of Chicago P, 1973.

Lewis, David Levering. *When Harlem Was in Vogue*. New York: Oxford UP, 1981.

Oliver, Lawrence J. *Brander Matthews, Theodore Roosevelt, and the Politics of American Literature, 1880–1920*. Knoxville: U of Tennessee P, 1992.

Price, Kenneth M., and Lawrence J. Oliver, eds. *Critical Essays on James Weldon Johnson*. New York: G.K. Hall, 1997.

Roediger, David R., ed. *Black on White: Black Writers on What It Means to Be White*. New York: Schocken, 1999.

Rottenberg, Catherine. "Race and Ethnicity in *The Autobiography of an Ex-Colored Man* and *The Rise of David Levinsky*: The Performative Difference." *MELUS* 29 (2004): 307–21.

Schulz, Jennifer Lea. "Restaging the Racial Contract: James Weldon Johnson's Signatory Strategies." *American Literature* 74 (2002): 31–58.

Van Vechten, Carl. "Introduction to Mr. Knopf's New Edition." *The Autobiography of an Ex-Coloured Man*. New York: Vintage, 1989. xxxiii–xxxviii.

CHAPTER FIFTEEN

Teaching Nella Larsen's *Quicksand*

EMILY M. HINNOV

My intention in a Harlem Renaissance class, in part, is to emphasize the point that the Harlem Renaissance is an integral movement of transatlantic modernism.[1] From the first day of class, I stress the point with my students that both black and white modernists relied upon the mask of primitivism to explore notions of the self; black artists of the Harlem Renaissance took on this identity performance to express their own unique culture as a rich experience of modern American life, just as white writers relied upon the problematic trope of primitivism to discover the self through a new kind of literature.[2]

To begin the discussion of Nella Larsen's *Quicksand* (1928), I note that Zora Neale Hurston's *Their Eyes Were Watching God* (1937) (the novel we end the semester with) concludes with Janie Crawford's whole vision of the horizon. The other side of the story is Larsen's *Quicksand*. While Hurston's later novel is a kind of *Bildungsroman* that students by and large respond enthusiastically and warmly to, Larsen's earlier work illustrates the destructive problem of whiteness and its function in the decline of her would-be tragic mulatta, Helga Crane. Students just don't feel that same warmth or enthusiasm for Helga; in fact, they are downright frustrated with her. Whereas Hurston's vision for Janie is expansive, Larsen's text reveals and condemns limiting configurations of race and gender discrimination. This comparison begs the question of how one modernist narrative of an African American woman's search for selfhood could close with such a positive image of communal wholeness whereas another ends with its heroine wholly entrapped by the hegemonic system of whiteness. Did Janie somehow escape or merely ignore the ever-present forces of racism and sexism, as some critics of Hurston's novel have argued? What follows is an explanation of how and why I set up Larsen's novel as a text that engenders resistance in its reader with suggestions for some ways of thinking about how to teach through that resistance.

As with all the other texts I teach in this course, I assign Biographical and Cultural Artifact Presentations whereby students must research, analyze, and explore particular persons/artifacts/documents that might help shed light on our understanding of literary texts. As we discuss Larsen's *Quicksand*, I assign a Biographical Presentation on Larsen herself, with particular focus on Larsen's own mixed ancestry and troubled relationship with her parentage.[3] I suggest that the presenter begin with George Hutchinson's definitive biography, Thadious M. Davis's exemplary biography, and Deborah A. McDowell's introduction to the Rutgers University Press edition that we use in class. I also assign related Cultural Artifact Presentations on Berlin Dada artist Hannah Höch's surrealist, often primitivist collages and Josephine Baker's famously exotic and sensual *danse sauvage* as important cultural markers of the Harlem Renaissance. We might also view these artistic creations as feminist representations of fragmented female identity within a modernist cosmopolitan context.[4] Some engaging discussions about race, class, sexuality, and artistic representations of Negro womanhood emerge from these presentations, which provide rich connections with Larsen's novel.

Through her portrayal of Helga Crane, Larsen undercuts primitivist stereotypes of black womanhood. As we learn from the Biographical Presentation, Larsen demands absolute social equality for African Americans and thereby dispels denigrating images of black or mulatta womanhood in her fiction. In order to prepare students for an understanding of Larsen's political purpose, I introduce short essays early on in the course that explore concepts of what it meant to be doubly denigrated (and doubly conscious) as a black woman in the 1920s, in particular Elise Johnson McDougald's "The Task of Negro Womanhood" and Marita K. Bonner's "On Being Young—a Woman—and Colored," both published in 1925. We consider these texts as representations of the contrasts inherent in expressions of African American female artistry in the Harlem Renaissance. This discussion is preceded by an earlier class conversation about the aesthetic and political implications of W.E.B. Du Bois's "Criteria of Negro Art," Langston Hughes's "The Negro Artist and the Racial Mountain," and Marcus Garvey's "Africa for the Africans," with particular focus on these male writers' proclamations of racial pride and its relationship to class and nation. I ask my students, as they compare the essays written by women, to consider what ways Bonner's and McDougald's perspectives on African American accomplishments and contributions, ideal womanhood, and the creation of art and culture differ from those of male writers. We often come to the conclusion that despite the rather upbeat nature of McDougald's piece, both Bonner and McDougald expose the difficulties of negotiating black womanhood in the male-dominated age of the New Negro; both writers advocate for African American womens' silent yet stoic suffering while they gather the power that will one day come to fruition in racial and sexual equality. Bonner's essay especially provides a fascinating pretext to the torment Helga Crane experiences throughout *Quicksand*.

As we begin with our close readings of Larsen's novel, I frame the conversation by suggesting that it is the devastating structures of racism that interrupt and disallow Helga Crane's engagement with whole selfhood or community in *Quicksand*. Although Helga continually rejects primitivist narratives that depict who she should be from a white (often male) perspective, she cannot move beyond or envision anything other than a romantic heterosexual fantasy to fulfill her life. The sorrowful ending of *Quicksand*, which undermines cultural conceptions of a celebratory primitivism intrinsic to the Harlem Renaissance, illuminates Larsen's political genius in fictional form. Instead of employing a Hurstonian joyful vision, Larsen (much like Bonner) shows us the stark reality of life for a black woman who struggles with white supremacist patriarchal tyranny. As part of an implied reading community, we are saddened to witness Helga's downward spiral. Nevertheless, Larsen's exclusive use of omniscient narration and repeated use of the passive voice distances Helga from her community of readers. Throughout the novel, then, Helga appears increasingly alienated from herself and, ultimately, as students no doubt notice, her reading audience. Indeed, students feel little connection to Helga, and tend to remain aloof in response to her behavior. Our assessment of Larsen's novel, sparked by short writing assignments based on close textual analysis, intense small and large group discussion, and collaborative critical thinking, shows students the value of an affective reading of *Quicksand*.[5]

There are a number of important scenes in Larsen's novel that I feel are necessary to discuss with students in detail by modeling the kind of close reading I want them to be able to do in their papers. It's best to start at the beginning with the opening scene of *Quicksand*, when Helga notably expels herself from Naxos's white-worshipping community in search of a place where she can belong. Like Hughes, she despises the middle-class codes of proper blackness (which apparently means behaving through codes of whiteness) embraced at the school. Having rejected whitewashed blackness, Helga looks instead for something more "authentically" black and familial—sort of like Langston Hughes's "low-down folks" (41). Helga's chief obstacle to finding wholeness is that she has no self-affirming story of her own life to carry her through the trials of interfacing with a white supremacist world. The first words she utters in the novel, fatefully, are "No, forever!" (3). As I point out, this two-word declaration foretells Helga's ongoing refusal to form any meaningful relationship with the ever-distant community around her, or to create an assenting narrative of self. As students read on, they become increasingly detached from Helga as she simultaneously falls further into the quicksand that consumes her. Without a coherent language to tell the narrative of her past or to imagine her future, Helga is left without a sense of self, family, or community.

This incommunicative divide does not stop Helga, at first, from looking for community elsewhere, bringing us to the next key passage in the novel. For a luxuriant yet brief time during her first visit to New York, she feels a sense of wholeness within her surrounding community in the "primitive jungle" of "Harlem, teeming black Harlem" (43). Throughout the novel, Larsen shows Helga's repeated attempts to reconverge with her ostensible primitivist past, even while she feels distanced and separate from it. A prime example occurs in the well-known Harlem nightclub scene: "She was drugged, lifted, sustained, by the extraordinary music" but then "the shameful certainty that not only had she been in the jungle, but that she enjoyed it ... began to taunt her" (59). Critics have interpreted Helga's reticence as a resistance to being categorized as a typically "savage" and oversexed black female,[6] and I too contend in our class discussion of this passage that Helga's total abandon would only reinscribe the sensationalized stereotype of the black primitive and exotic female. Here I also remind students that Larsen's own personal dilemma, as a biracial woman writer expected to answer the call of Harlem Renaissance literature, is reflected in her portrayal of Helga Crane.

Once in Copenhagen, Helga again struggles with her racialization as an exoticized, hypersexual woman—a construction produced by the whiteness of her surveyors—much like the fragmented figures in Hannah Höch's Dada collages or the supersensual Josephine Baker. From the moment she arrives in Copenhagen, she behaves like a "Silent, unmoving" (65) exotic museum piece, similar to Bonner's Buddha figure in "On Being Young—a Woman—and Colored." Helga participates in the literal construction of her body (as sexual, exotic, and available to men) that eventually cements her status as an unspeaking, captivating object in Olson's portrait.

In the last of Helga's suffocating, self-deluding, and ultimately remote behavior, she lies in agony, a debilitated and once again pregnant mother of five. Here we see that marriage and motherhood, instead of representing a traditional kind of feminine completion, are together only another link in the chain that binds Helga Crane from enjoying connectedness or wholeness. Her fate could not be more different from Janie Crawford's; we can only conclude that Helga, utterly lacking in voice, vision, or communal wholeness, ends her story in a position of total extinction.

As I tell my class, Deborah McDowell notes that feminist scholars' gynocritical approach to the literary canon in the 1970s initially left Larsen out. Thanks to the efforts of such black feminist critics as Thadious Davis, the reprinting of

Larsen's novels in the mid-1980s has gained Nella Larsen a new audience of feminist admirers who have begun to fully recognize her as a visionary modern novelist. Larsen's *Quicksand* reveals to her contemporary and present community of readers the profound tragedy of a black woman who cannot grasp any kind of wholeness within self or community. Yet what I most want for my students to realize is that Helga Crane's unrealizable (and even universal) need to imagine a balanced sense of self with regard to race and gender insists that audiences fill in this gap through an affective kind of reading.[7] Most importantly, because Helga is unable to speak from her oppressed subject position, readers might recall that unspoken voice. Larsen, therefore, forces her readers to look within their own lives for an ethics that would have supported Helga in her process of becoming a whole self. If we, as a class, can imagine a more compassionate connection between reader and protagonist within a literary text, then perhaps we can understand the complexities and resistances of Helga's way of (un)knowing herself. Finally, I suggest to my students that we can then view Larsen's novel as a complication of modernist narratives of gender, race, and community *and* as a vital call for social justice that Hurston answers in her own novel, written a decade later in the aftermath of the Harlem Renaissance. The work of Nella Larsen lends itself to this kind of affective analysis of literature and the ways in which our dynamic, intersubjective reading can transform our views of both self and community. My greatest hope as I teach *Quicksand* is that my students can become just such a redemptive reading community.

NOTES

1. I teach "The Harlem Renaissance: New Boundaries of Gender, Race, Region, and Form" as an interdisciplinary undergraduate course. Our study focuses on literary discourses of raced and gendered identity, cultural nationalism, modernist aesthetics, and primitivism in writings of the Harlem Renaissance.
2. For more on key concepts from the theoretical conversation focusing on black aesthetics as central to the formation of modernism, see especially Sieglinde Lemke's argument that there is no modernism without primitivism. See also Hackett and Marcus.
3. Born in Chicago in the 1890s to a black West Indian father (who died when Larsen was a young girl) and a Danish mother, Larsen spent her early life in the midst of "modern buildings and technological innovations ... [and] transformations of identity [that were] possible given the fluidity of western and immigrant lives in an expanding city" (Davis 4). She encountered the "behavioral codes and color snobbery [used] to establish class distinction" (5) in New York City, where she met and married research physicist Dr. Elmer Samuel Imes in 1919. Larsen soon labeled herself a "mulatta," was trained as a librarian at the New York Public Library, and became good friends with Carl Van Vechten, the white novelist and critic who became one of her most prominent literary mentors. Largely as a result of the success of her novels, Larsen was the first black female creative writer to win the Guggenheim (in 1930), but her third novel was never published.

4. For an excellent resource on images by Höch, see *The Photomontages of Hannah Höch*.

5. I ask students to come to each class with a 1-2 page reading response that offers textual support for their ideas and asks questions and/or provides suggestions for discussion. The major writing assignments for this class are as follows: Close Reading of Literary Text paper (students perform a line by line analysis of a short story, long poem, or passage of a novel), Analysis of Nonfiction Text paper (students reflect, through close reading of an essay, on how the chosen nonfiction piece echoes, represents, explores, or challenges concepts associated with the Harlem Renaissance), and finally the Researched Comparative paper. Their task for the Researched Comparative paper is to choose a central thematic issue, topic, element, or narrative technique associated with writing of the Harlem Renaissance and to draw a comparison about the way two authors handle it in their work.

6. Focusing on the portrayal of female sexuality in Nella Larsen's novels, Deborah McDowell argues that, "because she gave her characters sexual feelings at all, she has to be regarded as something of a pioneer, a trailblazer in the Afro-American female literary tradition" (xxxi). Similarly, Kimberly Monda contends that "Racist white society's assumptions about black women's sexual availability help explain Helga Crane's sexual repression, and also remind us of Larsen's courage in attempting to portray her heroine's sexual desire" (25). Claudia Tate reads Helga Crane as "an aggressive and defensive seductress, implicated in her own tragic fate" (9).

7. George Hutchinson aptly speaks to Larsen's implicit connection between the treatment of race in her novel and the value of ethics: "Never embracing Jean Toomer's idea of a 'new race,' Larsen rather exposed the violence of racialization as such—the force that had divided her from her mother—in the attempt to make it ethically insupportable, an affront to humanity" ("Nella Larsen" 345).

WORKS CITED

Baker, Jr., Houston A. *Modernism and the Harlem Renaissance*. Chicago: U of Chicago P, 1987.

Bonner, Marita K. "On Being Young, a Woman, and Colored." Patton and Honey 109–12.

Davis, Thadious M. *Nella Larsen: Novelist of the Harlem Renaissance: A Woman's Life Unveiled*. Baton Rouge: Louisiana State UP, 1994.

Du Bois, W.E.B. *The Souls of Black Folk*. 1903. New York: Johnson, 1968.

———. "Criteria of Negro Art." Patton and Honey 47–51.

Garvey, Marcus. "Africa for the Africans." Patton and Honey 83–89.

Hackett, Robin. *Sapphic Primitivism: Productions of Race, Class, and Sexuality in Key Works of Modern Fiction*. New Brunswick: Rutgers UP, 2004.

Hughes, Langston. "The Negro Artist and the Racial Mountain." Patton and Honey 40–44.

Hurston, Zora Neale. *Their Eyes Were Watching God*. 1937. New York: Harper, 1998.

Hutchinson, George. *The Harlem Renaissance in Black and White*. Cambridge: Harvard UP, 1995.

———. *In Search of Nella Larsen: A Biography of the Color Line*. Cambridge: Harvard UP, 2006.

———. "Nella Larsen and the Veil of Race." *American Literary History* 9 (1997): 329–49.

Larsen, Nella. *Quicksand* and *Passing*. 1928 and 1929. Ed. Deborah E. McDowell. New Brunswick: Rutgers UP, 1986.

Lemke, Sieglinde. *Primitivist Modernism: Black Culture and the Origins of Transatlantic Modernism*. Oxford: Oxford UP, 1998.

Marcus, Jane. *Hearts of Darkness: White Women Write Race*. New Brunswick: Rutgers UP, 2004.

McDougald, Elise Johnson. "The Task of Negro Womanhood." Patton and Honey 103–08.

Monda, Kimberly. "Self-Delusion and Self-Sacrifice in Nella Larsen's *Quicksand*." *African American Review* 31 (1997): 23–39.

Patton, Venetria K., and Maureen Honey, eds. *Double-Take: A Revisionist Anthology of the Harlem Renaissance*. New Brunswick: Rutgers UP, 2001.

The Photomontages of Hannah Höch. Organized by Peter Boswell et al. Minneapolis: Walker Art Center, 1996.

Tate, Claudia. *Psychoanalysis and Black Novels: Desire and the Protocols of Race*. New York: Oxford UP, 1998.

CHAPTER SIXTEEN

Teaching Claude McKay's *Home to Harlem*

TOM LUTZ

In many ways, Claude McKay's *Home to Harlem* (1928) teaches itself. That is, it is quite self-consciously and unambiguously a map to a social world, one that the text assumes is only slightly familiar to its readers. The novel functions, in other words, as its own ethnography. The main thematic issues of the text are discussed within it, and again, these are approached fairly obviously and explicitly. A few of these issues, though, require students to have some contextual knowledge.

I like to start any course on the Harlem Renaissance with two texts, both of them short films produced just before the crash: Bessie Smith's *St. Louis Blues* (16 minutes, 1929) and Duke Ellington's *Black and Tan* (19 minutes, 1929). Both are narrative films with a musical performance at their core, and both, I suggest to students, make implicit arguments about African American art, about the relation of the lived experience of African Americans to their artistic creation. These two very different arguments about African American cultural production help me introduce students to the major debates within and between the African American intellectual and artistic communities of the 1920s: arguments about jazz, primitivism, assimilation, incrementalism, representation, and the other debates that pitted the "New Crowd" against the "Old Crowd." I understand these arguments to animate all the complex cultural products of the Renaissance, especially the novels, and perhaps nowhere quite as explicitly as in Claude McKay's fiction from the late 1920s, especially *Home to Harlem* and *Banjo* (1929). McKay, like any good literary artist, tries to represent both sides of these arguments, but he tends to list in one particular direction. I think it is necessary to understand his position to appreciate both the force and the failure of his fiction.

The two films have similar basic structures. In both, the performers play themselves in a schematic yet realist fictional story. They both start with a narrative section that sets up the musical performance, and in both the music is performed within that narrative. Both involve what are purported to be the real-life struggles of the artists themselves, or allegorical versions of those real-life struggles. In both, the music is shown to be a direct response to the problems these artists face.

Bessie Smith's film opens with a craps game on the floor of an apartment building hallway. The janitor takes bribes to let them play. A flashy player named Jimmy comes in and wins a lot of money. A beautiful woman flirts with him a little, blowing on his dice for luck. Jimmy takes her into a furnished room. What would Bessie say? she asks, and it becomes clear they are in Bessie's room and Jimmy is supposedly Bessie's boyfriend. Jimmy says not to worry about Bessie, he can do whatever he wants. Meanwhile Smith comes into the hallway and the gamblers sheepishly suggest that she go to her room to see who is there. When she does, she is furious at his betrayal and punches the other woman while he looks on, amused. The other woman runs out, after which Jimmy starts to leave. Bessie pleads with him not to leave her, reminding him that she gives him money and buys him clothes. He laughs, pushes her to floor, and tries to walk out. Smith, abject, cleaves to his leg until he literally kicks her off. He leaves, she takes a swig of gin, and then she starts to sing "St. Louis Blues." The rest of the film is the song; a cut takes us into a club with Smith leaning on the bar, still singing, sipping a beer. The crowd provides backup. Jimmy comes into the bar, dances with Bessie only in order to steal more money from her, and then leaves again, laughing. Bessie launches into the refrain once more.

The Duke Ellington film begins with Ellington and his trumpet player, Arthur Whetsol, sitting at an upright piano in what seems to be Ellington's apartment. Ellington plays from a handwritten score and explains to Whetsol when the brass and winds will come in. Whetsol, reading from Ellington's score, plays along with him until they are interrupted. Piano movers come to repossess his piano, and Fredi Washington, the dancer, gives them a bottle of gin to lie to their employer and say no one was home, allowing them to keep the piano for a few more days. Washington has a heart ailment and is not supposed to dance anymore, but she convinces Ellington that she is well enough and gets them a job in a nightclub. The center of the film is that nightclub performance with Ellington's orchestra, Washington, and a number of other dancers. She has a relapse during her dance and collapses. The last section of the film is Ellington playing at her death bed as she dies.

The Smith film provides a very strong and clear argument that her music, and perhaps the blues itself, arises spontaneously from the experience of the singer. Smith plays herself as a victim in the film, and there is literally only one moment between her abject victimhood and her production of song, a moment just long enough for a single action, a swig from a bottle of gin. Her art results, naturally, spontaneously from her abjection, no more premeditated or mediated than a stiff drink. The other patrons in the bar, moved by her plight, join in. The dancing in the film is similarly impulsive; Jimmy enters the bar, feels good, and does a wild solo dance in response, simply expressing (or so it suggests) how he feels. When he again abuses Smith, she again immediately sings her tragic plight, the Greek chorus of bar patrons spontaneously backing her up. African American cultural production, the film represents, flows immediately and unrehearsed from the depths of black experience.

The Ellington film takes the opposite tack. The film insists from the first scene that his music does not flow spontaneously in response to some lived experience: Like European orchestral music, it is thought through, it is composed, it is arranged, it is rehearsed. Ellington is not denying oppression, as the film also asserts immediately that his music is produced under conditions of economic deprivation—Ellington can barely hold on to his piano, and Washington needs to go back to work even if it quite literally kills her. Ellington shows that African American music can be a response to the tragedies of black life under such conditions; the "Black and Tan Symphony" is a funeral march, and Ellington weeps as he plays the last verse. But the music itself is created in the same way that Euro-American music is—through standard forms of notation, arrangement, and careful rehearsal. The dancing makes the same point. In this era, dancers such as Bojangles Robinson and Josephine Baker were applauded for their pure improvisatory exuberance and fed the myth: Robinson claimed that his famous stair dance was created in an instant of joy at meeting the president. The Ellington film again begs to differ; it features a troupe of tap dancers whose moves are so tightly rehearsed that they dance in absolutely perfect unison, so perfect, in fact, that they look like they're glued to each other, six in a row, back to front, with a fraction of an inch separating each leg from the next dancer's; if one dancer impulsively expressed a personal emotion they would all fall down. And Washington's story seems directly aimed at audiences and critics who understood dancing like hers to be an unmediated expression of pure feeling. We see her backstage dizzy, depressed, and failing, but when she comes on stage she seems happy, even overjoyed. Her dance is an act, a choreographed representation of spontaneous self-expression, not actual spontaneous self-expression.

These filmic arguments were related to the cultural-political polemics of the day. Smith's "St. Louis Blues" is everything the Black Bourgeoisie, the Old Crowd, didn't want to see in African American art. Gambling, drinking, domestic violence, thievery, abjection: This is exactly the kind of representation of lower-class immorality that Old Crowd types such as Jessie Redmon Fauset and W.E.B. Du Bois argued should be avoided, since it reinforced white racist stereotypes. The Ellington film makes the minor lower-class characters illiterate, comic buffoons and concentrates on the problems and dilemmas of the educated, "refined" characters such as Ellington and Washington, just as novelists such as Fauset did. Claude McKay, on the other hand, was often on Smith's side, happy to represent all facets of lower-class black life, including the criminal and degraded. *Home to Harlem* and *Banjo* feature brothels, knife fights, gigolos, loan sharks, drunken brawls, and drugs, just for starters, and the heroes of these tales, Jake and Banjo, are not exactly willing to wait for weddings to have sex, nor are they averse to mind-altering substances. Du Bois famously complained that he wanted to take a bath after reading *Home to Harlem* and thought that jazz and blues themselves were degraded forms of music that were imperfectly evolved. For McKay, this is the attitude of "a dyed-in-the-wool pussy-footing professor," as he called Alain Locke (qtd. in Lewis 153). McKay believed that the bourgeois complaints against his work were part of an enormous cultural mistake.

McKay believed in the value of what was then commonly referred to as the "primitive." This word, as many who have taught the period know, causes a lot of problems in the classroom, with minority students in particular prone to take offence, and it takes some doing to introduce the word and concept. McKay considered D.H. Lawrence "a spiritual brother" and believed, along with Sherwood Anderson, H.L. Mencken, and a host of others in the 1910s and 1920s, that the deadening weight of civilization was choking off people's primitive, vital life force. McKay argued, in his fiction and criticism, that African American quotidian and artistic culture was an antidote to such overcivilization. All night dancing was better than civilized bedtime, the "colorful" speech of the uneducated was more vibrant than the anglicized speech of overcivilized Negroes, and the improvised banjo and fiddle more satisfying than the player piano and traditional symphony. McKay does not deny the value of European forms, either musical, linguistic, or social, but he firmly tips the balance toward the "earthy people," whose continued existence, and continued expression, he represents as heroic and salutary.

To make these points I turn to some of McKay's nonfiction: "Our age is the age of Negro art," he wrote in *The Negroes in America* (1922–1923). "The slogan of the aesthetic world is 'Return to the Primitive.' The Futurists and Impressionists are agreed in turning everything upside-down in an attempt to achieve the wisdom of the primitive Negro" (63). Thus he represents the primitive as a hopeful future, not as an embarrassing past. In this he is taking a position contrary to the critique of African American folk forms made by people such as Fauset, Du Bois, and some white critics who saw all primitivist culture as a rejection and refutation of progress. In McKay's review of the first all-black Broadway musical *Shuffle Along* (1921), he rails against conservative critics who declare that

> Negro art … must be dignified and respectable like the Anglo-Saxon's before it can
> be good. The Negro must get the warmth, color, and laughter out of his blood, else

the white man will sneer at him and treat him with contumely. Happily the Negro retains his joy of living in the teeth of such criticism; and in Harlem, along Fifth and Lenox avenues, in Marcus Garvey's hall with its extravagant paraphernalia, in his churches and cabarets, he expresses himself with a zest that is yet to be depicted by a true artist. (*Passion* 63)

McKay argues that African American performance is in demand the world over because it expresses the "irrepressible exuberance and legendary vitality of the black race" (*Banjo* 324), and that exuberance and vitality are at least in part due to the fact that the black race has not been fully deadened by civilized living.

Arguments about primitivism and civilization are at the heart of the cosmopolitan novel of the 1920s, as in the writing of Lawrence, Ernest Hemingway, F. Scott Fitzgerald, William Faulkner, Willa Cather, T.S. Eliot, Edith Wharton, and the other writers of the Harlem Renaissance. Take this well-known passage from Lawrence's *Women in Love* (1920), in which Birkin contemplates a statue of an African woman:

> She knew what he himself did not know. She had thousands of years of purely sensual, purely unspiritual knowledge behind her ... Thousands of years ago, that which was imminent in himself must have taken place in these Africans; the goodness, the holiness, the desire for creation must have lapsed. ... Is our day of creative life finished? Does there remain to us only the strange awful afterwards of the knowledge in dissolution, the African knowledge, but different in us, who are blond and blue-eyed from the North? (253–54)

In Sherwood Anderson's *Dark Laughter* (1925), black dock workers throw parcels and words around, feeling their bodies and work and words all in harmony and "unconscious love of inanimate things lost to whites" (106). Anderson, himself influenced by Lawrence, uses the free laughter of the "uncivilized Negro soul" to provide ethical commentary on the ridiculousness of civilized morality. And both of these writers were in turn important influences on McKay.

For Lawrence and Anderson, primitive vitality and primitive wisdom had been lost, and theirs was a primitivism drenched in nostalgia. For white writers such as Carl Van Vechten and Hemingway and black writers such as McKay and Nella Larsen, the cultural worlds of the primitive and the civilized coexisted, mingled, created hybrids, and would continue to do so. McKay loved Lawrence, he said, because he represented "all of the ferment and torment and turmoil, the hesitation and hate and alarm, the sexual inquietude and the incertitude of this age, and the psychic and romantic groping for a way out" (*Long Way* 247). Bourgeois respectability was the illness bred by modernity, primitivism the cure.

At times in his fiction, McKay makes more programmatic statements. "Could he not see what Anglo-Saxon standards were doing to some of the world's most interesting peoples?" he asks in *Banjo*. "Some Jews ashamed of being Jews ... The Irish objecting to the artistic use of their own rich idioms." This is nothing but the "inferiority bile of non-Nordic minorities," he goes on. "Educated Negroes ashamed of their race's intuitive love of color, wrapping themselves up in respectable gray, ashamed of Congo-sounding laughter, ashamed of their complexion (bleaching out), ashamed of their strong appetites. ... Rather than lose his soul," he concludes in Lawrentian fashion, "let intellect go to hell and live instinct!" (164–65). And in an embrace of the primitive much older than Lawrence, as the Fiedler thesis made clear, McKay often sides with those who want to shuck civilization entirely and head off into the wilderness. In the final passage of *Banjo*, Banjo tells Ray that they would be better off without the civilizing force of women. "Don't get soft ovah any one wimmens, pardner. Tha's you' big weakness. A woman is a conjunction. Gawd fixed her different from us ... Come on, pardner. Wese got enough between us to beat it a long ways from here" (326).

At other times, McKay tempers these primitivist yearnings, and Ray, a kind of shadow protagonist in both novels, represents this more cosmopolitan option. Ray wants to be more like Jake and Banjo, feeling that he has become overcivilized himself. But he also is proud of his reading (for which McKay provides regular catalogues) and his ability to move in several worlds. He is not, in fact, completely ready to "live instinct" if that in fact does require the loss of intellect, but it is instinct that needs saving in the industrial society, not intellect.

McKay's representation of music is one of the places he works through these issues, and so I like to play students quite a bit of music besides that in the two films. I also show them a lot of sheet music covers, band photos, and other short films, including Louie Armstrong's *Rhapsody in Black and Blue* (1932) in which a West Indian husband, conked on the head by his American-born wife for his laziness, dreams that he has become the King of Jazzmania and sits on a throne in a soap-bubble-filled heaven where Armstrong plays music for him. Armstrong is dressed in an animal skin, and his playing at the primitive is, I argue, much like McKay's. The film is irrepressibly modern, from its opening phonograph to its film techniques to Armstrong's jazz and diction. But it embraces the primitive at the same time. In a similar way, it is when McKay is describing jazz and blues that his text becomes most obviously modernist, as in this passage from *Home to Harlem*:

> Oh, "blues," "blues," "blues." Red moods, black moods, golden moods. Curious syncopated, slipping-over into one mood, back-sliding back to the first mood. Humming in harmony, barbaric harmony, joy-drunk, chasing out the shadow of the moment before. (54)

In their abandonment of syntax, neologizing freedom, and combination of vernacular and literary diction, such passages about music announce their own modernism. McKay rejected most modern innovations in poetic form in his own poetry; according to Wayne F. Cooper, he believed that "'real' poetry adhered to Victorian poetic conventions, and that the modernists substituted novelty for discipline and incomprehensibility for beauty" (166). But in those sections of his novels in which he describes music, he grants himself the modernists' freedoms from formal convention. Readers are offered a verbal representation of the freedom from "civilized" constraints that makes for and is made by jazz and blues, and these passages are supposed to give readers a taste of the "joy-drunk" response to music the characters feel. The more primitive those characters are, the less trammeled the appreciation, and the more modernist the prose needs to become in order to represent it. Like Smith, he believed in representing all of life in all its squalor and poetry; like Ellington, he looked at culture from a thoroughly cosmopolitan perspective; and like Armstrong, he thought the highest state to be the kind of primitive "joy-drunk" that the most modern jazz could instill.

WORKS CITED

Anderson, Sherwood. *Dark Laughter*. New York: Boni, 1925.

Black and Tan. Dir. Dudley Murphy. In *Hollywood Rhythm*.

Cooper, Wayne F. *Claude McKay: Rebel Sojourner in the Harlem Renaissance: A Biography*. Baton Rouge: Louisiana State UP, 1987.

Fiedler, Leslie A. *Love and Death in the American Novel*. New York: Criterion, 1960.

Hollywood Rhythm vol. 1. DVD. Kino Video, 2001.

Lawrence, D.H. *Women in Love*. 1920. Cambridge: Cambridge UP, 1987.

Lewis, David Levering. *When Harlem Was in Vogue*. New York: Penguin, 1981.

McKay, Claude. *A Long Way from Home*. 1937. New York: Arno, 1969.

———. *Banjo; A Story Without a Plot*. New York: Harper, 1929.

———. *Home to Harlem*. 1928. Boston: Northeastern UP, 1987.

———. *The Negroes in America*. 1922–1923. Ed. Alan L. McCleod. Trans. Robert J. Winter. Port Washington, New York: Kennikat, 1979.

———. *The Passion of Claude McKay: Selected Poetry and Prose, 1912–1948*. Ed. Wayne F. Cooper. New York: Schocken, 1973.

Rhapsody in Black and Blue. Dir. Aubrey Scotto. In *Hollywood Rhythm*.

St. Louis Blues. Dir. Dudley Murphy. In *Hollywood Rhythm*.

CHAPTER SEVENTEEN

Teaching *The New Negro*

MICHAEL SOTO

When I took a Harlem Renaissance course as a graduate student, my instructor, Henry Louis Gates Jr., held up a copy of *The New Negro* (1925) on the first day of class and called it the "Bible of the Harlem Renaissance."[1] Needless to say, I took note of the description. In the years since that moment, my growing understanding of the book and its place in African American and U.S. cultural history confirmed and gave added dimension to Gates's phrase, which is particularly apt if we consider *The New Negro* as a contribution to "culture" in the sense supplied by Matthew Arnold, that is, as a form of expression transcending everyday experience and shaping social mores. More than anything else, when I teach *The New Negro* I want my students to appreciate the book as an intervention not just in African American letters, but also in American race relations and social organization more broadly.

I have little doubt that Gates referred to *The New Negro* as a figurative Bible strategically, with a sense of how the comparison might register among the broad range of students present, from first-year undergraduates to graduate students. To brand-new college students, the reference would quickly indicate the text's monumental role in shaping America's understanding—then and now—of the New Negro movement and the Harlem Renaissance. Graduate students would take the phrase with a grain of salt, hoping to discern the various interests (aesthetic, economic, political) served by the volume. This bifurcated set of reactions mirrors the two key roles *The New Negro* might play in a course syllabus. On the one hand, the book might be assigned to undergraduates or advanced high school students as an anthology of the movement's poetry, drama, fiction, nonfiction prose, and art; after all, this was its original role, and in fact *The New Negro* regularly served as a textbook in "Negro Literature" and "Negro History" courses from the 1930s to the 1960s. It is worth noting that as an anthology, *The New Negro* is rather nar-row in scope and oddly prescriptive. (As its original subtitle, "An Interpretation," suggests, the book resembles a manifesto as much as a "disinterested" assembly of texts and visual images.) As such, it helps to point out what *The New Negro* omits, particularly in comparison to such contemporaneous titles as *The Book of American Negro Poetry* (1922), *Caroling Dusk* (1927), and *Negro* (1934), or in com-parison to today's many anthologies of African American literature. On the other hand, advanced undergraduates and graduate students should investigate the text more pointedly; they should explore the book's publishing and reception histo-ries, its contribution to intellectual history, and its ideology; they should unpack the "Bible's" theology, so to speak. I'll provide a few ideas about how these goals might be accomplished below.

Because few students (including graduate students) will have heard of Alain Locke (1886–1954), the book's editor and guiding voice, I always introduce *The New Negro* by way of a quick biographical sketch. (Ross Posnock and Johnny Washington address Locke's contributions, respectively, to intellectual history and to philosophy.) The most salient details of Locke's life—born into the black middle class of Philadelphia, undergraduate and graduate degrees from Harvard, first African American Rhodes scholar, a distinguished career as a philosopher at Howard—can be quickly summarized. I find it more important to share the sobriquets (often taking the form of evocative metaphors) heaped upon Locke by his contemporaries and by more recent critics. Charles S. Johnson, in his account of the famous Civic Club dinner in 1924, was the first of countless writers and critics to call Locke the "dean of the movement" ("Debut" 143). In his Harlem Renaissance memoir, *The Big Sea* (1940), Langston Hughes counted Locke among the "three people who midwifed the so-called New Negro literature into being" (218). More pejoratively (and more memorably), Wallace Thurman, in his Harlem Renaissance roman à clef, *Infants of the Spring* (1932), satirized Locke in the person of Dr. A.L. Parkes as "a professor of literature in a northern Negro college ... who, also ... played mother hen to a brood of chicks, having appointed himself guardian angel to the current set of younger Negro artists" (180). And Claude McKay, in a letter protesting Locke's editorial treatment of the Jamaican's poetry (Locke excluded "Mulatto" from *The New Negro* and changed the title of "The White House," curbing the poem's political ire), charged that Locke was "a dyed-in-the-wool, pussy-footing professor" (qtd. in Lewis 153). More recently, Nathan Irvin Huggins described Locke as a "dapper, gentle, nut-brown man" (56), and David Levering Lewis identified Locke as "fanatic on culture, and by 'culture' he meant all that was not common, vulgar, or racially distasteful" (149).

The sheer enormity of *The New Negro* prohibits any single interpretation of or critical approach to its varied contents. (For insightful analyses of individual titles in the volume, I recommend George Hutchinson's *The Harlem Renaissance in Black and White* and Barbara Foley's *Spectres of 1919*.) Instead, I would like to point out seven ways to approach *The New Negro*, including activities that might be assigned to individual students or small groups of students in advanced seminar settings, or that might form (in more or less sequential order) components of a lecture before a larger class.

Approach 1: Describe the intellectual and political context for the New Negro ideology. As numerous critics and historians have noted, the phrase "New Negro" in the late nineteenth century signaled everything from brash criminals to political firebrands to Booker T. Washingtonian accommodationists. Alain Locke radically revised the public meaning of the phrase and in so doing recast the meaning of African American intellectual identity in narrowly culturalist terms. Discussion questions: Based on Locke's "Foreword" and "New Negro" essay, how would you expect a New Negro man or woman to dress and act in social situations? Where would he or she live, and what would her or his home look like? What books would line the shelves? In contrast, how might we describe the life of an Old Negro? For more perspective and historical detail, see Gates, Huggins, and Foley.

Approach 2: Describe the events leading up to the publication of The New Negro, *including the Civic Club dinner in November 1924 and the publication of the* Survey Graphic *Harlem number in March 1925.* Locke very cannily put together an impressive roster of contributors to *The New Negro*, but the volume was the result of much debate and joint effort in the months leading up to its release. When *Opportunity* editor Charles S. Johnson organized a dinner party to honor young African American artists and writers (most prominently Jessie Fauset, whose *There is Confusion* [1924] recently appeared), he leaned heavily on Locke. Among the many distinguished guests—black, white, and otherwise—was Paul Kellogg, editor of the social advocacy journal *Survey*, which published an illustrated *Survey Graphic* number each month. Kellogg was so impressed by the talent and energy at the dinner that he asked Locke to edit a Harlem issue. Even before the *Survey Graphic* Harlem number was released, Albert Boni obtained the rights to reprint its contents in a more expansive book. Discussion questions: Who were Paul Kellogg and Albert Boni, and why were they interested in "New Negro" identity? Which subjects did the *Survey* address, and what was its usual approach to covering them? If available at the library, show and describe one or two issues of the *Survey Graphic* published before the Harlem number. What type of books did Albert and Charles Boni publish during the 1920s? A comprehensive list of titles can be obtained from the Library of Congress online catalog (www.loc.gov). For more perspective and historical detail, see Lewis and Hutchinson.

Approach 3: Compare and contrast the Survey Graphic *Harlem number and* The New Negro. Students respond very actively when they're given a chance to discuss the "look" and "feel" of the *Survey Graphic* and *The New Negro*.[2] *The New Negro* is more comprehensive in two obvious ways: size (452 pages compared to the *Survey Graphic's* 103, which includes many pages of advertising) and editorial content (emphasizing national Negro culture and institutions rather than just the Harlem enclave). The shift reveals something about the target audiences: *The New Negro* was designed for a Negro college audience, whereas the *Survey Graphic* was read by those engaged in social work. *The New Negro* dispensed with some (but not all) of Winold Reiss's controversial illustrations; many of the remaining illustrations were reproduced as color plates and supplemented with the work of his protégé Aaron Douglas. Discussion questions: What do the ads in the *Survey Graphic* tell us about its readers, and how does this compare with the readership that we might presume for *The New Negro*? Which titles from the *Survey Graphic* are omitted from or changed in *The Negro*, and what overall effects do the changes create? How does the art change from the *Survey Graphic* to *The New Negro*? How do changes to individual titles (e.g., "Youth Speaks"/"Negro Youth Speaks"; "The Making of Harlem"/"Harlem: The Culture Capital") impact the message of the two collections? What gets added to *The New Negro*, and to what effect? For more perspective and historical detail, see Carroll, Hutchinson, and Foley.

Approach 4: What aesthetic theories does The New Negro *advance?* Even when they appear to be merely descriptive, several titles in *The New Negro* take aesthetic stances that are more accurately labeled normative (if contradictory). For example, art collector and philanthropist Albert C. Barnes asserts that "Negro art ... is a sound art because it comes from a primitive nature upon which a white man's education has never been harnessed" (19). Poet and editor William Stanley Braithwaite favors instead "poetry that is racial in substance, but with the universal note, with the conscious background of the full heritage of English poetry" (38) and fiction, such as Jean Toomer's *Cane* (1923), that is simultaneously "objective," poignant, and transmuting (44). Similarly, Locke equates "thoroughly modern" (even "ultra-modern") expression with a "lusty vigorous realism" (50). Here and elsewhere, *The New Negro* provides a theoretical yardstick with which to measure the volume's more strictly creative contents. Discussion questions: How does the visual art in *The New Negro* fare against Barnes's analysis? How does the book's poetry and fiction measure up to Braithwaite's and Locke's vision for literary expression? What do Arthur A. Schomburg and Arthur Huff Fauset contribute to our understanding of African American culture? How do these writers contradict one another? For more perspective and historical detail, see Hutchinson.

Approach 5: Assess the role of visual art and graphic design in The New Negro. *The New Negro* is a visually ambitious title, with several drawings by Aaron

Douglas, whose work is now synonymous with the Harlem Renaissance; with drawings as well by Miguel Covarrubias and W.V. Ruckterschell; with several reproduced title pages and musical scores; with photographs of numerous African masks and sculptures; and with a frontispiece and color portraits (in the original edition) and bold, deco-style designs by Winold Reiss. Taken individually, particularly as a counterpoint to nearby texts, these illustrations deserve attention and interpretation on their own terms. Taken as a whole, the illustrations present a compelling way to understand individual, racial, and national identity in the wake of artistic modernism and technosocial modernity. For more perspective and historical detail, see Carroll and Nadell.

Approach 6: Race versus Class, Gender, and Sexuality in The New Negro. I have rolled these three important issues into a single category simply because class, gender, and sexuality are treated very narrowly (strategically so) in *The New Negro*. Each of these identity categories deserves more substantial consideration than a single paragraph would suggest. From the very outset, Locke came under fire for *The New Negro's* evasiveness on questions of class, and feminist scholars have brought similar scrutiny to the text on questions of gender. Additionally, when students are made aware of the fluid sexual identities of many of *The New Negro's* contributors—Cullen, Grimké, Hughes, Locke, McKay, and Nugent immediately spring to mind, but the entire collection bears consideration in this way—individual titles, and the larger concern of New Negro identity, take on added and intriguing dimensions. For more perspective and historical detail, see Hull, Stavney, and Foley.

Approach 7: American Cultural Nationalism and Pan Africanism in The New Negro. Whenever two or more persons take up questions of racial identity, there is likely to be at least some disagreement. And while Locke largely avoided the work of confrontational radicals in assembling *The New Negro*, the book nevertheless yields far-ranging and sometimes contradictory views from its multiracial, multiethnic, and international roster of contributors. When anthropologist Melville J. Herskovits studied what's unique about Harlem life, he concluded that "In Harlem we have to-day, essentially, a typical American community. ... In other words, it represents, as do all American communities it resembles, a case of complete acculturation" (354; 360). Countee Cullen's "Harlem Wine," Claude McKay's "The Tropics in New York," and W.A. Domingo's "Gift of the Black Tropics" offer their own competing versions of African American (or more precisely transnational, Afro-diaspora) life in Harlem. Meanwhile, W.E.B. Du Bois, in "The Negro Mind Reaches Out," extends his question "How does it feel to be a problem?" across the four corners of the globe, assessing the connection between race and colonial oppression. These few examples (and we could easily add many more) demonstrate that *The New Negro* offers no simple answer to the question,

"What does it mean to be a New Negro in U.S. and world culture?" For more perspective and historical detail, see Hutchinson and Edwards.

Anyone familiar with *The New Negro* will quickly recognize that this is by no means an exhaustive list of approaches to the book. Still, should the book find its way into the classroom—and it truly *should*—then it would be difficult if not impossible to avoid the issues they raise. Best of all, students who are drawn to Harlem Renaissance courses often take up one or more of these approaches with no other prompting than *The New Negro* itself.

NOTES

1. Editions of *The New Negro* were released in 1925, 1968, and 1992. The latter release, a modestly priced paperback reprint of the original 1925 edition with a new introduction by Arnold Rampersad, is the only version still in print. (Unfortunately, the book's many color prints are reproduced in black and white, and Winold Reiss's portraits have been omitted.) At present, the rights to the title are held by Touchstone, an imprint of Simon & Schuster.
2. The full text of the journal can be found online at the University of Virginia Library Electronic Text Center (etext.lib.virginia.edu/harlem/). A reprint of the journal is also available from Black Classics Press.

WORKS CITED

Carroll, Anne. *Word, Image, and the New Negro: Representation and Identity in the Harlem Renaissance.* Bloomington: Indiana UP, 2005.

Cullen, Countee, ed. *Caroling Dusk: An Anthology of Verse by Negro Poets.* New York: Harper, 1927.

Cunard, Nancy. *Negro.* London: Wishart, 1934.

"Debut of the Younger School of Negro Writers." *Opportunity* 2.17 (May 1924): 143–44.

Edwards, Brent Hayes. *The Practice of Diaspora: Literature, Translation, and the Rise of Black Internationalism.* Cambridge: Harvard UP, 2003.

Gates, Henry Louis Jr. "The Trope of a New Negro and the Reconstruction of the Image of the Black." *Representations* 24 (1988): 129–55.

Huggins, Nathan Irvin. *Harlem Renaissance.* New York: Oxford UP, 1971.

Hughes, Langston. *The Big Sea.* 1940. Introduction. Arnold Rampersad. New York: Hill and Wang, 1993.

Hull, Gloria T. *Color, Sex, and Poetry: Three Women Writers of the Harlem Renaissance.* Bloomington: Indiana UP, 1987.

Hutchinson, George. *The Harlem Renaissance in Black and White.* Cambridge: Harvard UP, 1995.

Johnson, James Weldon, ed. *The Book of American Negro Poetry.* New York: Harcourt, 1922.

Lewis, David Levering. *When Harlem Was in Vogue.* New York: Penguin, 1979.

Locke, Alain, ed. *The New Negro.* 1925. Introduction. Arnold Rampersad. New York: Touchstone, 1992.

Nadell, Martha Jane. *Enter the New Negroes: Images of Race in American Culture.* Cambridge: Harvard UP, 2004.

Posnock, Ross. *Color and Culture: Black Writers and the Making of the Modern Intellectual*. Cambridge: Harvard UP, 1998.

Stavney, Anne. "'Mothers of Tomorrow': The New Negro Renaissance and the Politics of Maternal Representation." *African American Review* 32 (1998): 533–61.

Thurman, Wallace. *Infants of the Spring*. New York: Macaulay, 1932.

Washington, Johnny. *Alain Locke and Philosophy: A Quest for Cultural Pluralism*. Westport, CT: Greenwood, 1986.

CHAPTER EIGHTEEN

Teaching George S. Schuyler's *Black No More*

RITA KERESZTESI

In June 1926, the *Nation* published a provocative short essay by George S. Schuyler, "The Negro-Art Hokum," a piece so controversial that the editors felt the need to follow it up by inviting Langston Hughes to address the topic of "Negro" art again a week later. Reading the two articles back to back offers a thought-provoking starting point for discussing Schuyler's novel *Black No More* (1931).[1] In "The Negro-Art Hokum" Schuyler states that national belonging and class status trump the primacy of racial content in art, an argument that sparked Hughes's impassioned manifesto on the Black aesthetic and racial pride, "The Negro Artist and the Racial Mountain." During his writing career, Schuyler's political views moved from the left to the right; he embraced conservative political views on integration and issues of social welfare during the Civil Rights era.[2]

Schuyler emphasizes the Americanness of the "Negro," an argument that is consistent with the Harlem Renaissance's integrationist agenda, such as Du Bois's program of the "Talented Tenth," and with his articulation of "double consciousness" as a struggle between racial and national belonging, and Schuyler challenges assumptions of racial separatism propagated by Hughes and Marcus Garvey. Schuyler opens his piece with the following provocative statement:

> Negro art there has been, is, and will be among the numerous black nations of Africa; but to suggest the possibility of any such development among the ten million colored people in this republic is self-evident foolishness. (36)

Schuyler then develops his notion of cultural difference that is more influenced by geographical location and class status than by the cultural essentiality and specificity of race or ethnicity. He was, and still is, perceived as an iconoclast in his analysis of cultural differences that owe more to the attributes of upbringing and the surrounding social environment than to the primacy of racial belonging.

In his opinions Schuyler echoes the arguments that critique a unified black consciousness on grounds of national, cultural, and geographical differences. Schuyler's contemporary, the Jamaican-born W.A. Domingo, whose essay "Gift of the Black Tropics" was anthologized in Alain Locke's *The New Negro* (1925), critiques African Americans when as a Caribbean immigrant he is grouped with other West Indians regardless of nationality, an attitude that mirrors whites' assumptions that all blacks in the United States are African Americans. Domingo is incensed by "[t]his indiscriminating attitude on the part of native Negroes":

> To the average American Negro, all English-speaking black foreigners are West Indians, and by that is usually meant British subjects. There is a general assumption that there is everything in common among West Indians, though nothing can be further from the truth. (91)

Domingo's argument points to differences between the immigrant communities of the African Diaspora: Besides the groups from the British West Indies, there are also the "Spanish-speaking Negroes from Latin America" (91), as well as those from the French West Indies and Africa.

Both Domingo and Schuyler critique nondiscriminative groupings of black peoples under the category of race and the assumption of perceived essential similarities. While Domingo explains the national differences between immigrant populations of the African Diaspora through analyses of cultural differences, Schuyler argues against the racial essentialism involved in ignoring the Americanness of blacks in favor of a unified African character. When discussing the cultural production of American "Negroes"—such as the spirituals, the blues, ragtime, and jazz—he questions the common racial content of the music and names the geographical locale and the commonality of class status as its sources. He states: "Aside from his color, which ranges from very dark brown to pink, your American Negro is just plain American. Negroes and whites from the same localities in this country talk, think, and act about the same" (37). Schuyler takes the controversial stance that there are no separate African or European characters, only social groups that share a locale and similar economic and cultural environments. While this is a statement that deserves attention, especially because of its focus on issues of class in connection to those of race, nevertheless, Schuyler makes an in-the-face assumption that opposes Garvey's racial separatism and Du Bois's later Pan-Africanism, or the Afrocentric ideas articulated by scholars such as the Jamaican-born historian J.A. Rogers or the Senegalese Cheikh Anta Diop. But, more specifically, Schuyler opposes the notion of racial purity—of African

Americans, Caucasians or American Indians—and the rhetoric of racially specific cultures. But his genetic pragmatism did not prevent him from taking pride in the accomplishments of peoples of African descent. He was one of the first supporters of J.A. Rogers, an early historian and theorist of Afrocentrism. Schuyler, for example, encouraged Rogers to compile his writings and publish *The World's Greatest Men of African Personages* (1931) and *The World's Greatest Men of Color 3000 B.C. to 1946* (1947). As Schuyler explained to Ishmael Reed and Steve Cannon in an interview a few years before his death: "The first man to do that [Afrocentric writing of history], of course, was J.A. Rogers. He preceded all these people and was a better researcher and scholar" (qtd. in Leak 142). By drawing attention to economic, social, and cultural factors besides those of race and skin color, Schuyler points out the damaging effects of stereotyping by whites. Schuyler states:

> The mention of the word "Negro" conjures up in the average white American's mind a composite stereotype of Bert Williams, Aunt Jemima, Uncle Tom, Jack Johnson, Florian Slappery, and the various monstrosities scrawled by the cartoonists. Your average Aframerican no more resembles this stereotype than the average American resembles a composite of Andy Gump, Jim Jeffries, and a cartoon by Rube Goldberg. (37)

It is important to note here that Bert Williams wore blackface as a double mask: a West Indian immigrant from the Bahamas pretending to be an African American who put on the mask of blackness according to racist white stereotypes.

In his short essay Schuyler develops a quite daring definition of race that argues with both black separatism and white supremacy: "Again, the Aframerican is subject to the same economic and social forces that mold the actions and thoughts of the white Americans. He is not living in a different world as some whites and a few Negroes would have us believe" (37). His evidence for the similarities enlist examples of food, work conditions, clothing, language, Christian religious practices, fraternal affiliations, schooling, housing, consumer goods (cars, cigarettes, Hollywood movies), and "the same puerile periodicals"; "in short, when he [the African American] responds to the same political, social, moral, and economic stimuli in precisely the same manner as his white neighbor, it is sheer nonsense to talk about 'racial differences' as between the American black man and the American white man" (38). Schuyler's analysis of the commodification of American culture is reminiscent of the Frankfurt School's Marxist reading of the loss of the "aura" of artistic authenticity in the modern world of "mechanical reproduction." Schuyler anticipates a postmodern America where the normalization of consumer culture makes racial and ethnic differences negligible and susceptible to pastiche. While Hughes's conclusion of a similar analysis leads to the celebration of racial differences preserved in folk culture and by "the low-down folks, the so-called common element" (41), they both sound the alarm of what

Hughes calls "this urge within the race toward whiteness" by the black middle class, "the desire to pour racial individuality into the mold of American standardization, and to be as little Negro and as much American as possible" (40). Hughes concludes his essay with a rallying call to the celebration of blackness: "We know we are beautiful. And ugly too. … We build our temples for tomorrow, strong as we know how, and we stand on top of the mountain, free within ourselves" (44).

As Hughes crafts a manifesto for immediate action, Schuyler cautions against the dangers of black separatists aligning themselves with the fanatics of white supremacy:

> This nonsense [of the "Negro-art hokum"] is probably the last stand of the old myth palmed off by Negrophobists for all these many years … that there are "fundamental, eternal, and inescapable differences" between white and black Americans. That there are Negroes who will lend this myth a helping hand need occasion no surprise. It has been broadcast all over the world by the vociferous scions of slaveholders, "scientists" like Madison Grant and Lothrop Stoddard, and the patriots who flood the treasury of the Ku Klux Klan; and is believed, even today, by the majority of free, white citizens. (38–39)

To make his stand on the issue of racial separatism absolutely clear, Schuyler goes on to state: "On this baseless premise, so flattering to the white mob, that the blackamoor is inferior and fundamentally different, is erected the postulate that he must needs be peculiar; and when he attempts to portray life through the medium of art, it must of necessity be a peculiar art" (39).

If read in response to the white supremacist notion of the separation of races based on assumed biological differences, Schuyler's article voices a reasonable interpretation of race that takes into account class status and cultural upbringing. His evidence for such an argument, though, is somewhat shaky. He assumes an equality of opportunities for blacks and whites: "And that education and environment were about the same for blacks and whites" (38). But read closely, Schuyler's analysis is projected to the future of a next generation, a rather hopeful assumption that with education and similar social environments, the differences between blacks and whites would be negligible. Thereby, he dehistoricizes racial differences and projects a utopic vision of race.

In a later piece concerning "Negro-art" Schuyler is much more explicit about his support for racially inspired literature. In "Instructions for Contributors" (1929), published in *The Sunday Evening Quill*, he advises prospective writers as follows:

> Stories must be full of human interest. Short, simple words. No attempt to parade erudition to the bewilderment of the reader. No colloquialisms such as "nigger," "darky," "coon," etc. Plenty of dialogue, and language that is realistic. … Above all,

however, these characters must live and breathe, and be just ordinary folks such as the reader met. The heroine should be of the brown-skin type.

All matter should deal exclusively with Negro life. Nothing will be permitted that is likely to engender ill feelings between blacks and whites. The color problem is bad enough without adding any fuel to the fire. (qtd. in Ervin 152)

In his "Instructions" Schuyler promotes a racially motivated literature that is respectful in its representation of African Americans but not inflammatory to whites. His disillusionment with putting art in the hands of Race Men is reminiscent of the disillusionment Frankfurt School philosophers felt when propagating the separation between art and politics for the sake of maintaining art's independence from the propagandistic use of political rhetoric. In that light, his novel, *Black No More*, written only a year later, is a case study for his proposed aesthetic ideals.

Black No More can be best read as Schuyler's fictional exploration of the race problem and the definition of race, a kind of companion piece to his two previously discussed articles. The novel's genre is multifaceted. It can be read as a who's who satire of the Harlem Renaissance, a roman à clef, and a fictional retrospective similar to Wallace Thurman's *Infants of the Spring* (1932) or Countee Cullen's *One Way to Heaven* (1934). Ishmael Reed, in his introduction to the Modern Library edition of the novel, calls it "the most scathing fiction about race written by an American" (x). Reed views the novel as a science fiction fantasy—Schuyler was the first African American to write in that genre—that explores the solution to the race problem, what Du Bois labeled "the problem of the Twentieth Century" (*Souls* 5). Schuyler proposes the most inflammatory solution of the time: miscegenation, a genetic versus cultural assimilation into white society (what he calls "chromatic democracy" [44] in his novel). In light of the alternatives, such as moving the whole African American population back to Africa, imagined not only by Garvey but also by white supremacists (obviously motivated by opposite reasons), or the American version of the "final solution" of lynching African Americans out of existence on American soil (as the parable of the imagined Happy Hill, Mississippi community does in Schuyler's novel), the acknowledgment of de facto miscegenation seems like a rather logical alternative. In Schuyler's opinion, as stated through Dr. Junius Crookman's character, the problem of miscegenation is already mute: "when you consider that less than twenty percent of our Negroes are without Caucasian ancestry and that close to thirty percent have American Indian ancestry, it is readily seen that there cannot be the wide difference in Caucasian and Afro-American facial characteristics that most people imagine" (15).

Thus, for Schuyler the assumption of the existence of "pure" races in the twentieth-century United States is as fantastic as the solution of whitening all blacks. While Schuyler disagrees with his contemporaries, both black racial militants and white supremacists, about the existence of racial purity in genetic terms, he does not deny the importance of Black racial nationalism for the sake of political ends or to fight racism in the United States. He imagines a scientific as opposed to a cultural or political solution to the race problem. With his satire he managed to tap into the most visceral fears of white supremacy, the intermixing of the races. Naming his primary target audience, he dedicates the novel to Caucasians "who can trace their ancestry back ten generations and confidently assert that there are no Black leaves, twigs, limbs or branches on their family trees" (xvii). Schuyler takes on the most fundamental value of the American nation: white supremacy that is supported by Christian doctrine. The author calls Caucasians to task: What would be the consequences if white supremacy would achieve its wish and turn the whole nation white? With Dr. Junis Crookman's treatment at Black-No-More clinics, African Americans are turned white in three days: "It looked as though science was to succeed where the Civil War had failed" (10). With the combination of "electrical nutrition and glandular control" (11), African features and hair are also changed in the process. While the speech patterns remain the same, according to Schuyler's analysis of racial and class differences, those won't matter since dialect is regional as opposed to being race specific: "The educated Haitian speaks the purest French and the Jamaican Negro sounds exactly like an Englishman. There are no racial or color dialects; only sectional dialects" (14). Therefore, in Schuyler's speculative fiction, if racism is fueled by differences in skin color, the solution then is to make everyone white.

Consistent with his "Negro-Art Hokum" argument, the novel follows an economic line of logic: Race is really just a ploy for maintaining economic differences in the United States—hence his emphasis on class as opposed to racial issues in that article. In the novel, he picks up the issue of race, on the minds of all white supremacists, black cultural assimilationists, and black separatists of his time. Through the plot he takes on not only Northern and Southern whites, but also key players and issues of the Harlem Renaissance movement represented by Du Bois's Talented Tenth and Garvey's Back-to-Africa agenda. In a strikingly modern and still relevant critique of the inevitable corruptive forces of power and politics, whether in big government or race-based bureaucratic organizations, he narrows all, often contradictory, arguments to the lowest common denominator: Prejudice is based on the profitability of artificially maintained differences (of race or class status). Under the conditions of capitalism, the only stable value is that of profitability. Thereby, in the early twentieth-century United States everyone and everything is up for sale. In a remarkably astute assessment he names capitalism as the culprit for racism: He articulates the connection between whiteness and a materialistic approach to all aspects of life. Once his main character Max Disher crosses over into white society, he is not only bored and isolated, he also finds the world of Anglo-Saxon whites to be a "hard, materialistic, grasping, inbred society" (43). In Schuyler's opinion, middle-class African Americans are not immune to the materialism of white capitalism, calling it "the almost European atmosphere of every Negro ghetto," once the opportunity comes to move into the middle class via turning white: "The happy-go-lucky Negro of song and story was gone forever and in his stead was a nervous, money-grubbing black, stuffing coin in sock" (63). Such assessment of the black middle class is very similar to Hughes's critique in "The Negro Artist and the Racial Mountain," impersonated by the character of the "Philadelphia clubwoman" who has succumbed to the "old subconscious" that "white is best" (43). While Hughes approaches the issue of "American standardization" from an aesthetic and racially motivated perspective, Schuyler adds the economic dimensions of class and capitalism to the debate.

In Schuyler's novel, there are very few people who can resist the temptation of money in favor of staying true to one's convictions and beliefs—in this case, to blackness. The only character who remains immune to the temptations of a better life or huge sums of money is Madeline Scranton, "the last black gal in the country" (156). She does not go through the whitening process, even after the last holdouts to the cause of the Race (such as the Du Bois and Garvey characters) are whitened. In this farce on authenticity, racial or cultural, she is the only "real Negro" (180) left, and she becomes the model for the new trend, along with Max Disher's mix-raced son:

> Everybody that was anybody had a stained skin. A girl without one was avoided by the young men; a young man without one was at a decided disadvantage, economically and socially. A white face became startlingly rare. America was definitely, enthusiastically mulatto-minded. (179)

But, the turning of the ideal from white to dark skin does not stop prejudice and discrimination. Only their target has changed: "as a result of his [an eminent anthropologist's] long research among the palest citizens, he was convinced that they were mentally inferior and that their children should be segregated from the others in school" (178).

The novel ends with the cycle starting all over "AND SO ON AND SO ON" (176). Once everyone's skin has become white, the new trend is to darken one's skin to distinguish oneself in a sea of lily-white faces: "If it were true that extreme whiteness was evidence of the possession of Negro blood, of having once been a member of a pariah class, then surely it were well not to be so white!" (177). Due to Crookman's innovative scientific, as opposed to social, political, or cultural, solution to the race problem that had eliminated—visually—all African Americans in the nation (hence the plan to move their operations to the

Caribbean where whiteness still holds its cash value), the country that had based its identity on white supremacy cannot function anymore: According to the novel's race-based economy, the political system has collapsed and businesses that cater to racial discrimination have failed. The massive collapse of political and economic institutions proves that both are fundamentally dependent on the presence of African Americans as scapegoats and as producers as well as consumers of goods and, therefore, on the maintenance of the color line. Schuyler's speculative fiction plays out the impossibility of whiteness without its black other as referent. But he goes on to state, consistent with his class-based analysis, that not only African Americans but also the underclass in general are indispensable to the functioning of a competitive market, that is, to the profitability and necessity of poverty for imperialism to keep its local national markets viable.

Schuyler's two early texts, "The Negro-Art Hokum" and *Black No More*, function as companion pieces to enter the debate on race and the black aesthetic not in opposition but as complementary to contemporary debates. As Jane Kuenz argues, if put within the context of a white supremacy that accepted African Americans only as laborers but not as citizens, a category reserved only for those of Anglo-Saxon descent and regulated by the phantasmagoric "one-drop-of-blood" rule, then it "should not be surprising ... that ... George Schuyler might be wary of the peculiar, the racial, and the different in African-American life and art" (181). She continues:

> In other words, while Schuyler's novel seems to erase race by redefining it as a version of class, it ends up only highlighting the nonidentity of those terms: in the world of *Black No More*, "blackness" can always reemerge within class in the form of the threat of alienated labor or as the comforts unavailable in this alienated world. (188)

Along the Frankfurt School's Marxist line of argumentation concerning the generalized threat of commodification (even though he was one of the early critics of Marxism as a viable path for African Americans), Schuyler cautions that under the conditions of capitalism and emergent imperialism, anything, including the authenticity of race and most certainly culture, can be co-opted, bought, and sold.

NOTES

1. Several debates took place about the distinctness of "Negro" art during the Harlem Renaissance. Besides those by Schuyler and Hughes, other articles concerning "Negro" art and literature include: William Stanley Braithwaite, "The Negro in American Literature" (1925); Alain Locke, "The New Negro" (1925); Amy Jacques Garvey, "On Langston Hughes: I Am a Negro—Beautiful" (1926);

W.E.B. Du Bois, "Criteria of Negro Art" (1926); Richard Wright, "Blueprint for Negro Writing" (1937); and Zora Neale Hurston, "Characteristics of Negro Expression" (1935). These essays are collected in Patton and Honey.

2. For a discussion of Schuyler's life and views, see Ferguson, Leak, and Schuyler, *Conservative*.

WORKS CITED

Domingo, W.A. "The Gift of the Black Tropics." 1925. Patton and Honey 90–95.

Ervin, Hazel Arnett. *The Handbook of African American Literature*. Gainseville: UP of Florida, 1994.

Ferguson, Jeffrey B. *The Sage of Sugar Hill: George S. Schuyler and the Harlem Renaissance*. New Haven: Yale UP, 2005.

Hughes, Langston. "The Negro Artist and the Racial Mountain." 1926. Patton and Honey 40–44.

Kuenz, Jane. "American Racial Discourse, 1900–1930: Schuyler's *Black No More*." *Novel* 30 (1997): 170–92.

Leak, Jeffrey B., ed. *Rac[e]ing to the Right: Selected Essays of George S. Schuyler*. Knoxville: U of Tennessee P, 2001.

Patton, Venetria K., and Maureen Honey, eds. *Double-Take: A Revisionist Harlem Renaissance Reader*. New Brunswick: Rutgers UP, 2001.

Schuyler, George S. *Black and Conservative: The Autobiography of George S. Schuyler*. New Rochelle: Arlington House, 1966.

———. *Black No More*. 1931. New York: Modern, 1999.

———. "The Negro-Art Hokum." 1926. Patton and Honey 36–39.

CHAPTER NINETEEN

Teaching Wallace Thurman's *Infants of the Spring*

ELISA GLICK

In a memorable declaration about his "pet hates," Wallace Thurman declared that he despised "all Negro uplift societies, Greta Garbo, Negro novelists including myself, Negro society, New York state divorce laws, morals, religions, politics, censors, policemen, sympathetic white folk" (Anderson 209). This statement encapsulates many of the things I find engaging about *Infants of the Spring* (1932), which is, like its author, witty and irreverent, defiantly nonconformist, frankly controversial, and suspicious of all forms of sentimentality and dogmatism. In my experience teaching at a large Midwestern public university, I have found that a wide range of students, including those at both the graduate and undergraduate levels, appreciate just these qualities in *Infants of the Spring*. Perhaps this is because today's students identify with Thurman's passionate defense of individuality and nonconformity over and against the dictates of political correctness. As Ray—the novel's ethical touchstone—declares, "Let each seek his own salvation. To me, a wholesale flight back to Africa or a wholesale allegiance to Communism or a wholesale adherence to an antiquated and for the most part ridiculous propagandistic program are all equally futile and unintelligent" (Thurman 240).

While an affinity for the protagonists' rebelliousness and iconoclasm may offer students a more accessible entrée into the novel's world, *Infants* challenges us as teachers to present the complex intellectual, aesthetic, and social convictions that undergird its bohemianism. As recent criticism on the novel demonstrates, *Infants* has generated increased interest among scholars due to the novel's openly queer content and themes (Blackmore; Cobb; Ganter; Glick; Kelley; Knadler; Silberman). Critiquing the "powerful current of homophobia in black letters" in a 1993 essay entitled "The Black Man's Burden," Henry Louis Gates Jr. reminds us that the Harlem Renaissance "was surely as gay as it was black, not that it was exclusively either of these" (233). By now, most of us are aware that the major figures of the movement were gay or bisexual: Alain Locke, Langston Hughes, Countee Cullen, Claude McKay, Richard Bruce Nugent, and, of course, Wallace Thurman. Let me emphasize at the outset that this chapter does not argue in favor of a queer reading of the novel. If Thurman makes queer aesthetics and erotics central to his project—as I think he clearly does—then our challenge is how to productively incorporate this knowledge into our pedagogy. With this in mind, I address two central questions in this essay: How might *Infants* complicate or change our thinking about what the Harlem Renaissance was? How do we as teachers negotiate questions of identity, race, and desire in our classrooms?

I am aware that, for some instructors, addressing issues of queer sexuality may present new challenges. For this reason, I want to consider what some of these challenges might be and possible ways to address them. It is my hope that all instructors—regardless of their race, ethnicity, sexuality, or gender—will teach this novel in their courses. While this may seem like a facile point, it seems to me worth articulating because *Infants* is fundamentally concerned with disrupt-ing notions of authenticity. Indeed, Thurman challenges the notion that who we are—including our affiliations and aspirations—can be encapsulated by identity categories such as race and sexuality; furthermore, he refuses to treat these mark-ers of identity as stable and fixed. This is not to say that the categories of race and sexuality have no social reality for Thurman—their hierarchies and prescriptions fundamentally shape the imaginative possibilities of his work, as the author him-self is keenly aware. My point here is that the logic of Thurman's novel contains an important insight for us as teachers—namely, that we are inevitably positioned both inside and outside the definitions, categories, and discourses we seek to illuminate.

Because I teach sexuality and gender studies and am an "out" gay faculty member, colleagues sometimes contact me for advice about a variety of concerns related to sexuality. They ask how to present gay authors in their classes or in their own research, or how to help a student who seems to be struggling with her sexuality or suffering from the negative consequences that are too often attendant to the coming-out process. Straight-identified graduate students have shared with me their concerns about whether or not they are authorized to teach courses on gay and lesbian literature. As I tell these students, I am disinclined to think of any instructor or, for that matter, any literary text as representative of a singular or unified tradition or community. Nevertheless, I don't want to minimize the challenges we face as teachers when we venture into new pedagogical territory. I vividly remember my own early forays in teaching when, as a white graduate student, I questioned my own ability and qualifications to teach about African American traditions. Of course, non–African American faculty who teach the Harlem Renaissance (or other forms of African American literature and culture) have to address more than their own concerns about whether they might be perceived as incompetent cultural interlopers. I think the "open secret" of multiculturalism is that some of our students and colleagues see the category of experience—which produces, as Zora Neale Hurston has put it, our understanding of "what it feels to be colored me"—as a prerequisite for teaching about cultural difference.

Approaching these issues from another angle, I want to argue that an instructor who is outside a particular tradition or community is sometimes exactly the right person to expose the effects of reified ideologies of difference. This is not because of some false notion of objectivity, but because all traditions—and our engagements with them—are inevitably multiple and contradictory. As educators, we can seize opportunities to put into play those questions of identity, difference, and representation that are fundamental to the project of the Harlem Renaissance itself. With this in mind, I would encourage instructors not to present *Infants* (or other explicitly queer African American literature) as part of a minority or alternative canon within the Harlem Renaissance, but rather as work that productively engages the central political commitments and aesthetic/erotic energies that the black arts movement calls forth. I see this approach as a useful and important corrective to a longstanding and oppressive cultural logic that opposes race and sexuality (Harper; McBride; Mercer and Julien; Somerville). For teachers of the Renaissance, I would suggest that Thurman directs our attention to a crucial manifestation of this opposition between queerness and blackness: the tendency to depict Harlem's queer dandy or bohemian aesthete as a "race traitor" whose decadence threatened to tarnish the image of the "New Negro."

It is precisely such logics of exclusion that *Infants of the Spring* seeks to call into question. This claim emerges with particular clarity when we contextualize the author and his work within the broader black arts movement, a step that seems to me crucial for any teacher of this text. Students will find it useful to know that Thurman is widely recognized as the leader of the Renaissance's second generation, a self-consciously unconventional and "decadent" colony of artists and writers. The movement's epicenter was a rent-free rooming house at 267 West 136th Street, famously called "Niggerati Manor" by Zora Neale Hurston and memorialized as such in *Infants*. In addition to Hurston, this vanguard group of artists included Langston Hughes, Aaron Douglas, and Richard Bruce Nugent. Organized and edited by Thurman, the magazine *Fire!!* (1926)—which included poetry by Countee Cullen and Hughes, illustrations by Nugent and Douglas, drama by Hurston, and fiction by Thurman, Hurston, and Nugent—is commonly read as a defining moment in which this younger generation of artists separated from the bourgeois, race-building politics of Harlem's Old Guard. Writing about a Harlem milieu that included jazz and blues, prostitution, drug use, homosexuality, and bisexuality, Thurman departed from the code of what had previously been considered appropriate representations of African American identity and culture. As Steven Watson asserts, one critic called *Fire!!* "effeminate tommyrot"—thus decrying what was seen as the movement's fall into decadence and excess (92). As I have argued elsewhere, Thurman's queer black dandy strategically appropriates the nineteenth-century, European tradition of decadence (whose principle figures were J.K. Huysmans and Oscar Wilde) in order to critique the primitivism implicit in the New Negro's quest for authenticity.

Although frequently interpreted as a satire of the Harlem Renaissance and its most recognizable personalities, *Infants* materializes a form of parody that is more generous than satire—something closer to a camp sensibility. For me, it is the democratic leveling of camp irony that makes the novel so fascinating and complex, positioning its author in an apparent contradiction. For Thurman appreciates and even at times identifies with the artists (e.g., Paul Arbian) and politics (e.g., "race consciousness" and "race pride") that his work boldly sends up. Ray's awareness of his own implication in the systems he critiques conveys Thurman's attention to the problem of complicity, as well as the political limitations of Ray's individualistic philosophy. In *Infants*, everyone (including Ray) is implicated in the perpetuation of the "Negro problem": earnest Communists and bourgeois opportunists; white supremacists and kindly, white "Negrotarians"; Du Boisian proponents of "uplift" and hedonistic proponents of free love and decadence; African Americans who cross the color line in order to pass for white and those who would judge them as race traitors; white thrill-seekers who fetishize African Americans as exotic/primitive; and African Americans who themselves reproduce primitivist notions of blackness.

If some critics have described *Infants'* iconography as bleak and pessimistic, this is perhaps due to the protagonists' complicity with the inequities of racial stratification. However, despite the cynicism that is integral to Thurman's vision, *Infants* is ultimately neither pessimistic nor fatalistic about art, politics, or social change. To the contrary, there is a strong ethical dimension in the protagonists' desire to challenge social hierarchies and norms of race and sexuality by ushering into being a utopian world of art, sensuality, and freedom.

Like the inhabitants of "Niggerati Manor," Thurman's bohemian cohort refused to adhere to bourgeois dictates of black respectability, the Old Guard's party line of "racial uplift," and the notion that African American artists must privilege an "authentic" construction of blackness grounded in either African art or African American folk traditions. In so doing, Thurman and his "queer" circle did not retreat from politics and history into a separate realm of aesthetics and pleasure but instead made art, lifestyle, and culture sites of political engagement. Seventy-five years after its publication, *Infants of the Spring* remains a vital testament to the ongoing challenges posed by such engagements.

WORKS CITED

Anderson, Jervis. *This Was Harlem: A Cultural Portrait, 1900–1950.* New York: Farrar Straus Giroux, 1982.

Blackmore, David. "'Something ... Too Preposterous and Complex to Be Recognized or Considered': Same-Sex Desire and Race in *Infants of the Spring.*" *Soundings* 80.4 (Winter 1997): 519–29.

Cobb, Michael L. "Insolent Racing, Rough Narrative: The Harlem Renaissance's Impolite Queers." *Callaloo* 23.1 (2000): 328–51.

Ganter, Granville. "Decadence, Sexuality, and the Bohemian Vision of Wallace Thurman." *MELUS* 28.2 (Summer 2003): 83–104.

Gates, Henry Louis. "The Black Man's Burden." *Fear of a Queer Planet: Queer Politics and Social Theory.* Ed. Michael Warner. Minneapolis: U of Minnesota P, 1993. 230–38.

Glick, Elisa F. "Harlem's Queer Dandy: African-American Modernism and the Artifice of Blackness." *Modern Fiction Studies* 49.3 (Fall 2003): 414–42.

Harper, Phillip Brian. *Are We Not Men?: Masculine Anxiety and the Problem of African-American Identity.* New York: Oxford UP, 1996.

Kelley, James. "Blossoming in Strange New Forms: Male Homosexuality and the Harlem Renaissance." *Soundings* 80.4 (Winter 1997): 499–517.

Knadler, Stephen. "Sweetback Style: Wallace Thurman and a Queer Harlem Renaissance." *Modern Fiction Studies* 48.4 (Winter 2002): 898–936.

McBride, Dwight. "Can the Queen Speak? Racial Essentialism, Sexuality and the Problem of Authority." *Callaloo* 21.2 (1998): 363–79.

Mercer, Kobena, and Isaac Julien. "Race, Sexual Politics and Black Masculinity: A Dossier." *Male Order: Unwrapping Masculinity.* Eds. Rowena Chapman and Jonathan Rutherford. London: Lawrence and Wishart, 1988. 97–165.

Silberman, Seth Clark. "Lighting the Harlem Renaissance *AFire!!*: Embodying Richard Bruce Nugent's Bohemian Politic." *The Greatest Taboo: Homosexuality in Black Communities.* Ed. Delroy Constantine-Simms. Los Angeles: Alyson, 2000. 254–73.

Somerville, Siobhan B. *Queering the Color Line.* Durham: Duke UP, 2000.

Thurman, Wallace. *Infants of the Spring.* 1932. Boston: Northeastern UP, 1992.

Watson, Steven. *The Harlem Renaissance: Hub of African-American Culture, 1920–1930.* New York: Pantheon, 1995.

CHAPTER TWENTY

Teaching Jean Toomer's *Cane*

NATHAN GRANT

Jean Toomer's great collection of poetry and short prose, *Cane*, has been thought by many to be the signal work of the Harlem Renaissance. Taken together, the pieces evoke the post-Reconstruction South, its consciousness of its recent slave past, and the social organization and spiritual aspirations of its black and white folk. But perhaps the most interesting continuing debate about *Cane* since its appearance in 1923 is whether it is in fact a novel. The short pieces that comprise *Cane*, and several of those lesser-known works that did not, were everywhere among the pages of the "little magazines" of the modernist 'teens and 'twenties; for example, "Calling Jesus" (originally published as "Nora") and "Harvest Song" first appeared in *Double Dealer* in 1922; "Fern" appeared in *Little Review* in 1923; "Seventh Street" was first printed in *Broom* in 1922; and "Bona and Paul" was, though not yet published, a story written as early as 1918. With this evidence, it is difficult to imagine a master prose work—a novel—with as variegated a history as *Cane*'s. Yet the question at the very horizon of this debate—"What's a novel?"—has sustained the discussion for so many years. Even more interesting is the fact that much contemporary criticism on *Cane* is the kind that one would find of the novel, beginning with an assumption of the work's "essential unity." Though critic Robert Bone classifies *Cane* with Richard Wright's *Native Son* (1940) and Ralph Ellison's *Invisible Man* (1952), Toomer's work reads like neither of these. Accordingly, students at either the upper-division college or Masters level should enjoy continuing this debate in the classroom by looking at *Cane*'s component parts.

First, it is likely that some students will argue that a novel is defined partly by its faithfulness to narrative and its resistance to poetry. *Cane*, however, is one of those texts in the midst of an already long list of texts that can be considered modernist—that is, those texts that have broken with the rigorous symmetry that characterized the aesthetic standards of the Victorian era. Toomer's selection of poems, appearing as they do before each short prose work in every case except that of "Karintha," can be thought of as replicating the epigrams that often appeared at the headings of chapters of Victorian novels, and perhaps most specifically, at the heads of the chapters of W.E.B. Du Bois's *The Souls of Black Folk* (1903). With their paths having crossed at Georgia Douglas Johnson's salon in Washington D.C. on more than one Saturday night, one can imagine the seasoned scribe Du Bois handing the mantle to the young expressionist as well as infusing the anxiety of influence; there could thus be enough for speculation on the rather close similarity, for example, between Toomer's poem "Song of the Son" in *Cane* and Du Bois's earlier "Song of the Smoke."

The most useful edition of *Cane* I have found is the Norton Critical Edition, edited by Darwin T. Turner, which supersedes the older Liveright edition (and includes the still useful introduction by Turner). In this newer edition, students can evaluate the text in the light of much correspondence between Toomer and other principals of the period, as well several critical essays prominent both then and now. I should reiterate that the best audience for *Cane* would begin at the upper-division level, but I should do so with the caveat that some students, even in this population, may find the text a bit daunting. A bit of background on issues regarding Sigmund Freud, stream of consciousness, expressionist theater, and modernism should prepare most students for *Cane*'s curiously evocative nature. Guides for these include Freud's *The Interpretation of Dreams* (1900), which, for its discussions of language in psychoanalysis, would be essential as a lens on expressionist writing. The broad strokes of modernism are finely painted by Peter Childs's *Modernism* (2000), and twentieth-century modernism as lived experience is well explicated by Walter Kalaidjian's *American Culture between the Wars: Revisionary Modernism and Postmodern Critique* (1993). Among biographies, *The Lives of Jean Toomer: A Hunger for Wholeness* (1987), by Cynthia Earl Kerman and Richard Eldridge, is less concerned with Toomer as writer than as spiritual seeker; among other things that this volume will reveal are the details surrounding Toomer's devotion of a good deal of his life to studying the teachings of the Russian mystic Georges Gurdjieff, and in the 1930s, his becoming the foremost practitioner and teacher of Gurdjieffianism in the United States. Charles Scruggs and Lee Vandemarr's *Jean Toomer and the Terrors of American History* (1998) focuses not only on *Cane* but also on Toomer's journalistic and other writings to make assessments on Toomer's impact on American culture and racial politics. All of these are rich and important studies for beginning work on Toomer's background and will give significant dimension to the brief notes on Toomer that follow.

Nathan Pinchback Toomer was born on December 26, 1894 to Nathan Toomer and Nina Pinchback, the daughter of Pinckney Stewart Benton Pinchback, formerly governor of Louisiana and the first governor of a Southern state who was of African descent. Of significant renown there and in the venues of the national black aristocracy, colloquially known as the "Colored 400," Pinchback had little regard for Nathan Toomer, probably a Georgia farmer who also may have had a shady, duplicitous past. After Nathan left Nina in 1895, Pinchback, who dominated virtually every aspect of his adult daughter's life, agreed to support Nina and her son on the condition that the boy's name be changed. Thus began a series of name changes that would characterize Toomer's entire life; after becoming Eugene Pinchback Toomer as a young child, Toomer later changed his first name to Jean, probably after reading Romain Rolland's *Jean-Christophe* (1904–1912), a semi-autobiographical novel about the life of a fictional composer whose dedication to his art alienates him from society. While one should be careful about using psychobiographical elements to interpret imaginative works, it may be a fair observation that on one level *Cane* is Toomer's quest for his lost identity, and thus also a quest for the lost father. In 1921, while caring for his aging grandparents, Toomer became acting headmaster at an agricultural school in Sparta, Georgia. Linton S. Ingraham, the school's headmaster (and the model for the foppish Hanby in "Kabnis") was going North to seek contributions to the school and needed someone reliable to look after things. As a friend of Pinchback, Toomer became a likely candidate. In Ingraham's offer came not only the opportunity to relieve himself of the arduous task of caring for two cantankerous grandparents, but also the chance to search for the father missing since his infancy and thus complete his testament of youth.

The richly evocative tone of *Cane* derives from Toomer's discovery of black rural life in Georgia, and aspects of the "quest for the father" as well. "Karintha," the story that begins *Cane*, actually appears first in Toomer's "Natalie Mann," a play staged by the Howard Players in Washington D.C. in 1922 after his return from Georgia but ultimately rejected for production. In this play, the protagonist Nathan Merilh (recall that Nathan was Toomer's father's first name, as well as his own) seeks to have his girlfriend Natalie realize her truest self-potential. "Karintha" is the story he has written for her, and he will risk his art by presenting the story to his white fellow artists for their critiques. These artists, as Nathan Merilh gleefully remarks, are collectively known as "Young America" (or the "young Aesthetes"), the cadre of writers and intellectuals of the period with whom Toomer associated: Among them were Paul Rosenfeld, Gorham Munson,

Alfred Kreymborg, Hart Crane and Kenneth Burke. This "gift of the father" as sacrificed to white criticism mirrors the questioning by Jean Toomer of whites and blacks he met, of what might possibly have become of Nathan Toomer in all the years preceding.

As a corollary to this notion, the stories in *Cane*'s Part I are all entitled (excepting the last, "Blood-Burning Moon") with names of women, who like Nina, are abused and wandering. The stories in Part II (excepting "Avey") are otherwise titled, but the protagonists are fractured, class-conscious, embittered men. In "Kabnis" we find what is normally called the "absorption" in *Cane* of all the male characters, and perhaps some aspects of some of the female ones as well; Ralph Kabnis appears to possess a glimmer of self-consciousness, manifest in his aborted efforts to announce himself to the world, which represents the human failure of purpose caused by the unendurable weight of racism.

Students will likely be unfamiliar with the poverty of black rural Georgia as seen through Toomer's eyes. They may have the most resistance to "Karintha," in which it is apparent that the young girl is learning about sexuality through both limited economics and sexual abuse, but ultimately lose all sympathy for the character after they learn that she has murdered her child. Moreover, silences in the text as to quite *why* she has killed the child and the lack of expressions of remorse can make her monstrous to most readers. Class discussion has invariably led to invocations of sanctions against her, including prison or capital punishment, and it may be useful to give background to Karintha's plight by discussing the rural South in the first years of the twentieth century. Another effective measure would be to stop discussion of the story and have students write about what to them would constitute the most dreadful privation—either as an at-home assignment, or as a brief listing they may make in class. Then the instructor could construct situations involving certain everyday choices and ask whether students in their new environs could make better choices than did Karintha. My experience has been that students gradually develop a sense of what truly grinding poverty is like, and why Karintha succumbs to her terrible choice—and also why she seems not to express the sorrow that students feel inevitably accompanies such an event. It seems useful to discuss that in the presence of poverty is the absence of choice, and that the absence of *every* choice can vitiate emotion.

This is an element of "Karintha" that appears to recur throughout Part I. Absent or limited choices affect Becky, Carma, Fern, and Esther in various ways (and seem to have different valences for "Avey" in Part II); if students are not satisfied with the facts of poverty as an explanation for Karintha's actions, one can look to "Blood-Burning Moon" or "Kabnis" for answers. Where the lives of every black man or woman can turn on the whim of white intolerance, could Karintha, in her obviously heinous act, have actually saved her child from a possibly worse fate? In this light, the silences regarding her motivations seem to become all the more dark and more sinister—but for reasons that may have less to do with Karintha than first thought.

Part II of *Cane* can perhaps engender a discussion of class (particularly as crossed with race), which can be a useful one especially since many American students yet appear not to have developed a vocabulary for class. "Seventh Street" and its violently sexualized metaphors ironically set the stage for the more genteel, "dicty" mood of Part II, wherein the characters, particularly the male characters, are largely immobilized by the fact of class-consciousness. Useful for this discussion is a close look at "Theater," in which John, deceived by his untested talents as a writer on the one hand and his repressed sexuality on the other, denigrates Dorris, the showgirl to whom he is vaguely attracted. The fundamental yet irreducible connection that black men have to black women in the Washington D.C. and Chicago portion of *Cane* is forged in an interracialism that continuously echoes the "unconscious rhythms, black reddish blood [thrust] into the white and whitewashed wood of Washington" in "Seventh Street." The echo matures to a crescendo in "Bona and Paul," wherein Paul's classic confusion is manifest in his racialized performance; just as the nameless protagonist in James Weldon Johnson's 1912 novel, *The Autobiography of an Ex-Colored Man*, only vaguely realizes, Paul's tortured relationship to the white Bona reflects his confused fidelity to both art and race.

In the third and final section, Ralph Kabnis, as discussed above, is the presumptive aggregate of all the characters in *Cane*. One possible view of this character's value is that he has been horrified by the effeteness of the men and dismayed by the frustrations of the women in the preceding sections. Kabnis is fearful of the possibility of his being lynched and as a result cannot affirm a uniquely black, pan-historical voice in order to stand against that possibility. Toomer, having himself migrated many times, from South to North and across the Midwest to New York, and then having returned later to Washington D.C. and then moved on to Georgia, also has Kabnis follow a South-North-South trek, thus completing, with social, psychological, and philosophical gaps (note the semicircles that mark the heads of each section), an American odyssey of race and the conflicts and confluences of class.

Barbara Clare Foley has noted that there is every reason to believe that "Kabnis" is at least partly autobiographical; the particularly horrific lynching as told to Kabnis by Layman and Halsey might well have mirrored an actual incident, leading to perhaps several other murders, in Sparta, Georgia, in the early 1920s ("Land"). Lewis, who serves a brief function as Kabnis's ego ideal, may have been, according to Foley, a Walter White figure, as White had been commissioned by the National Association for the Advancement of Colored People

(NAACP) to investigate lynchings in the South during this period. In this connection, there may be for Kabnis, as well as perhaps for Toomer, the opportunity to strike a definitive blow for justice, but Kabnis's decision appears to be to reject the succinct yet time-honored teachings of Father John, who, allied with the goodness and purity of the young Carrie Kate, can make the attempt to forge a new beginning and write a different future. It may be useful at this juncture to try to have students determine for themselves whether Toomer offers a similar rejection, feeling that the stories of the postslavery South, themselves forged in the antebellum period, formed a folk spirit that was "walking in to die on the modern desert," as Toomer wrote in an autobiographical fragment (*Wayward* 123). To this end, it may also be useful to mention that *Cane* enjoyed a revival during the Black Consciousness/Black Arts Movement of the 1970s as a text that left an evocative literary record of the dangers of black life through the turn of the twentieth century, thus marking the landscape of the Civil Rights era for possible correctives.

I began coyly enough by suggesting a reentry into the continuing debate as to whether *Cane* is in fact a novel. Perhaps nothing I say below, then, will settle it; nevertheless, I believe a case should be made for *Cane*'s structural unity, and thus its admission to the ranks of the genre. If Ian Watt in *The Rise of the Novel* (1957) is correct, then any novel's expression of the movements of contemporary life is effected "through a more largely referential use of language than is common in other literary forms" (32). *Cane*, through its combination of genres (i.e., the poem and short sketch) and of other effects, would seem to display the early twentieth-century South through just these means. But it seems to be the fact of the combination of such disparate genres—poetry and short prose—that determines many of the positions that disallow *Cane*'s novelistic status. Several commentators on *Cane* and modernism, such as Robert M. Crunden in *Body and Soul* (2000), say flatly that *Cane* "is not a novel" (29). But then, in Crunden's case and others, there is no precise definition of what a novel *is*. Similarly restrictive definitions would deny novelistic status to some of the most intriguing works of the twentieth century, such as Alain Robbe-Grillet's *Jealousy* (1957), Toni Cade Bambara's *The Salt-Eaters* (1982), and Christine Brooke-Rose's *Thru* (1992); in addition, the antinovel novel that appeared just the year before *Cane*, James Joyce's *Ulysses*, perhaps indeed gave the world more novel than that for which it might ever be prepared. In each case, the echo of the original meaning of the word "novel," the "new little thing," is heard and is thus ever capable of advancing the frontier of the modern. It is in this connection that the very rebellion against traditional depictions of human experience is often its own statement of human complexity. Surely the South of Jean Toomer's tempestuous era must be anchored in this notion.

WORKS CITED

Bone, Robert. *The Negro Novel in America*. New Haven: Yale UP, 1958.

Childs, Peter. *Modernism*. London: Routledge, 2000.

Crunden, Robert M. *Body and Soul: The Making of American Modernism*. New York: Basic, 2000.

Foley, Barbara. *Spectres of 1919: Class and Nation in the Making of the New Negro*. Urbana: U of Illinois P, 2003.

———. "In the Land of Cotton: Economics and Violence in Jean Toomer's *Cane*." *African American Review* 32 (1998): 181–98.

Freud, Sigmund. *The Interpretation of Dreams* rev. ed. 1900. Trans. James Strachey. New York: Avon, 1967.

Kalaidjian, Walter B. *American Culture Between the Wars: Revisionary Modernism and Postmodern Critique*. New York: Columbia UP, 1993.

Kerman, Cynthia Earl, and Richard Eldridge. *The Lives of Jean Toomer: A Hunger for Wholeness*. Baton Rouge: Louisiana State UP, 1987.

Scruggs, Charles, and Lee VanDemarr. *Jean Toomer and the Terrors of American History*. Philadelphia: U of Pennsylvania P, 1998.

Toomer, Jean. *Cane*. 1923. Ed. Darwin T. Turner. New York: Norton, 1988.

———. *The Wayward and the Seeking: A Collection of Writings by Jean Toomer*. Ed. Darwin T. Turner. Washington D.C.: Howard UP, 1980.

Watt, Ian. *The Rise of the Novel*. Berkeley: U of California P, 1957.

CHAPTER TWENTY-ONE

Teaching Carl Van Vechten's *Nigger Heaven*

EMILY BERNARD

The word *nigger*, you see, sums up for us who are colored all the bitter years of insult and struggle in America: the slave-beatings of yesterday, the lynchings of today, the Jim Crow cars, the only movie show in town with its sign up FOR WHITES ONLY, the restaurants where you may not eat, the jobs you may not have. The unions you cannot join. The word *nigger* in the mouths of foremen on the job, the word *nigger* across the whole face of America!

—LANGSTON HUGHES, *THE BIG SEA*

These are lines from *The Big Sea* (1940), the autobiography of Langston Hughes, and I recalled them easily when I received an e-mail from a student in a graduate course on the Harlem Renaissance I taught recently. The student, I'll call him Kevin, had written to respond to the book we were discussing that week, Carl Van Vechten's 1926 novel, *Nigger Heaven*. In his e-mail, Kevin wrote, "I hated every time the word was uttered by a Caucasian counterpart in class, and I was actually going to boycott the class last Thursday as a protestation." Kevin didn't have to tell me what word he meant; I knew.

You know, too.

I had multiple and contradictory reactions to Kevin's e-mail that, as I began thinking about them, seemed, to me, to be intimately connected to questions about the relationship between race and art that dominated intellectual discourse of the Harlem Renaissance and continues to have a significant place in public and private conversations about race and representation—who can say what about black people. My recent experience of teaching *Nigger Heaven* to a mixed-race group of generally thoughtful and insightful students brought me a great distance.

Whereas, several months before we actually read the book, I wondered whether *Nigger Heaven* actually merited the time and attention I had planned to give it, now I feel strongly that not only are courses that include discussions of the literature of the Harlem Renaissance incomplete without it, but also that continuing public battles over the role of the black artist and the purpose of black art are enriched when contemporary arguments generated by *Nigger Heaven* are brought into them.

While my student Kevin was alarmed every time the word "nigger" was used during our class discussion of *Nigger Heaven*, I was probably equally amazed at how often it was not. I found that no student, white or nonwhite, wanted to say the word "nigger" in class. A few followed my lead and used the actual word but not before prefacing their usage with a disclaimer about how uncomfortable it made them to say it. For the most part, the students resorted to using the phrase, "the n-word." Besides "the n-word," the phrase in heaviest circulation that day in our discussion was "n-word heaven."

Both phrases were awkward, without rhythm, and, to boot, "N-word Heaven" was just *not* the title of the book. I recalled a story about a Harlem Renaissance conference during which a prominent black female scholar of African American literature refused to say "nigger," or "nigger heaven," and used, instead, the same awkward stand-in phrase that we were employing. At the time I heard the story, those verbal acrobatics seemed ridiculous; they seemed ridiculous now, too, but I couldn't see any way out of it. How could I possibly insist that my students say the word "nigger"? What would be gained by such a demand? But our gentle side-stepping was solving nothing. Still, to insist seemed cruel.

My classroom discomfort was not unique. We were only enacting a now-common modern ritual made most public in the 1995 trial, *The People v. Orenthal James Simpson*, where, to quote Ann duCille, "the quintessentially American word 'nigger' was recreated in the public imagination as the unspeakable thing never spoken—a word so extraordinary, so far outside common usage, so rabidly racist and un-American that it could be only alluded to as the 'N word.' He who would say 'nigger' would also plant evidence to frame an innocent black man" (6).

Here, duCille refers to the revelation during the trial that the prosecution's star witness, Los Angeles police detective Mark Fuhrman, had perjured himself on the witness stand when he testified that he had not used the word "nigger" in ten years, when he had actually been taped using it forty-two times, "repeatedly and with relish," Randall Kennedy describes in his book, *Nigger*. Amid allegations of malevolent police work, what has actually and finally branded Mark Fuhrman an irrecoverable racist in the imagination of the American public is his articulation of the word "nigger," a word whose very expression was considered such an act of rhetorical violence that it could not even be uttered in the courtroom of the Simpson trial—the fragile locution, "the n-word," the same clumsy phrase we were using that day in class, was employed instead. Looking back at the trial, considering, once again, its impact on the American psyche, it is no wonder that my students were anxious about saying the word "nigger" out loud. Far from individual, their discomfort was a nation's discomfort.

But surely something was being lost in the careful but imprecise language we were using. Something essential was not being sidestepped at all, but brought that much further into relief. In part, I had condoned the sidestepping in order to avoid getting lost in a discussion about the title of the book. But then I realized that such a conversation was not only inevitable, it might well be the most important discussion to have. I asked my students directly why they were not saying the word; could they imagine it as capable of signaling anything other than racial hatred? I brought in Judith Butler's *Excitable Speech* and cited her quotation of Richard Delgado's conclusion that: "Words such as 'nigger' and 'spic' are badges of degradation even when used between friends: *these words have no other connotation*." Butler responds to Delgado, writing:

> And yet, this very statement, whether written in his text or cited here, has another connotation; he has just used the word in a significantly different way. Even if we concede—as I think we must—that the injurious connotation is inevitably retained in Delgado's use, indeed, that it is difficult to utter those words or, indeed, to write them here, because they unwittingly recirculate that degradation, it does not follow that such words can have *no other connotation*. Indeed, their repetition is necessary … in order to enter them as objects of another discourse. (100)

I offered that Butler's argument applied to the rhetorical hurdles we were facing in class. One student suggested that our discussion was ahistorical; that times had changed and the meaning of the word had changed with it. He cited the popularly held assumption that "nigga," a recently coined term, had rescued the term "nigger" from past associations with white racism and transformed it exclusively into a term of endearment. I quoted Judith Butler again: "The possibility of decontextualizating and recontextualizing such terms through radical acts of public misappropriation constitutes the basis of an ironic hopefulness that the conventional relation between word and wound might become tenuous and broken over time" (100). In other words, I told them, the term "nigga," and all the discourse in favor over it, is an expression of that hopefulness. But the recent case of the oratorical gymnastics in the O. J. Simpson trial, as well as our current discomfort with the term, was proof enough for me that the moment of severance between word and wound had not yet arrived. As a final test, I asked them, "What if Carl Van Vechten had titled his book 'Nigga Heaven'? Would it then be easier for you to say the actual title?" Everyone was quiet until one student, the same student who had advocated in favor of the term "nigga," said, "No white person should ever, ever say that word." So much for changing times and evolving terminology.

Despite the years and the experiences that distinguish them, Carl Van Vechten was keenly aware of what my student meant; he, too, believed no white person should say the word. That was why he included a footnote at the first usage of the word "nigger" in the book: "While this informal epithet is freely used by Negroes among themselves, not only as a term of opprobrium, but also actually as a term of endearment, its employment by a white person is always fiercely resented. The word Negress," the footnote continued knowledgeably, "is forbidden under all circumstances" (26). Van Vechten included this footnote because he hoped it would reveal that his own motives were not malicious, but it rather indicated his ambitions to, in Judith Butler's phrase, enter the word "nigger" as an object of "another discourse." This moment was also meant to demonstrate Van Vechten's personal familiarity with black cultural idioms and underscore his status as an honorary insider in black circles. The larger and unintended irony of this footnote resides in Van Vechten's apparent belief that his employment of this racial epithet in the body and title of his book would be viewed as exceptional by black readers and go toward confirming publicly his authority in intimate inter-personal circles as a black cultural insider.

Later, after he was surprised and even hurt by the negative reaction his book received from some black people, Van Vechten consistently claimed that he meant his title ironically. In an Afterword to the 1951 edition of *Nigger Heaven*, Van Vechten wrote:

> There have been those who have objected to the title. These objections have usually come from people who have not read the novel. The title is symbolic and ironic, even tragic. Before the book was published I had submitted the manuscript to two prominent Negro literary men, James Weldon Johnson and Rudolph Fisher, for their approval and disapproval and also to check up on errors. After it had passed the test successfully, it was submitted to the world.

Van Vechten uses the "authentic" blackness of Fisher and Johnson to justify himself here, in the same way that, in present-day scholarship, Van Vechten's relationship with Langston Hughes and Nella Larsen are often used to exonerate Van Vechten from charges of racism. If respected black writers such as Hughes and Johnson liked or at least approved of the title, the logic goes, then Van Vechten's intentions could not be racist. But both the "some of my best friends" defense, like the "irony" defense, seems to me too convenient, and ultimately insufficient. The fact is that Van Vechten used "nigger" in his title *because* it was—and is—a racial epithet. There was a transgressive pleasure he enjoyed in using a word "forbidden under all circumstances" to white people. This same transgressive pleasure was perhaps mutually experienced in correspondence between black writers such as Hughes and Larsen and Van Vechten, in which the word appears frequently. But what Larsen and Hughes "felt" about Van Vechten's use of the word is irrelevant when it comes to the word's historical meaning and continuing rhetorical power in our lexicon.

Are discussions about the word "nigger" still meaningful? Obviously, I think so. African Americans have been consumed with nomenclature since the inception of African presence in this country; in the history of African American intellectual discourse, the terms used to refer to us by white mainstream society have been understood as being inextricably connected to our social, political, and cultural standing in that society. But what I find remarkable about these discussions is how they simultaneously obscure *and* reveal the enormous histories of interracial discord represented by—and perhaps even lodged within—these terms. Similarly, I found that our class discussion about the title of *Nigger Heaven* distracted us from and yet spoke directly to what is perhaps most pernicious—and most important—about the book, which is its chilling vision of the black writer's options in the literary marketplace, a vision that, I will demonstrate, has present-day application.

The plot of *Nigger Heaven* revolves around a writer who can't write, a conceit Van Vechten used in his first novel, *Peter Whiffle* (1922). Byron Kasson is a recent transplant to New York from Philadelphia. Early in the novel, he meets Mary Love, a librarian at the Harlem branch of the New York Public Library, and their arrested romance serves as the novel's ostensible plot. Like other Harlem Renaissance novels, *Nigger Heaven* concerns the alienation its main characters experience from the larger black population that surrounds them. The bond that yokes Mary and Byron is their mutual sense of isolation, a lack of a spontaneous connection to blackness, figured as a "lost or forfeited birthright" (88), in a deliberate allusion to James Weldon Johnson's 1912 novel, *The Autobiography of an Ex-Colored Man*. Throughout *Nigger Heaven*, Mary Love asks herself some version of the question: "How had she, during the centuries, lost [the] vital instinct?" (91). This is the question around which the entire plot of *Nigger Heaven* revolves, and the answer is believed to reside outside of history and inside the psyches of individual characters.

In particular, *Nigger Heaven* wants its readers to understand that the alienation experienced by its protagonist, Byron Kasson, is a self-generated phenomenon. He is sensitive, vulnerable to every slight, real or imagined. Even his own father describes him as "touchy" and "inclined to ... feel any demonstration of sympathy from others as patronizing" (172). The novel is either not interested in or unable to resolve the dilemma that it constructs as Mary's identity, but it provides Byron with a ray of hope, inside of a paradox. In order to recover his birthright, Byron must write; but he cannot write until he has recovered his birthright, which is, according to the novel, an unmediated, unselfconscious relationship to "authentic" blackness.

Naturally, Byron's problems with writing are inextricably related to his troubled sense of his racial selfhood. Consider his first day of gainful employment in New York, when Byron takes a job as an elevator operator after his father cuts him off financially. The other operators are already friendly: "They spoke freely about their amorous adventures, about games of craps, about dives on Lenox Avenue, about Numbers." Byron's creative radar picks up the signals: "You want to be a writer, he adjured himself, and this is probably first-class material." Immediately, however, Byron concludes: "he could never feel anything but repugnance for these people, because they were black ... I can't bear to think of myself as a part of this, he sighed" (192). Sensing his disgust, the other workers begin to express their own mounting ill-will toward Byron, thus compounding Byron's sense of alienation from other black people.

Interestingly, it is his obsession with race that prevents Byron from being able to write about race, or anything else, for that matter. "The Negro problem seemed to hover over him and occasionally, like the great, black bird it was, claw at his heart." In *Nigger Heaven*, it is not Byron's preoccupation with race that is problematic but rather it is his attitude toward the utilization of this preoccupation, or rather his failure to transform his preoccupations into material that a white reading public can recognize as authentically black. Late in the novel, Byron is summoned to the offices of *American Mars*—based on *American Mercury*—by its editor, Russett Durwood—based on H.L. Mencken—to whom Byron had submitted a story he had, at long last, been able to compose. "I am very much interested in Negro literature; that's why I sent for you," Durwood tells him. He has some advice. "Why in the hell don't you write about something you know about?" Durwood asks and then embarks upon a virtual monologue on the "wealth" of material in Harlem.

I use the word "wealth" deliberately. I mean to refer back to Carl Van Vechten's infamous response to the 1926 *Crisis* survey, "The Negro in Art: How Shall He Be Portrayed?", in which he declared:

> The squalor of Negro life, the vice of Negro life, offer a wealth of novel, exotic, picturesque material to the artist ... The question is: Are Negro writers going to write about this exotic material while it is still fresh or will they continue to make a free gift of it to white writers who will exploit it until not a drop of vitality remains? (219)

Weeks after Van Vechten's words were in print, *Nigger Heaven* was published. To some, Van Vechten's words in the *Crisis* seemed a chilling revelation of his calculating intentions with *Nigger Heaven*. We may bristle at Van Vechten's brutal cynicism and essentialist language, but the outcome he describes above is a veritable cliché in the annals of African American culture. White spectatorship—and appropriation—is, finally, a central facet of African American cultural history.

After his encounter with Durwood, Byron is done for; it is not Durwood, however, but Byron's own attitude that does him in. He leaves Durwood's office in a lather. "He treated me that way because I am a Negro! was his subsequent conclusion. He wouldn't dare talk like that to a white man." Later, Byron comes to his senses: "Probably Durwood had been right. At any rate, he was now capable of the realization that Durwood had not intended to patronize him." Unfortunately, it's too late for this revelation to do him any good. As I have said, *Nigger Heaven* is only interested in Byron's sensitivity as an individual psychic distortion; nowhere does it allow for the possibility that Byron's "sensitivity" might have historical roots or be a logical response to the systemic realities of white racism. Byron's resistance to Durwood's suggestion that he "write what he know" presumes an ahistorical, authentic black identity that somehow inhabits Byron physically and spiritually. As editor of *American Mars*, Durwood's ideas about blackness are not benign; they have the power, at least to some degree, to chart the course of black writing, which has always been and continues to be a primary site of African American identity formation.

"Almost as soon as blacks could write, it seems, they set out to redefine—against already received racist stereotypes—who and what a black person was, and how unlike the racist stereotype the black original indeed actually could be" (131). These are Henry Louis Gates's words from his 1988 essay, "The Trope of a New Negro and the Reconstruction of the Image of the Black." Is the relationship between racial identity and writing still as urgent as Gates describes it here? "We are a new breed, free to write as we please, in part because of our predecessors, and because of the way life has changed." I quote these words, not from "The Negro Artist and the Racial Mountain" by Langston Hughes but from Terry McMillan's introductory essay to the 1990 anthology of contemporary African American fiction: *Breaking Ice*. McMillan's triumphant language recalls the victorious diction of "The Negro Artist and the Racial Mountain" exactly, as do the problems exhibited in her reasoning. "We build our temples for tomorrow, strong as we know how, and we stand on top of the mountain, free within ourselves" (694), Hughes proclaimed in his 1926 manifesto. The fact that Terry McMillan and Trey Ellis echo Hughes's decree so explicitly proves not that the progress Hughes reported has actually finally been achieved, but precisely the opposite. The more passionate the rhetorical need to announce the black author's freedom to "write as we please," the more what is being demonstrated is how far we are from that actual goal, I'm afraid; black writers are still told to "write what they know," and what it *is* that they know. As James Weldon Johnson explained in 1928, white influence and expectation, so intimately connected to black identity itself, cannot easily and simply be shrugged off. But what my class discussion of *Nigger Heaven* enabled, importantly, was an even more important larger discussion of the historic tension between African American writing and a white consumer audience: a central tension in African American literary history. This tension has been as stifling as it has been productive, and African American literature as we know it would never have existed in its absence.

WORKS CITED

Butler, Judith. *Excitable Speech: A Politics of the Performative*. New York: Routledge, 1997.
DuCille, Anne. *Skin Trade*. Cambridge: Harvard UP, 1996.
Gates, Henry Louis, Jr. "The Trope of the New Negro and the Reconstruction of the Image of the Black." *Representations* 24 (1988): 129–55.
Hughes, Langston. *The Big Sea: An Autobiography*. 1940. New York: Hill and Wang, 1993.
Johnson, James Weldon. *The Autobiography of an Ex-Coloured Man*. 1912. New York: Knopf, 1927.
Kennedy, Randall. *Nigger: The Strange Career of a Troublesome Word*. New York: Pantheon, 2002.
McMillan, Terry, ed. *Breaking Ice: An Anthology of Contemporary African-American Fiction*. New York: Penguin, 1990.
"Negro in Art: How Shall He Be Portrayed?" *Crisis* 31.5 (March 1926): 219–20.
Van Vechten, Carl. *Nigger Heaven*. 1926. Ed. Kathleen Pfeiffer. Urbana: U of Illinois P, 2000.
———. *Peter Whiffle: His Life and Works*. New York: Knopf, 1922.

CHAPTER TWENTY-TWO

Teaching Edward Christopher Williams's *When Washington Was in Vogue*

ADAM MCKIBLE

When Washington Was in Vogue, by Edward Christopher Williams, is the most recent addition to the canon of Harlem Renaissance literature. The first African American epistolary novel, *When Washington Was in Vogue* consists of letters written by Captain Davy Carr, a veteran of World War I and a recent arrival in the capitol, to a friend in Harlem. Davy's letters initially describe the lives and mores of Washington's black middle class, but as the novel progresses, he increasingly focuses on Caroline Rhodes, a vivacious flapper with whom he falls in love. Williams's novel was originally published anonymously in 1925–1926, but it was not released in book form until January 2004. I have had the opportunity to teach Williams's book a number of times since its publication, and I am happy to report that *When Washington Was in Vogue* is an engaging and accessible text that taught well in both a Harlem Renaissance elective and an American literature survey. My experience with the novel suggests that it is appropriate at the college level, would be a welcome addition in graduate courses, and might work at the high school level. The novel is essentially a love story with some intrigue and social commentary, and I hesitate to recommend it for high school students only because of my own lack of experience teaching at that level.

I begin teaching *When Washington Was in Vogue* by discussing Williams's biography and the history of his once-forgotten book.[1] Williams was born in Cleveland, Ohio on February 11, 1871 to Daniel P. Williams, a fair-skinned African American, and Mary Kilkary, a white woman from Ireland. Because of his parentage, Williams was fair enough to pass for white, but throughout his life he never concealed his racial heritage. After attending public schools in Cleveland, Williams matriculated to Adelbert College of Western Reserve University (now Case Western Reserve University), where he excelled in both academics and athletics. He was elected to Phi Beta Kappa, played a number of team sports, and was class valedictorian.

Shortly after graduating in 1892, Williams became an assistant librarian for the university, and in 1894 he was appointed head librarian of Western Reserve's Hatch Library, where he served until 1909. Williams was an innovative and dynamic figure who developed the library's collections and trained his colleagues in the latest techniques of library science. Deeply interested in what was then a relatively new field, Williams attended the New York State Library School in 1899–1900 to earn a master's degree, thus becoming the first professionally trained black librarian in America. He was also an active participant in library associations around the country. In 1902, he married Ethel Chesnutt, daughter of the writer Charles Waddell Chesnutt.

Williams resigned his post in 1909 for unknown reasons, but there are suggestions that white racism at Western Reserve might have prompted his decision. Relocating to the District of Columbia, Williams was named principal of the all-black M Street High School (now Paul Lawrence Dunbar High School), where he remained for seven years. During this time, Williams became increasingly involved in Washington's burgeoning African American literary community. In 1916, Williams returned to his original profession by becoming head librarian at Howard University, where he also taught courses in library science and foreign languages and literature. Williams remained at Howard until shortly before his death, and he also made regular visits to New York City to work at the 135th Street Branch Library in Harlem. He died on December 24, 1929.

Williams flourished as a writer while at Howard. He was a regular participant in various cultural organizations, founded a literary society, helped develop the talents of a number of writers, and often had regular contact with many of the now familiar figures of the Harlem Renaissance, including Jean Toomer, Georgia Douglas Johnson, and Zora Neale Hurston. During his years in Washington, Williams wrote three plays, which were performed at Howard, and a number of short stories. He also reputedly published essays and poems anonymously or under the pseudonym Bertuccio Dantino. Most significantly, he wrote "The Letters of Davy Carr: A True Story of Colored Vanity Fair," which ran anonymously and serially in *The Messenger* (1917–1928), a little magazine published by A. Philip Randolph and Chandler Owen in Harlem.

"The Letters of Davy Carr" appeared at a key juncture in *The Messenger*'s eleven-year history, and instructors interested in exploring the literary-historical context of the Harlem Renaissance or the role of that era's little magazines might want to pause to consider this subject. At the outset, *The Messenger* was a socialist publication that billed itself as "A Journal of Scientific Radicalism" and garnered the attention of several government agencies and officials, including such infamous Red-Baiters as U.S. Attorney General A. Mitchell Palmer and F.B.I. Director J. Edgar Hoover. In late 1923, however, the magazine made a dramatic shift by becoming an advocate of black capitalism and a showplace for the African American bourgeoisie. *The Messenger* turned back toward the left in June 1925, when Randolph began his involvement with the Brotherhood of Sleeping Car Porters. "The Letters of Davy Carr" started running in the magazine in January 1925, during its pro-business phase, and ended in June 1926, when Williams's bourgeois subject matter and deliberately old-fashioned style were at odds with the newly radicalized magazine.

"The Letters of Davy Carr" slipped into obscurity immediately after its publication, and received virtually no critical attention for the next seventy-five years.[2] I first encountered the unsigned text while working on my dissertation, when I read it on microfilm. Several years later, with the help of a former student and the invention of Google, I was able to link Williams to his creation. Working with another student on an independent study course, I began to organize my approach to editing and introducing Williams's rediscovered novel, which was published for the first time in book form by HarperCollins in 2004. When teaching the novel, I like to highlight my students' involvement in its development into a free-standing book, because this helps emphasize the collaborative nature of both education and publishing.

During my introductory comments on Williams's biography and book, my students inevitably ask why and how its title was changed to *When Washington Was in Vogue*, and I consider this a good opportunity to explore the ways in which editorial and marketing considerations influence literary development and transmission. As the novel was making its way to print, the sales department at HarperCollins worried that the word "letters" in the title would scare off potential buyers. A number of alternatives were tossed around by everyone involved in the process (my editor, my agent, the marketing department, and me) until we agreed that the book's title would be *When Washington Was in Vogue*, and that the cover would also contain the phrases "A Love Story" and "A Lost Novel of the Harlem Renaissance." This approach was chosen to attract multiple buyers. "A Love Story," it was felt, would appeal to a predominantly female readership; "A Lost Novel of the Harlem Renaissance" would attract African American buyers; and the title, which is a gloss on David Levering Lewis's seminal study *When Harlem Was in Vogue* (1981), would draw the attention of scholars and educators. This rather tenuous connection between Lewis's book and Williams's renamed novel may, in fact, be useful to teachers interested in pursuing or challenging Lewis's assertion that the Harlem Renaissance was ultimately an elitist "cultural nationalism of the parlor" dominated and domesticated by black and white civil rights leaders and patrons (xvi). Lewis draws this claim, and his title, from a chapter in Langston Hughes's autobiography, *The Big Sea* (1940), entitled "When the Negro Was in Vogue," which portrays the "Negro Vogue" in large part as a passing fancy of white readers and thrill-seekers. How, I ask in class, might Williams's book, which has no white characters and was published in a magazine with very few white readers, challenge the image of the Harlem Renaissance presented by Lewis and Hughes?

After we have examined Williams's biography and the publication of his novel, I ask my students to consider the book's narrator and point of view. Because it is an epistolary novel, *When Washington Was in Vogue* is told entirely from Davy Carr's perspective, and students might not immediately realize the ironic distance between Williams and his protagonist/narrator. Davy is, after all, a self-professed "mid-Victorian" (30) in a modernizing world, and his inability to recognize his feelings for Caroline owes a great deal to his disjunctive relationship to the changing times. As they probe this topic, students comment on Davy's strong sense of social propriety, his sometimes flowery or overrefined language, and the glacial progress of his emotional awareness. Through this discussion, they come to understand that Williams intends for his audience to read Davy Carr's letters with at least a modicum of skepticism, particularly when he is writing about women or his own emotional awareness.

However, while Davy might appear old-fashioned, his experiences represent two of the most important sociohistorical developments that contributed to the rise of the Harlem Renaissance: the Great Migration and black military service in World War I. As Davy mentions in his first letter, he and his correspondent, Bob Fletcher, are both from "the Sunny South" (9), and many of Davy's impressions of, and reactions to, life in Washington appear to be shaped by his upbringing "in a little provincial Southern city" (51). Instructors may want to pause on this detail, and they can draw comparisons between Davy and any number of similar characters from such texts as Rudolph Fisher's "City of Refuge" (1925), Jean Toomer's *Cane* (1923), and Wallace Thurman's *Infants of the Spring* (1932).

Davy and Bob were also officers serving in France during the war, an experience that Davy returns to repeatedly in his letters. As most historians of the Harlem Renaissance note, African American military service became a turning point in black political consciousness.[3] Returning veterans, who were treated with greater dignity in France than in the United States, came home expecting better treatment from the nation they had just defended, and they were a driving force behind the development of the "New Negro" or "New Negro Manhood" movement. In a course devoted to the Harlem Renaissance, one might compare Davy as a veteran with Jake Brown in Claude McKay's *Home to Harlem* (1928), particularly since Williams condemned that novel's author as a "filth monger" (qtd. in Lewis 227). McKay celebrates Jake as a heroic urban primitive unfettered by conventional morality, and his novel mocks characters who have pretensions to refinement. In contrast, Williams's novel foregrounds the sophistication and manners of Washington's most "highly cultivated people" (10) and condemns the untoward behavior of its few *demimonde* characters. These divergent approaches to portraying black life were disputed regularly during the Harlem Renaissance. They informed the debates surrounding McKay's novels as well as Carl Van Vechten's *Nigger Heaven* (1926), and teachers might want to invoke this divergence when considering the differing editorial approaches adopted by Alain Locke in his groundbreaking *The New Negro* (1925) and those employed in the publication of *Fire!!* (1926), the far racier little magazine issued by such younger figures of the Renaissance as Thurman, Hughes, Hurston, and Richard Bruce Nugent.

Davy's identity as a veteran can also be a useful point of departure in an American literature class; I teach *When Washington Was in Vogue* in conjunction with Ernest Hemingway's *The Sun Also Rises* (1926), which provides students with the opportunity to consider why the white Jake Barnes and the black Davy Carr might approach changing social norms so differently. How does Jake's modern alienation and rejection of middle-class social norms compare with Davy's more cohesive sense of self and his embrace of traditional behavior? Why might an African American character embrace some of the cultural shifts mourned by Hemingway's white characters? Conversely, might Jake and Davy have more in common than we might first imagine?

Having examined the novel in its historical and literary contexts, I focus my students' attention on the central concern of the text, namely, as Davy asks, "is the love of an up-to-date, modern girl worth having?" (44). At heart, *When Washington Was in Vogue* is indeed a love story, one that unites a rather conservative gentleman with a slightly younger woman possessing "all the best and the worst points of the modern flapper" (8). As students work their way through the book, they often wonder why Davy does not recognize his feelings for Caroline more quickly, which gives us the opportunity to ponder the conflicting gender norms and expectations in the novel. At this point, if not earlier, we also discuss the role of skin tone politics. Unlike Davy, who is fair enough to pass for white, Caroline is decidedly dark. Davy dwells on complexion and its consequences regularly in his letters to Bob, and even though he criticizes other light-skinned African Americans for their disdain of darker African Americans, I suspect that his relationship with Caroline is, in fact, adversely colored by color. In this sense, *When Washington Was in Vogue* amplifies a preoccupation with skin color and sexuality that can be found in numerous other Harlem Renaissance novels, including Thurman's *The Blacker the Berry* (1929) and Nella Larsen's *Quicksand* (1928).

Ultimately, Davy does decide that the love of a modern flapper is worth having, but he comes to this realization only after Caroline gives up much of the behavior that would classify her as a flapper in the first place. She stops smoking and drinking and starts moderating her behavior around Davy. With Caroline's transformation in mind, I distribute the following handout, which culls paragraphs from Christina Simmons's article, as well as my introduction and Emily Bernard's commentary to the novel:

Is *When Washington Was in Vogue* feminist or anti-feminist?

Christina Simmons, *Canadian Review of American Studies*: Carr's self-mocking tone does not fully undermine the message of moral and social caution that pervades the story: though Caroline "has a mind of her own, originality, and courage," as well as true inner beauty that far outshines the artificial "product of the beauty culturist's art," she also learns the lesson that young women must beware of male "sports"—slick and morally questionable ladies' men ... Caroline reins in her modern feminine assertiveness and modestly stops visiting Carr's room once she realizes that she's falling in love with him. Carr becomes irritable with Caroline's flirtatious independence and procession of boyfriends but remains self-deluded about the reasons for his mood until the end, when, about to leave Washington, he realizes that he, too, is in love. They have it out, make up, and kiss. Thus the story asserts the basic goodness and marriageability of the flapper while lightly mocking provincial moralism and, at the same time, confirms traditional dicta of feminine decorum and the need for masculine protection.

McKible: Whatever his actual age, Davy considers himself much older and rather old-fashioned in comparison with Caroline, who bobs her hair, wears abbreviated clothing, drinks bootleg liquor, and smokes cigarettes whenever her mother isn't looking. Williams's novel appears to share the anti-modernism of its protagonist, because as the novel progresses, Caroline alters her behavior to suit Davy's tastes and win his affection. Modern flappers may fascinate Davy Carr, but at the end of the day, he is far more comfortable in the company of women who behave according to traditional expectations. Although it is a delightful novel, *When Washington Was in Vogue* is not a particularly feminist novel.

Bernard: Even though, as Adam McKible asserts in his introduction, *When Washington Was in Vogue* is not a feminist novel, there are fascinating women everywhere in this book, frankly sensuous, free-thinking, plain-speaking women. ... All of the women in the Rhodes family are exceptional but Caroline is the "flower of the flock." Indeed, Caroline Rhodes may be among the most memorable characters in Harlem Renaissance fiction. Like Clare Kendry in *Passing*, she is a young woman who fails to heed conventional attitudes about decorum and female behavior. She smokes, makes off-color jokes, and glories in a variety of male company. When she is with Davy, she lodges sarcastic barbs, teases him into doing her schoolwork, and steals his cigarette holder. Davy's hesitant sensuality is outdistanced by Caroline's no holds barred approach to racy banter. Early in the novel, when Davy suggests the he might give her a spanking if she were his daughter, Caroline keeps the joke alive, inflecting Davy's "innocent" comment with raunchy sexual innuendo. To put it simply, Caroline Rhodes is a delight.

After allowing students some time to jot down their thoughts about these passages, we begin a discussion that serves as a culmination to our analysis of Williams's text.

During the class time devoted to *When Washington Was in Vogue*, we consider the novel's reception and publication, its historical and literary contexts, its formal aspects and major themes, and we conclude by asking to what extent (if at all) a novel that seems to be antimodern by virtue of its narrator and gender dynamics should be read ironically. Caroline's capitulation to Davy's unspoken expectations about womanly behavior may not entail the sort of tragic consequences Helga Crane faces when she marries Pleasant Green in Larsen's *Quicksand*, but is Caroline's transformation fortunate? Should we congratulate Caroline and Davy for making a happy match, or should we be at all skeptical about their future marriage? Is Williams's novel typical of the Harlem Renaissance in its portrayal of love and sexual norms, or does it diverge in this aspect from other novels of the Harlem Renaissance?

When Washington Was in Vogue elicits a spectrum of comments from my students. As happens with any other required text, some students love it while others hate it; some warm to it eventually while others become disappointed by the end. In this sense, Williams's novel is much like any other book we assign, I imagine. But in teaching *When Washington Was in Vogue*, I also garnered comments from my students that I have not often heard before. My African American students delight in reading a book about black life that does not dwell extensively on slavery or oppression; they were happy to read a love story that celebrates but does not sugar coat a black middle-class community. My white students are also grateful for this perspective, because it provides them with a way of conceptualizing black life that differs strongly from the often adverse images of African Americans that saturate popular culture.

Lost for decades, *When Washington Was in Vogue* is a welcome addition to the literature of the Harlem Renaissance and an exciting text for use in the classroom. The novel offers many insights into that era's multiple engagements with modernity, and it expands our geographical conceptualization of a literary and cultural phenomenon named for a specific place. Indeed, *When Washington Was in Vogue* demonstrates that Harlem was not the only center of Renaissance excitement in the 1920s.

NOTES

1. My introduction to the novel provides a brief biographical sketch. See also "Some Schoolmen," Porter, Davis, and Josey.
2. The one exception to this critical occlusion is Simmons. She discusses the novel as being authored anonymously.
3. The first chapter of David Levering Lewis's *When Harlem Was in Vogue* contains an excellent discussion of returning black veterans and the development of the Harlem Renaissance.

WORKS CITED

Bernard, Emily. Commentary. *When Washington Was in Vogue*. By Edward Christopher Williams. New York: Amistad, 2003.

Davis, Russell H. *Memorable Negroes in Cleveland's Past*. Cleveland: Western Reserve Historical Society, 1969.

Josey, E.J. "Edward Christopher Williams: Librarian's Librarian." *Negro History Bulletin* 33 (1970): 70–77.

Lewis, David Levering. *When Harlem Was in Vogue*. New York: Knopf, 1981.

McKible, Adam. Introduction. *When Washington Was in Vogue*. By Edward Christopher Williams. New York: Amistad, 2003.

Porter, Dorothy B. "Phylon Profile, XIV: Edward Christopher Williams." *Phylon* 7 (1947): 315–21.

Simmons, Christina. "Modern Marriage for African Americans, 1920–1940." *Canadian Review of American Studies* 30 (2000): 273–300.

"Some Schoolmen." *Crisis* 10 (July 1915): 118–20.

Williams, Edward Christopher. *When Washington Was in Vogue: A Love Story (A Lost Novel of the Harlem Renaissance)*. 1925–1926. New York: Amistad, 2003.

Part III.
Supplemental Materials

Historical Maps of Harlem

For Location of Hotels see Map, Page 146

Figure 1. CHIEF POINTS OF INTEREST IN UPPER MANHATTAN. From the *Automobile Blue Book* (1920). *Courtesy of the University of Texas Libraries, The University of Texas at Austin.*

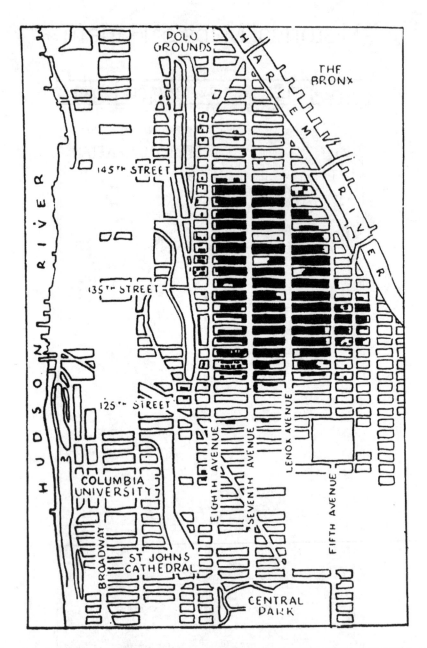

Figure 2. DETAIL FROM JAMES WELDON JOHNSON'S "THE MAKING OF HARLEM," SURVEY GRAPHIC HARLEM NUMBER (1925). The original caption reads: "This sketch map shows approximately where Negroes live in Harlem, according to a housing survey made in 1924 by the New York Urban League. The fringe of houses in which both Negro and white tenants live is not indicated." *Courtesy of Trinity University Library.*

Harlem Renaissance Syllabi

The first four syllabi suggest roughly ten weeks of material that might be incorporated into a longer (twelve- or fifteen-week) semester. The last syllabus suggests roughly four weeks of material for incorporation into an American or African American literature survey course. Most of the poetry, drama, and short fiction listed among the syllabi can be located in multiple sources; all of the poetry, drama, and short fiction can be found in Venetria K. Patton and Maureen Honey, eds., *Double-Take: A Revisionist Harlem Renaissance Anthology* (Rutgers, 2001).

HARLEM RENAISSANCE GENRES

This course introduces students to the multiplicity of literary genres that emerged from the Harlem Renaissance.

Non-fiction Prose/Manifestos

Week 1: Alain Locke, "The New Negro"; W.E.B. Du Bois, "Criteria of Negro Art"; George S. Schuyler, "The Negro-Art Hokum"; Langston Hughes, "The Negro Artist and the Racial Mountain"; Elise Johnson McDougald, "The Task of Negro Womanhood"

Poetry

Week 2: Poems by James Weldon Johnson, Georgia Douglas Johnson, Angelina Weld Grimké, Anne Spencer, Claude McKay

Week 3: Poems by Jean Toomer, Sterling Brown, Gwendolyn Bennett, Helene Johnson, and Mae Cowdery

Week 4: Poems by Countee Cullen and Langston Hughes

Drama

Week 5: Plays by Angelina Weld Grimké, Willis Richardson, Marita Bonner, and Bruce Nugent

Prose Fiction

Week 6: Short stories by Jessie Fauset, John Matheus, Rudolph Fisher, Wallace Thurman, and Dorothy West

Week 7: Edward Christopher Williams, *When Washington Was in Vogue* (epistolary novel)

Week 8: Jessie Fauset, *Plum Bun* (Bildungsroman, novel of manners, romance)

Week 9: George S. Schuyler, *Black No More* (science fiction, satire)

Week 10: Wallace Thurman, *Infants of the Spring* (Künstlerroman, "Queer" fiction)

BLACK AND WHITE MANHATTAN

This course investigates the role of intra- and inter-racial cooperation and conflict during the Jazz Age.

Week 1: James Weldon Johnson, *The Autobiography of an Ex-Colored Man*

Week 2: Waldo Frank, *Holiday*

Week 3: Jean Toomer, *Cane*

Week 4: Poems by Angelina Weld Grimké, Georgia Douglas Johnson, Claude McKay

Week 5: Jessie Fauset, *There is Confusion*

Week 6: Alain Locke, ed., *The New Negro*

Week 7: Poems by Gwendolyn Bennett, Sterling Brown, Countee Cullen, Langston Hughes, Helene Johnson

Week 8: Carl Van Vechten, *Nigger Heaven*

Week 9: Langston Hughes, *The Ways of White Folks*

Week 10: Nancy Cunard, ed., *Negro*

WOMEN OF THE HARLEM RENAISSANCE

This course looks at the major figures and themes associated with women's literature of the Harlem Renaissance.

Week 1: Alain Locke, "The New Negro"; A. Philip Randolph and Chandler Owen, "The New Negro—What is He?"; Zora Neale Hurston, "Characteristics of Negro Expression"; Marita O. Bonner, "On Being Young—a Woman—and Colored"; Alice Dunbar-Nelson, "Woman's Most Serious Problem"; Marion Vera Cuthbert, "Problems Facing Negro Young Women"

Week 2: Poems by Alice Dunbar-Nelson and Georgia Douglas Johnson

Week 3: Poems by Angelina Weld Grimké, Anne Spencer, and Jessie Fauset

Week 4: Plays by Georgia Douglas Johnson, Angelina Weld Grimké, May Miller, and Marita Bonner

Week 5: Short stories by Jessie Fauset, Zora Neale Hurston, and Nella Larsen

Week 6: Nella Larsen, *Quicksand*

Week 7: Short stories by Anita Scott Coleman, Gwendolyn Bennett, and Dorothy West

Week 8: Jessie Fauset, *Plum Bun*

Week 9: Poems by Gwendolyn Bennett, Gladys May Casely Hayford, Helene Johnson, and Mae Cowdery

Week 10: Zora Neale Hurston, *Their Eyes Were Watching God*

GAY AND LESBIAN WRITERS OF THE HARLEM RENAISSANCE

This course looks at the major figures and themes associated with gay, lesbian, bisexual, and transgendered writers and artists of the Harlem Renaissance.

Week 1: Wallace Thurman, *Infants of the Spring*

Week 2: Carl Van Vechten, *The Splendid Drunken Twenties*

Week 3: Bessie Smith, *Bessie Smith Songbook*

Week 4: Songs and poems by Bessie Smith, Ma Rainey, Gladys Bentley, and Mae Cowdery

Week 5: Poems by Angelina Weld Grimké and Alice Dunbar-Nelson

Week 6: Claude McKay, *Home to Harlem*

Week 7: Poems by Countee Cullen

Week 8: Poems by Langston Hughes and Claude McKay

Week 9: Bruce Nugent, *Gay Rebel of the Harlem Renaissance*

Week 10: Langston Hughes, *The Big Sea*

A HARLEM RENAISSANCE UNIT IN AN AMERICAN LITERATURE OR AFRICAN AMERICAN LITERATURE SURVEY

This unit introduces American literature or African American literature survey students to key issues of the Harlem Renaissance.

Week 1: Poems by Angelina Weld Grimké, Georgia Douglas Johnson, and Claude McKay

Week 2: Poems by Gwendolyn Bennett, Sterling Brown, Countee Cullen, Langston Hughes, and Helene Johnson

Week 3: Short stories by Jean Toomer, Zora Neale Hurston, Rudolph Fisher, and Dorothy West

Week 4: Nella Larsen, *Quicksand*

A Bibliography
for Teaching
the Harlem Renaissance

ANTHOLOGIES

Andrews, William L., ed. *Classic Fiction of the Harlem Renaissance*. New York: Oxford UP, 1994.

Cullen, Countee, ed. *Caroling Dusk: An Anthology of Verse by Black Poets of the Twenties*. 1927. Secaucus, New Jersey: Carol, 1993.

Gable, Craig, ed. *Ebony Rising: Short Fiction of the Greater Harlem Renaissance Era*. Bloomington: Indiana UP, 2004.

Gates, Henry Louis Jr. and Gene Andrew Jarrett, eds. *The New Negro: Essays on Race, Representation, and African American Culture, 1892–1938*. Princeton, New Jersey: Princeton UP, 2007.

Gates, Henry Louis Jr. and Nellie Y. McKay, eds. *The Norton Anthology of African American Literature* 2nd ed. New York: Norton, 2004.

Hatch, James V. and Leo Hamalian, eds. *Lost Plays of the Harlem Renaissance, 1920–1940*. Detroit: Wayne State UP, 1996.

Honey, Maureen, ed. *Shadowed Dreams: Women's Poetry of the Harlem Renaissance* rev. ed. New Brunswick, New Jersey: Rutgers UP, 2006.

Huggins, Nathan Irvin, ed. *Voices from the Harlem Renaissance*. New York: Oxford UP, 1976.

Johnson, James Weldon, ed. *The Book of American Negro Poetry* rev. ed. 1931. San Diego: Harcourt, 1983.

Knopf, Marcy, ed. *The Sleeper Wakes: Harlem Renaissance Stories by Women*. New Brunswick, New Jersey: Rutgers UP, 1993.

Lewis, David Levering, ed. *Portable Harlem Renaissance Reader*. New York: Penguin, 1994.

Locke, Alain, ed. *The New Negro*. 1925. New York: Atheneum, 1992.

Patton, Venetria K. and Maureen Honey, eds. *Double-Take: A Revisionist Harlem Renaissance Anthology*. New Brunswick, New Jersey: Rutgers UP, 2001.

Roses, Lorraine Elena and Ruth Elizabeth Randolph, eds. *Harlem's Glory: Black Women Writing, 1900–1950*. Cambridge, Massachusetts: Harvard UP, 1996.

Wintz, Cary D., ed. *The Harlem Renaissance, 1920–1940*. 7 vols. New York: Garland, 1996.

DICTIONARIES AND ENCYCLOPEDIAS

Aberjhani and Sandra L. West, eds. *Encyclopedia of the Harlem Renaissance*. New York: Facts on File, 2003.

Bloom, Harold, ed. *Black American Prose Writers of the Harlem Renaissance*. New York: Chelsea House, 1994.

Brown, Lois. *The Encyclopedia of the Harlem Literary Renaissance*. New York: Facts on File, 2006.

Harris, Trudier, ed. *Afro-American Writers from the Harlem Renaissance to 1940*. Detroit: Gale, 1987.

Kellner, Bruce, ed. *The Harlem Renaissance: A Historical Dictionary for the Era*. Westport, Connecticut: Greenwood, 1984.

Roses, Lorraine Elena and Ruth Elizabeth Randolph, eds. *Harlem Renaissance and Beyond: Literary Biographies of 100 Black Women Writers, 1900–1945*. Boston: G.K. Hall, 1990.

Wintz, Cary D. and Paul Finkelman, eds. *Encyclopedia of the Harlem Renaissance*. 2 vols. New York: Routledge, 2004.

Witalec, Janet, ed. *The Harlem Renaissance: A Gale Critical Companion*. 3 vols. Detroit: Gale, 2003.

GENERAL STUDIES AND ESSAY COLLECTIONS

Anderson, Paul Allen. *Deep River: Music and Memory in Harlem Renaissance Thought*. Durham, North Carolina: Duke UP, 2001.

Baker, Houston A., Jr. *Modernism and the Harlem Renaissance*. Chicago: U of Chicago P, 1987.

Balshaw, Maria. *Looking for Harlem: Urban Aesthetics in African American Literature*. London: Pluto, 2000.

Bloom, Harold, ed. *The Harlem Renaissance*. Philadelphia: Chelsea House, 2004.

Carroll, Anne Elizabeth. *Word, Image, and the New Negro: Representation and Identity in the Harlem Renaissance*. Bloomington: Indiana UP, 2005.

De Jongh, James. *Vicious Modernism: Black Harlem and the Literary Imagination*. Cambridge: Cambridge UP, 1990.

Dunn, Allen and George Hutchinson, eds. "The Future of the Harlem Renaissance: Special Issue." *Soundings* 80 (1997).

Edwards, Brent Hayes. *The Practice of Diaspora: Literature, Translation, and the Rise of Black Internationalism*. Cambridge: Harvard UP, 2003.

Fabre, Geneviève and Michel Feith, eds. *Temples for Tomorrow: Looking Back at the Harlem Renaissance*. Bloomington: Indiana UP, 2001.

Favor, J. Martin. *Authentic Blackness: The Folk in the New Negro Renaissance*. Durham, North Carolina: Duke UP, 1999.

Goeser, Caroline. *Picturing the New Negro: Harlem Renaissance Print Culture and Modern Black Identity*. Lawrence: UP of Kansas, 2006.

Huggins, Nathan Irvin. *Harlem Renaissance*. New York: Oxford UP, 1971.

Hutchinson, George, ed. *Cambridge Companion to the Harlem Renaissance*. Cambridge: Cambridge UP, 2007.

————. *The Harlem Renaissance in Black and White*. Cambridge: Harvard UP, 1995.

Johnson, Abby Arthur and Ronald Maberry Johnson. *Propaganda and Aesthetics: The Literary Politics of Afro-American Magazines in the Twentieth Century*. Amherst: U of Massachusetts P, 1979.

Krasner, David. *A Beautiful Pageant: African American Theatre, Drama, and Performance in the Harlem Renaissance, 1910–1927*. New York: Palgrave, 2002.

Lewis, David Levering. *When Harlem Was in Vogue*. New York: Viking, 1981.

Nadell, Martha Jane. *Enter the New Negroes: Images of Race in American Culture*. Cambridge: Harvard UP, 2004.

Schwarz, A.B. Christa. *Gay Voices of the Harlem Renaissance*. Bloomington: Indiana UP, 2003.

Sherrard-Johnson, Cherene. *Portraits of the New Negro Woman: Visual and Literary Culture of the Harlem Renaissance*. New Brunswick, New Jersey: Rutgers UP, 2007.

Smith, Katharine Capshaw. *Children's Literature of the Harlem Renaissance*. Bloomington: Indiana UP, 2004.

Tarver, Australia and Paula C. Barnes, eds. *New Voices on the Harlem Renaissance: Essays on Race, Gender, and Literary Discourse*. Madison, New Jersey: Fairleigh Dickinson UP, 2006.

Wall, Cheryl A. *Women of the Harlem Renaissance*. Bloomington: Indiana UP, 1995.

Watson, Steven. *The Harlem Renaissance: Hub of African-American Culture, 1920–1930*. New York: Pantheon, 1995.

Wintz, Cary D., ed. *Harlem Speaks: A Living History of the Harlem Renaissance*. Naperville, Illinois: Sourcebooks, 2007.

STERLING BROWN

Gabbin, Joanne V. *Sterling A. Brown: Building the Black Aesthetic Tradition*. Westport, Connecticut: Greenwood, 1985.

Rowell, Charles H. and Kendra Hamilton, eds. "Sterling A. Brown: A Special Issue." *Callaloo* 21 (1998).

Sanders, Mark A. *Afro-Modernist Aesthetics and the Poetry of Sterling A. Brown*. Athens: U of Georgia P, 1999.

Smethurst, James E. "The Strong Men Gittin' Stronger: Sterling Brown's *Southern Road* and the Representation and Re-creation of the Southern Folk Voice." *Race and the Modern Artist*. Ed. Heather Hathaway *et al*. Oxford: Oxford UP, 2003. 69–91.

COUNTEE CULLEN

Braddock, Jeremy. "The Poetics of Conjecture: Countee Cullen's Subversive Exemplarity." *Callaloo* 25 (2002): 1250–71.

Kelley, James. "Blossoming in Strange New Forms: Male Homosexuality and the Harlem Renaissance." *Soundings* 80 (1997): 498–517.

Shucard, Alan R. *Countee Cullen*. Boston: Twayne, 1984.

JESSIE FAUSET

Allen, Carol. *Black Women Intellectuals: Strategies of Nation, Family, and Neighborhood in the Works of Pauline Hopkins, Jessie Fauset, and Marita Bonner*. New York: Garland, 1998.

Pfeiffer, Kathleen. "The Limits of Identity in Jessie Fauset's *Plum Bun*." *Legacy* 18 (2001): 79–93.

Simmons, Christina. "'Modern Marriage' for African Americans, 1920–1940." *Canadian Review of American Studies/Revue Canadienne d'Etudes Américaines* 30 (2000): 273–300.

Tomlinson, Susan. "Visionary to Visionary: The New Negro Woman as Cultural Worker in Jessie Redmon Fauset's *Plum Bun*." *Legacy* 19 (2002): 90–97.

WALDO FRANK

Carter, Paul J. *Waldo Frank*. New York: Twayne, 1967.

Munson, Gorham B. *Waldo Frank: A Study*. Folcroft, Pennsylvania: Folcroft Library Editions, 1974.

Terris, Daniel. "Waldo Frank, Jean Toomer, and the Critique of Racial Voyeurism." *Race and the Modern Artist*. Ed. Heather Hathaway *et al*. Oxford: Oxford UP, 2003. 92–114.

LANGSTON HUGHES

Gates, Henry Louis, Jr. and K.A. Appiah, eds. *Langston Hughes: Critical Perspectives Past and Present*. New York: Amistad, 1993.

Mullen, Edward J., ed. *Critical Essays on Langston Hughes*. Boston: G.K. Hall, 1986.

Rampersad, Arnold. *The Life of Langston Hughes* 2nd ed. New York: Oxford UP, 2002.

Tracy, Steven C., ed. *A Historical Guide to Langston Hughes*. New York: Oxford UP, 2004.

JAMES WELDON JOHNSON

Fleming, Robert E. *James Weldon Johnson*. Boston: Twayne, 1987.

Levy, Eugene D. *James Weldon Johnson: Black Leader, Black Voice*. Chicago: U of Chicago P, 1973.

Price, Kenneth M. and Lawrence J. Oliver, eds. *Critical Essays on James Weldon Johnson*. New York: G.K. Hall, 1997.

Sundquist, Eric J. *The Hammers of Creation: Folk Culture in Modern African-American Fiction*. Athens: U of Georgia P, 1992.

NELLA LARSEN

Brickhouse, Anna. "Nella Larsen and the Intertextual Geography of Quicksand." *African American Review* (2001): 533–60.

Hutchinson, George. *In Search of Nella Larsen: A Biography of the Color Line*. Cambridge: Harvard UP, 2006.

Rabin, Jessica G. *Surviving the Crossing: (Im)migration, Ethnicity, and Gender in Willa Cather, Gertrude Stein, and Nella Larsen*. New York: Routledge, 2004.

Sherrard-Johnson, Cherene. "'A Plea for Color': Nella Larsen's Iconography of the Mulatta." *American Literature* 76 (2004): 833–69.

CLAUDE MCKAY

Cooper, Wayne F. *Claude McKay: Rebel Sojourner in the Harlem Renaissance: A Biography*. Baton Rouge: Louisiana State UP, 1987.

Gosciak, Josh. *The Shadowed Country: Claude McKay and the Romance of the Victorians*. New Brunswick, New Jersey: Rutgers UP, 2006.

Hathaway, Heather. *Caribbean Waves: Relocating Claude McKay and Paule Marshall.* Bloomington: Indiana UP, 1999.

Lutz, Tom. "Claude McKay: Music, Sexuality, and Literary Cosmopolitanism." *Black Orpheus: Music in African American Fiction from the Harlem Renaissance to Toni Morrison.* Ed. Saadi A. Simawe. New York: Garland, 2000. 41–64.

THE NEW NEGRO

Carroll, Anne Elizabeth. *Word, Image, and the New Negro: Representation and Identity in the Harlem Renaissance.* Bloomington: Indiana UP, 2005.

Foley, Barbara. *Spectres of 1919: Class and Nation in the Making of the New Negro.* Urbana: U of Illinois P, 2003.

Watts, Eric King. "African American Ethos and Hermeneutical Rhetoric: An Exploration of Alain Locke's *The New Negro.*" *Quarterly Journal of Speech* 88 (2002): 19–32.

GEORGE S. SCHUYLER

Ferguson, Jeffrey B. *The Sage of Sugar Hill: George S. Schuyler and the Harlem Renaissance.* New Haven: Yale UP, 2005.

Haslam, Jason. "'The Open-Sesame of a Pork-Colored Skin': Whiteness and Privilege in *Black No More.*" *Modern Language Studies* 32 (2002): 15–30.

Kuenz, Jane. "American Racial Discourse, 1900–1930: Schuyler's *Black No More.*" *Novel* 30 (1997): 170–92.

Peplow, Michael W. *George S. Schuyler.* Boston: Twayne, 1980.

WALLACE THURMAN

Carter, Linda M. "Wallace Thurman (1902–1934)." *African American Authors, 1745–1945: A Bio-Bibliographical Critical Sourcebook.* Ed. Emmanuel S. Nelson. Westport, Connecticut: Greenwood, 2000. 387–95.

Ganter, Granville. "Decadence, Sexuality, and the Bohemian Vision of Wallace Thurman." *MELUS* 28 (2003): 83–104.

Glick, Elisa F. "Harlem's Queer Dandy: African-American Modernism and the Artifice of Blackness." *Modern Fiction Studies* 49 (2003): 414–42.

Herring, Terrell Scott. "The Negro Artist and the Racial Manor: *Infants of the Spring* and the Conundrum of Publicity." *African American Review* 35 (2001): 581–97.

Singh, Amritjit, ed. *The Collected Writings of Wallace Thurman: A Harlem Renaissance Reader.* New Brunswick, New Jersey: Rutgers UP, 2003.

JEAN TOOMER

Fabre, Geneviève and Michel Feith, eds. *Jean Toomer and the Harlem Renaissance.* New Brunswick, New Jersey: Rutgers UP, 2001.

Grant, Nathan. *Masculinist Impulses: Toomer, Hurston, Black Writing, and Modernity*. Columbia: U of Missouri P, 2004.

Kerman, Cynthia Earl and Richard Eldridge. *The Lives of Jean Toomer: A Hunger for Wholeness*. Baton Rouge: Louisiana State UP, 1987.

Thompson Cager, Chezia. *Teaching Jean Toomer's* 1923 Cane. New York: Peter Lang, 2006.

CARL VAN VECHTEN

Bernard, Emily. "What He Did for the Race: Carl Van Vechten and the Harlem Renaissance." *Soundings* 80 (1997): 531–42.

Coleman, Leon. *Carl Van Vechten and the Harlem Renaissance: A Critical Assessment*. New York: Garland, 1998.

Kellner, Bruce. *Carl Van Vechten and the Irreverent Decades*. Norman: U of Oklahoma P, 1968.

Worth, Robert F. "*Nigger Heaven* and the Harlem Renaissance." *African American Review* 29 (1995): 461–73.

EDWARD CHRISTOPHER WILLIAMS

Asim, Jabari. "Lost and Found: A Tale of the Washington Renaissance." *Crisis* 111 (Jan./Feb. 2004): 58–59.

Josey, E.J. "Edward Christopher Williams: Librarian's Librarian." *Negro History Bulletin* 33 (1970): 70–77.

Porter, Dorothy B. "Phylon Profile, XIV: Edward Christopher Williams." *Phylon* 7 (1947): 315–21.

Simmons, Christina. "Modern Marriage for African Americans, 1920–1940." *Canadian Review of American Studies* 30 (2000): 273–300.

WEBSITES

Academy of American Poets. *A Brief Guide to the Harlem Renaissance*. n.d. 9 Jan. 2008. <http://www.poets.org/viewmedia.php/prmMID/5657>

ARTSEDGE/John F. Kennedy Center. *Drop Me Off in Harlem*. 2003. 9 Jan. 2008. <http://artsedge.kennedy-center.org/exploring/harlem/artsedge.html>

D.C. Public Library. *The Black Renaissance in Washington, D.C.* 2003. 9 Jan. 2008. <http://029c28c.netsolhost.com/blkren/>

Institute of International Visual Artists. *Rhapsodies in Black*. 1997. 9 Jan. 2008. <http://www.iniva.org/harlem/home.html>

John Carroll University. *Harlem Renaissance Multimedia Resource*. n.d. 9 Jan. 2008. <http://www.jcu.edu/harlem/index.htm>

Kirschenbaum, Matthew G. and Catherine Tousignant. *Harlem: Mecca of the New Negro: A Hypermedia Edition of the March 1925* Survey Graphic *Harlem Number*. 1996. 9 Jan. 2008. <http://etext.lib.virginia.edu/harlem/>

Library of Congress. *African American Odyssey: World War I and Postwar Society*. 1998. 9 Jan. 2008. <http://memory.loc.gov/ammem/aaohtml/exhibit/aopart7.html>

McMillian, Angela. *Library of Congress: A Guide to Harlem Renaissance Materials*. 2006. 9 Jan. 2008. <http://www.loc.gov/rr/program/bib/harlem/harlem.html>

Reuben, Paul P. "Chapter 9: Harlem Renaissance—An Introduction." *PAL: Perspectives in American Literature—A Research and Reference Guide*. 2007. 9 Jan. 2008. <http://web.csustan.edu/english/reuben/pal/chap9/9intro.html>

Schomburg Center for Research in Black Culture. *Harlem, 1900–1940: An African-American Community*. 2001. 9 Jan. 2008. <http://www.si.umich.edu/CHICO/Harlem/index.html>

MULTIMEDIA RESOURCES

Africa to America to Paris: The Migration of Black Writers. Dir. Jacques Goldstein and Blaise N'Djehoya. Videocasette. Films for the Humanities and Sciences, 1997.

Against the Odds: The Artists of the Harlem Renaissance. Dir. Amber Edwards. Videocassette. PBS Home Video, 1995.

Anthology of Negro Poetry. Ed. Arna Bontemps. Folkways Records, 1954.

Brother to Brother. Dir. Rodney Evans. DVD. Wolfe Video, 2005.

From These Roots: A Review of the Harlem Renaissance. Dir. William Greaves. Videocassette. William Greaves Productions, 1974.

Harlem Nights. Dir. Eddie Murphy. Videocassette. Paramount, 1994.

Harlem Renaissance: The Music and Rhythms That Started a Cultural Revolution. Dir. Marino Amoruso. DVD. Kultur, 2004.

In Black and White. Dir. Russ Karel. Videocassette. Films for the Humanities and Sciences, 1997.

I Remember Harlem. Dir. William Miles. Videocassette. Films for the Humanities and Sciences, 1991.

Looking for Langston: A Meditation on Langston Hughes (1902–1907) and the Harlem Renaissance. Dir. Isaac Julien. Videocassette. Water Bearer Films, 1992.

Midnight Ramble: Oscar Micheaux and the Story of Race Movies. Dirs. Bestor Cram and Pearl Bowser. Videocassette. PBS Video, 1994.

Murder in Harlem. 1935. Dir. Oscar Micheaux. Videocassette. Timeless Multimedia, 1993.

Powell, Richard J. et al. *Rhapsodies in Black: Art of the Harlem Renaissance*. Berkeley: U of California P, 1997.

Rhapsodies in Black: Music and Words from the Harlem Renaissance. Rhino, 2000.

Without Fear or Shame: 1920–1937. Dir. Sam Pollard. Videocassette. PBS Video, 1999.

Contributors

Emily Bernard is associate professor of English and ALANA U.S. Ethnic Studies at the University of Vermont. Her first book, *Remember Me To Harlem: The Letters of Langston Hughes and Carl Van Vechten*, was a *New York Times* Notable Book of the Year. Her current project, *White Shadows: Carl Van Vechten and the Harlem Renaissance*, will be published by Yale University Press in 2009.

Patrick S. Bernard is associate professor in the English Department at Franklin & Marshall College, where he teaches African American, American, and African Literatures. His primary research interests are call and response, literature and music, especially in the Harlem Renaissance, literary theory and cultural studies, and the Black Diaspora. His latest publications include "Mapping the Woman's Body: Race, Sex, and Gender in Mariama Ba's *Scarlet Song*" (*Women's Studies*), "Travel Culture as Performance in Richard Wright's *Black Power*" (*Langston Hughes Review*), "Magical Realism and History in *The Last Harmattan of Alusine Dunbar*" (*A Critical Introduction to Sierra Leone Literature*), and "The Cognitive Construction of the Self in *Their Eyes Were Watching God*" (*CLCWeb*).

Elisa Glick is assistant professor of English and Women's and Gender Studies at the University of Missouri, where she teaches courses on gender and sexuality studies, critical theory, and fin de siècle and twentieth-century literature and culture. In 2006, she was one of three faculty members to receive the Provost's Outstanding Junior Faculty Teaching Award. Her essay on Wallace Thurman, Richard Bruce Nugent, and the figure of the African American dandy, "Harlem's Queer Dandy," appears in *Modern Fiction Studies* (2003). She has also published articles in *Cultural Critique, Feminist Review,* and *GLQ.* Her forthcoming book, *Materializing Queer Desire: Oscar Wilde to Andy Warhol* (SUNY, 2008), studies queer dandyism and its relation to the sphere of the commodity in modern literature and culture.

Nathan Grant is an associate professor of English at the State University of New York at Buffalo, has taught both graduate and undergraduate courses in American and African American literature, and is the author of *Masculinist Impulses: Toomer, Hurston, Black Writing and Modernity* (Missouri, 2004).

Laura Harris is author of *Notes from a Welfare Queen in the Ivory Tower: Poetry, Fiction, Letters, and Essays* (Face to Face, 2002), a title nominated for the American Library Association 2002 Stonewall Book Award. Harris publishes in the areas of literary criticism, feminist and queer studies, and African diaspora studies. She edited *Femme: Feminists, Lesbians, and Bad Girls* (Routledge, 1997) and her article publications are found in venues such as the *Journal of Lesbian Studies* and *African American Review.* Harris is associate professor of English, World Literature, and Black Studies at Pitzer College.

Amber Harris Leichner is a Ph.D. student at the University of Nebraska-Lincoln in American Literature and Women's and Gender Studies focusing on the recovery of early twentieth-century women writers. She received her B.A. in English at Montana State University-Billings and her M.A. in English and Women's Studies at the University of Nebraska-Lincoln.

Emily M. Hinnov is currently assistant professor of English and Women's Studies at Bowling Green State University's regional branch campus, Firelands College. She has published articles on Virginia Woolf and a chapter on Sylvia Townsend Warner. She is currently working on a book-length study of transatlantic literary and visual representations of community in the interwar years.

Maureen Honey is professor of English at the University of Nebraska-Lincoln, where she teaches courses on Women in Popular Culture, Twentieth Century Women Writers, Women of the Harlem Renaissance, and Diverse Women Writers of the Early Twentieth Century. She is the editor, among other things, of *Shadowed Dreams: Women's Poetry of the Harlem Renaissance* (Rutgers, 1989 and 2006), *Bitter Fruit: African American Women in World War II* (Missouri, 1999), and the co-editor of *Double-Take: A Revisionist Harlem Renaissance Anthology* (Rutgers, 2001).

Rita Keresztesi, an associate professor of English at the University of Oklahoma, is the author of *Strangers at Home: American Ethnic Modernism between the World Wars* (2005). Her research and teaching focus on African American and

Afro-Caribbean literary and cultural studies. She is currently working on a second book titled *Diasporic Dialogues/From New Negro to Black Power*.

Dorothea Löbbermann teaches American literature at Humboldt-University, Berlin. She has worked extensively on African American literature and culture, particularly on the Harlem Renaissance, as well as on questions of place and (urban) spaces, of movement and travel, of identities and representation. Her books include *Memories of Harlem: Fiktionale (Re)Konstruktionen eines Mythos der zwanziger Jahre* (Campus, 2002), *Other Modernisms in an Age of Globalization*, co-edited with Djelal Kadir (Winter, 2002), and *CinematoGraphies: Visual Discourses and Textual Strategies in 1990s New York City*, co-edited with Günter H. Lenz and Karl-Heinz Magister (Winter, 2006). She is currently working on a project on Figurations of Homelessness.

Tom Lutz teaches at the University of California, Riverside and is director of the MFA in Creative Writing and Writing for the Performing Arts at UCR's Palm Desert Graduate Center. He co-edited *These 'Colored' United States: African American Essays from the 1920s* (Rutgers, 1996) and is the author of *Doing Nothing* (FSG, 2006), *Cosmopolitan Vistas* (Cornell, 2004), *Crying* (Norton, 1999), and *American Nervousness, 1903* (Cornell, 1991). He has written for newspapers, magazines, academic journals, radio, film, and television in the U.S. and abroad.

William J. Maxwell is associate professor of English and Interpretive Theory at the University of Illinois, Urbana-Champaign, where he teaches modern American and African American literature. He is the author of *New Negro, Old Left: African American Writing and Communism between the Wars* (Columbia, 1999) and the editor of Claude McKay's *Complete Poems* (Illinois, 2004). He is now at work on a book for the Princeton University Press entitled *FB Eyes: How J. Edgar Hoover's Ghostreaders Framed African American Literature*.

Adam McKible is associate professor of English at John Jay College of Criminal Justice in New York, where he teaches American and African American literature. He most recently co-edited, with Suzanne Churchill, *Little Magazines and Modernism: New Approaches* (Ashgate, 2007). He also rediscovered and introduced *When Washington Was in Vogue*, by Edward Christopher Williams (HarperCollins, 2004), and he is the author of *The Space and Place of Modernism: The Russian Revolution, Little Magazines, and New York* (Routledge, 2002) as well as various essays on little magazines and African American literature.

Martha Jane Nadell is associate professor of English at Brooklyn College, City University of New York. She is author of *Enter the New Negroes: Images of Race in American Culture* (Harvard, 2004) and has published essays in such places as *The*

Chronicle of Higher Education (2005) and *A Companion to Modernist Literature and Culture* (Blackwell, 2006).

Lawrence J. Oliver is professor of English and associate dean in the College of Liberal Arts at Texas A&M University (College Station). His research and teaching areas are late-nineteenth- and early-twentieth-century American literature and African American literature. His publications include *Critical Essays on James Weldon Johnson* (G.K. Hall, 1997), co-edited with Kenneth M. Price.

Hans Ostrom is professor of English at the University of Puget Sound. He is author of *A Langston Hughes Encyclopedia* (Greenwood, 2002) and co-editor of *The Greenwood Encyclopedia of African American Literature* (5 volumes, 2005). His most recent book is *The Coast Starlight: Collected Poems 1976-2006* (Dog Ear, 2006).

Anita Patterson is associate professor of English and director of American Studies at Boston University. She teaches courses on American literature, modernism, and black literature of the Americas, and is author of *From Emerson to King: Democracy, Race, and the Politics of Protest* (Oxford, 1997) and *Race, American Literature and Transnational Modernisms* (Cambridge, 2008).

Kathleen Pfeiffer is associate professor of English and coordinator of the American Studies Concentration at Oakland University in Rochester, Michigan. She is author of *Race Passing and American Individualism* (Massachusetts, 2003) and she introduced and edited the re-issues of Carl Van Vechten's *Nigger Heaven* (Illinois, 2000) and Waldo Frank's *Holiday* (Illinois, 2003). She is currently working on *Brother Mine: The Correspondence of Jean Toomer and Waldo Frank* and *Selected Letters of Waldo Frank*.

James Smethurst is associate professor of Afro-American Studies at the University of Massachusetts Amherst. He is the author of *The New Red Negro: The Literary Left and African American Poetry, 1930-1946* (Oxford, 1999) and *The Black Arts Movement: Literary Nationalism in the 1960s and 1970s* (North Carolina, 2005). He is also the co-editor of *Left of the Color Line: Race, Radicalism and Twentieth-Century Literature of the United States* (North Carolina, 2003) and *Radicalism in the South since Reconstruction* (Palgrave Macmillan, 2006).

Michael Soto is associate professor of English and director of the McNair Scholars Program at Trinity University, where he teaches courses on twentieth-century American literature and cultural history. He is author of *The Modernist Nation: Generation, Renaissance, and Twentieth-Century American Literature* (Alabama, 2004) and *Resources for Teaching the Bedford Anthology of American Literature* volume two (Bedford/St. Martin's, 2008). He is presently at work on a social history of the Harlem Renaissance.

Claudia Stokes teaches at Trinity University and is the author of *Writers in Retrospect: The Rise of American Literary History, 1875-1910* (North Carolina, 2006). She is also co-editor (with Michael A. Elliott of Emory University) of *American Literary Studies: A Methodological Reader* (New York, 2003).

Susan Tomlinson is assistant professor of English at the University of Massachusetts Boston, where she teaches courses in the Harlem Renaissance, early African American Literature, and gender and modernism. Her publications include articles on Jessie Fauset (*Legacy*) and Zona Gale (*Modern Fiction Studies*). She is completing a book-length manuscript, *Keeping It Decent: Jessie Fauset, Virtue, and the Crisis of New Negro Womanhood.*

Index

AFRICAN AMERICAN LITERATURE AND CULTURE

EXPANDING AND EXPLODING THE BOUNDARIES

General Editor
Carlyle V. Thompson

The purpose of this series is to present innovative, in-depth, and provocatively critical literary and cultural investigations of critical issues in African American literature and life. We welcome critiques of fiction, poetry, drama, film, sports, and popular culture. Of particular interest are literary and cultural analyses that involve contemporary psychoanalytical criticism, new historicism, deconstructionism, critical race theory, critical legal theory, and critical gender theory.

For additional information about this series or for the submission of manuscripts, please contact:

> Peter Lang Publishing, Inc.
> Acquisitions Department
> 29 Broadway, 18th floor
> New York, New York 10006

To order other books in this series, please contact our Customer Service Department:

> (800) 770-LANG (within the U.S.)
> (212) 647-7706 (outside the U.S.)
> (212) 647-7707 FAX

Or browse online by series:

> www.peterlang.com